Ambition and Arrogance

Photograph Courtesy of the
Archives of The Catholic University of America

AMBITION
AND ARROGANCE

Cardinal William O'Connell of Boston
and the American Catholic Church

By
Douglas J. Slawson

Cobalt
PRODUCTIONS

Portions of this book appeared previously in " 'The Boston Tragedy and Comedy': The Near-Repudiation of Cardinal O'Connell," *Catholic Historical Review 77* (October 1991), and in *The Foundation and First Decade of the National Catholic Welfare Council* (Washington, D.C.: The Catholic University of America Press, 1992). The author gratefully acknowledges The Catholic University of America Press for permission to reprint from the article.

Publisher's Cataloging-in-Publication
(Provided by Quality Books, Inc.)

Slawson, Douglas J.
    Ambition and arrogance : Cardinal William O'Connell of Boston and the American Catholic Church / by Douglas J. Slawson.
    p. cm.
    Includes bibliographical references and index.
    ISBN-13: 978-0-9787855-0-5
    ISBN-10: 0-9787855-0-9

    1. O'Connell, William, 1859–1944. 2. Cardinals—Massachusetts—Boston—Biography. 3. Americanism (Catholic controversy) 4. National Catholic Welfare Council (U.S.) 5. Catholic Church—United States—History—20th century. 6. United States—Church history—20th century.   I. Title.

BX4705.O3S63 2007   282'.092
                QBI06-600387

Cover is based on a photograph of William H. O'Connell when he was assistant pastor at St. Joseph's Church in Boston's West End.

For my wife Linda

Contents

Preface

IN 1913, THE BISHOPS OF NEW ENGLAND began an eleven-year, on-again-off-again drive for the removal from office of their metropolitan archbishop, Cardinal William Henry O'Connell of Boston. Their reasons were several and longstanding. An ambitious man, O'Connell had risen to power at a time when the Vatican was increasingly making itself the center and focus of Catholic life. Even as this centralization was occurring, some clergy and laypeople in the United States sought to accommodate their church to American circumstances and viewed the American Catholic church as the model for the future church worldwide.

After Pope Leo XIII condemned a theological distortion of this "Americanism," O'Connell portrayed himself as the Vatican's man in the ecclesiastical province of New England, reputed to be rife with adherents of the Americanist movement. His branding of others as opponents of Rome was the means he used to lift himself onto the archiepiscopal seat of Boston. Potent Vatican allies, whose friendship he had cultivated during his years in Rome, helped in this grasp for power. His rise in this fashion marked him as the first of a new breed of American prelate: one who advanced through Vatican connections.

His ascendancy through Roman, rather than American, channels alienated him from the bishops of the province and from many prelates in the American hierarchy. Deepening this estrangement were his attempts to bring Roman discipline to New England and the revelation of scandals touching his administration in Boston. With regard to money, O'Connell had an elastic conscience that permitted him to use his office for personal gain. Worse was his countenancing of the moral wrongdoing of two priests who lived with him, one of them his nephew. These scandals caused his suffragans—the bishops who belonged to his province—and others around the country to seek his removal.

The height of the drive for O'Connell's ouster coincided with a new movement to give national expression to American Catholicism. The bishops of the country had recently organized themselves as the National Catholic Welfare Council, an assembly intended to introduce collaborative leadership in the church. Never friendly to the idea, O'Connell viewed the council as a rival to his authority and power as a cardinal. It was too collegial and too tied to the Sulpician Fathers, who had been quiet, but ardent, promoters of the Americanist movement. The cardinal's detestation of the Sulpicians was absolute and unyielding. Their connection with the National Catholic Welfare Council caused him to view the organization as Americanism resurrected. When his suffragans chose to use the council as the instrument for his repudiation, O'Connell maneuvered its destruction by the Vatican. Its demise was brief because the hierarchy petitioned Rome to reconsider the case. In the ensuing years, O'Connell sought to minimize the council and assert his authority over the American church.

This book is not a new or full-scale biography of O'Connell. Rather, its scope is quite limited: it is the history of a tragic and regrettable episode of ecclesiastical corruption, of a man who betrayed his calling, his office, and his church. It is the tale of a cleric who, when opportunity presented itself, ambitiously sought power and then arrogantly used it to his advantage. It is the story of a man who forced his way to the top and then attempted to become spokesman of the American Catholic church.

Although O'Connell is the protagonist, the volume is, in another sense, a collective biography of those who resisted him. It tells the tale of bishops, priests, and laypeople who did not share O'Connell's vision of the church and were distraught by the scandalous behavior of his regime. To be sure, some Bostonians gloried vicariously in O'Connell's celebrity, but for others the offensiveness of his administration prompted a range of reactions, from temperate denunciation to ridicule to outrage. A number of bishops and priests relentlessly pursued his removal from office because of his misuse of it. They were ultimately unsuccessful because of O'Connell's masterful ability to mobilize his Roman power base and because of an absence of will at the highest level.

This study of O'Connell has much in common with present-day

events in the American Catholic church, particularly in Boston where the scandal over pedophile priests first came to light. O'Connell, Boston's first cardinal, and Bernard Law, one of the city's more recent ones, were both promoters and defenders of Vatican policy. Both covered up the sexual transgressions of priests. Both were the objects of campaigns for their removal from office. While Law ultimately resigned and went to live in Rome, O'Connell survived. To borrow from the title of one of Barbara Tuchman's books, the present story may serve as a "Distant Mirror" against which to view current affairs. There are lessons still to be learned from the past—and the present.

The primary sources used in this study are in multiple languages. Although the majority are in English, a significant number are in Italian, with a lesser amount in French, and a still smaller number in Latin. Throughout the endnotes, I have cited all unpublished sources, including foreign-language ones, in English. Published sources, however, are cited in the language of origin.

Because the story ranges over so many years, with so many characters, I have provided a list of participants in the saga in order to help the reader keep track of who is who.

The publication of a book is truly a group effort. I would like to take this opportunity to render thanks to some of those who have helped to bring this volume forward. I am indebted to Father Stafford Poole, C.M., and Father Gerald Fogarty, S.J., who read drafts and offered helpful suggestions. Any fault that remains in the book is mine, not theirs. Special thanks to my publisher, Cobalt Productions; editor Annie Ross, for her thoughtful reading and careful editing of the manuscript; the distributor, Independent Publishers Group, especially Cynthia Murphy, for professional guidance and support; publicist Mary Ann Lauricella of Lauricella Public Relations Co., for expert advice and work; and William Whitehead of Wm. Whitehead Design for the creative cover and layout of the book. Finally, I would like to thank my wife Linda for her support, encouragement, and constructive criticism during the several years that it took for this book to come to fruition.

Douglas J. Slawson

History repeats itself because no one was listening the first time.
—*Anonymous*

It is history that holds you accountable.
—*John Wheelwright in* A Prayer for Owen Meany
by John Irving

Hope is the other side of history.
—*Marcia Cavell*

The Early Years

WILLIAM HENRY O'CONNELL entered the world in Lowell, Massachusetts, on 8 December 1859, the last of eleven children born to John and Brigid (Farrelly) O'Connell. The couple had migrated with six children from Ireland during the potato famine. They settled first in New York where a seventh child was born, then soon relocated in Lowell, the birthplace of the remaining four children. Never poor, the family possessed modest means and added to them over time, ensuring a modicum of financial security. Through self-improvement and hard work, William's older brothers provided this stability after the untimely death of their father in 1865. Ultimately the family owned four homes and rented flats to increase income.[1]

The youngest O'Connell received a public education in a society dominated by Protestant Yankees who held Catholics in low regard. At the age of fifteen or sixteen, though still lacking a clear notion "of God's will in my regard," William O'Connell sensed that he might have a vocation to the priesthood. On graduating from high school, he decided to attend St. Charles' College in Ellicott City, Maryland, an institution run by the priests of St. Sulpice, usually referred to as Sulpicians, a French community founded and dedicated to preparing men for the ministry.[2]

In his published *Recollections,* he was generally positive about the experience, recounting the awe he felt about being in a Catholic school with religious symbols everywhere and fondly remembering three of his teachers, Fathers Pierre Denis, John B. Menu, and John Tabb. Gently critical of Sulpician discipline, he noted that each student had a spiritual director with whom he met weekly and from whom he received advice and "scrupulous" direction to be carried out in the coming week. "The result in the main was a pretty serious group of youngsters,

1

perhaps indeed too serious for their age," recalled O'Connell. "In any event, the discipline was good for all of us, even if at times we had inner feelings that perhaps our teachers were expecting rather too much in too short a while." The student body consisted of "a mixed company of the rough-and-ready type and the more refined and sensitive," all of whom got along. On the field there were plenty of sports to "work off the animal spirits," and in the chapel there was "great piety" with little "pietism akin to hypocrisy."[3]

O'Connell remained at St. Charles' for two and half years. According to his *Recollections*, midway through the third year he suffered "a very serious breakdown" from hitting the books too hard. Rather than risk his health, he opted to return home for rest and care, a decision blessed by the college president.[4] At least that was how O'Connell remembered it.

In later years, a Sulpician who was there at the time had a different recollection of the future cardinal's departure. Arsenius Vuibert recalled that O'Connell belonged to a group known to other students as the "Sewing Circle." On one occasion, the circle was satirized in poetry and the verse was posted on the bulletin board in the recreation hall. Incensed, O'Connell complained to the college president with the expectation that the culprit would be discovered and punished. Instead, the president encouraged O'Connell to let the matter drop, as did his confessor.[5] The young New Englander left the college never to return.

Though the truth about the motivation for his departure from St. Charles' is probably destined to escape history, historians do know that he came to detest the Sulpicians. If Vuibert's account is correct, O'Connell glossed over with genial recollections of fonder days what he considered as a youth to be unfair treatment at the hands of the Sulpicians. If O'Connell's memory is correct, Vuibert unfairly traced the root of the New Englander's later animosity to an unrequited slight against a lad. Certain to history is that the later friction between O'Connell and the Sulpicians was rooted in a difference over ecclesiology, that is, the theological understanding of the nature of the church.

O'Connell completed his post-secondary education at the Jesuit-run Boston College, to which he commuted daily by train from his home in Lowell. His teachers were Americans, rather than Frenchmen as at St. Charles'. Though he admired the latter in "a rather distant and awesome way," he found the former more congenial and possessed of broader vision and greater intellectual freedom.[6] As will be seen, his comparison of the two institutions at the time of his elevation to the cardinalate was dramatically more caustic and closer to his true feelings about the Sulpicians.

After O'Connell's graduation from college in 1881, he presented himself as a candidate for the priesthood to Archbishop John Williams of Boston, who sent him to Rome for theological studies at the American College, a residence house for students from the United States. The students attended classes at the Urban College of the Congregation for the Propagation of the Faith (commonly called Propaganda), the Vatican department in charge of mission countries in whose number America was still counted. In Rome, O'Connell developed a love for the center of Catholicism and made the acquaintance of two professors, Francesco Satolli and Antonio Agliardi. Later in life, he and Satolli became fast friends, and their relationship served the New Englander well.[7]

After ordination in 1884, O'Connell returned to Boston with "Rome . . . still tugging at my heart strings."[8] His first assignment took him to St. Joseph's church in Medford, where he served for two years, until his transfer to St. Joseph's in Boston's West End. There he ministered for nine. Hard work characterized his priesthood. For relaxation he enjoyed recapturing the experience of Italy. On days off, he and a friend from the American College pretended they were back in Rome. Hiring a coach to drive them around the milldam and Back Bay, they conversed in Italian "like a couple of cardinals taking their airing" in the Eternal City, and finished the day at the Hotel Victoria with dinner, complete with Chianti and fine cigars.[9]

These early years foreshadowed elements that serve in three ways as prologue to the chapters that follow. The first two were interrelated: O'Connell's trouble with the Sulpicians (and those they educated) and his identification with the Roman expression of Catholicism. In fact, the two were interchangeable. As will be seen, the Sulpicians favored the ecclesiastical rights and religious expressions of the local church over the centrist tendency that focused attention on the rights of the Vatican and the Roman expressions of Catholicism. Thus, O'Connell's anti-Sulpicianism and his Romanism were interdependent attitudes that would define his relationship to the American Catholic church.

The third element, ambition and the drive for self-improvement evident in his brothers, remained hidden in O'Connell during his early years. Expressed as worldliness in his mature years, these character traits would be no less defining of the youngest member of the family. They probably owed to an Irish middle-class desire for respectability amidst Yankee Brahmin society. In any case, allegations of impiety and lust for money pursued him throughout his episcopal career.

CHAPTER 1

The Ecclesiastical Milieu
Romanism Versus Americanism

HISTORIAN JAMES GAFFEY CORRECTLY OBSERVED that William Henry O'Connell's "unalterable ultramontanism . . . revealed the essence of the man."[1] Ultramontanism, meaning "beyond the mountains," refers to a nineteenth-century movement that focused the attention of European Catholics across the Alps to the papacy in Rome. Finding its earliest and longest lasting support among laypeople and priests, the movement sought to counter unwanted government interference with the independence of local bishops and local religious expression by emphasizing the pope's authority, and by extension the Roman curia's, over the entire church.[2]

At mid-century, the Vatican itself began fostering ultramontanism through a multifaceted strategy. It encouraged the proliferation of national seminaries in Rome where young men from around the world might imbibe the Roman view. It intervened in the affairs of local churches through papal nuncios (ambassadors to governments) and apostolic delegates (papal representatives to the hierarchies of nations). It sought to curtail the meeting of national councils of bishops. Finally, it promoted men to the episcopacy who were Roman-trained and/or tractable to Vatican views, while setting aside the candidates recommended by local bishops. Pope Pius IX's declaration of the doctrine of the Immaculate Conception in 1854 highlighted papal prerogative, and the definition of papal infallibility in 1870 solidified the movement. Historian Roger Aubert has noted that the desire of extreme ultramontanists to silence opposition to papal prerogative "led them to propagate a simplistic ecclesiology in which, for example, the Church was presented as 'the society of the faithful governed by the pope'. . . [in which] the teaching function of the bishops was limited to the transmission to the faithful of teaching handed down by the Holy See."[3]

Throughout life, O'Connell staunchly held to a rigid, centrist model of the church that focused on the papacy and sharply distinguished between the spiritual and temporal spheres. His first recorded public utterance on the subject came in a sermon on "The Supremacy of the Pope," delivered in 1895. In it, O'Connell summarized the teaching expounded by the First Vatican Council in the constitution *Pastor Aeternus* (*The Eternal Shepherd*, 1870), which set forth papal infallibility. He held that "in things spiritual" the pope possessed "authority and jurisdiction over the entire Church." This involved two separate ideas: first, that the Vatican was the center of religious unity, and, second, that it was the fountain of all spiritual authority. As the center of unity, the pope bound the faithful together in the family of Christ. "As the source of authority he alone impart[ed] either directly or indirectly all spiritual jurisdiction. He is the chief shepherd, all others from the lowliest to the highest are subject to his spiritual sway." This was the divinely ordained pattern of the church. "Whether we like it, or not; think it reasonable, or not . . . its existence is absolute."[4] In saying this, O'Connell voiced the current church teaching without exaggeration.

His application was less restrained, bordering on the simplism described by Aubert. O'Connell believed that a bishop must have his eyes riveted on Rome. At a celebration of his becoming a cardinal (1912), he enlarged on the spiritual and authoritative centrality of the papacy. The church's universality demanded that a bishop "every day of his life . . . feel that whatever he does has the approval of Rome." O'Connell saw himself as the embodiment of the ideal prelate, proclaiming "my filial devotion to the head of the Church has full possession of my mind and heart as the only defensible ground upon which to think or act in relation to my duty toward my Clergy and my people." "If today I were called upon to say why Christ's Vicar has lavished upon me so many and so great proofs of his affection and regard," he concluded, "the only answer I could give is this, that he has read the most secret motives of my heart and soul, the one mainspring which has guided me in all I have done or attempted to do, namely, the most simple and implicit confidence in the guidance of Peter's Successor, and the most absolute determination . . . to model my regime as a Christian bishop along the lines of his slightest wish in whatever concerned faith and morals, or the discipline of ecclesiastical life."[5]

O'Connell's willingness to take the pope's wish as command was a distinctive trait of the Boston prelate. Late in life he attributed all his success to obedience: "I performed what I had to do under the direction of those to whom I was responsible. In fact, like a good soldier, all my life I have accepted orders from my superiors and obeyed them faithfully to the best of my ability."[6]

He lived, with a notable lapse here and there, by the code of obedience and demanded it of others. The chain of command ran from pope to bishop to priest to people. "The Church," he reminded his flock in 1912, "is not a democracy. In it each member has his well-defined place. The great body of the faithful are the followers, the disciples of Christ. They hear and obey the law of Christ. They neither teach nor command. . . . In a word, the faithful are to be taught, to be led, to be fed."[7] The church was a divinely constructed pyramid with the pope at the peak and the laity at the base; everything operated from the top down. Laymen were receivers, acted upon and acted for, but not acting of themselves.

Confining the church's operation to the spiritual realm, O'Connell believed that Christ had founded it "to save souls and carry on His divine work in the world."[8] This had little or nothing to do with the secular sphere. Believing that "usually only harm comes to the Church from meddling irresponsibly with parties and politicians," O'Connell limited Catholic influence in politics to the defense of religious rights and forbade priests to mix in state affairs. The bishop alone had the authority to speak for the church in matters political; no cleric or layman was to take this duty upon himself.[9]

A final aspect of O'Connell's ecclesiology was the exalted nature of Roman education. A product of the Urban College in Rome and later rector of the American College there, O'Connell came to believe that study in the Eternal City imparted a purer form of doctrine than was elsewhere available. There, one imbibed quintessential Catholicism, untainted by national interests. "The Roman mind is the Church's mind and the mind of Christ," he wrote. "The Roman mind is neither

Italian, nor French, nor German, nor American. It is catholic." In his view, anyone who lived or studied in Rome without acquiring this mentality "must indeed be hopelessly dull."[10]

His attitude may have owed something to the Thomistic revival begun by Pope Leo XIII, who promoted the philosophy of Thomas Aquinas in an effort to secure Catholic theology against inroads by the modern philosophies of Immanuel Kant and Georg Hegel. O'Connell began studies soon after the pontiff declared Thomism the official system of the church and brought Professor Francesco Satolli from Perugia to spearhead the movement. The only textbooks allowed at the Propaganda College where American students attended class were Thomas Aquinas's *Summa Contra Gentiles* (*A Summary in Opposition to the Gentiles*) and *Summa Theologiae* (*A Summary of Theology*). In light of O'Connell's devotion to the papacy and the fact that Thomistic thought bore the stamp of papal approval, it is not surprising that he saw it as the "solid, substantial, and perennial" philosophy of the church, and identified it with true doctrine.[11]

Not every churchman in America shared O'Connell's vision. The early years of his priesthood witnessed the rise of the Americanist movement, led by such prelates as Archbishop John Ireland of St. Paul; Bishop John Keane, rector of The Catholic University of America; and Monsignor Denis O'Connell, rector of the American College in Rome. Sensing harmony between the principles of Catholicism and those of the United States, these men believed that the age of the Old World was about to give way to the age of the New: a world of democracy, individualism, activity, and social concern. America incarnated the future. If the universal Catholic church was to survive, it would have to adapt to the New World and the new age. The responsibility for guiding it along this path devolved on the American church.[12]

The clearest articulation of the Americanist platform came in Ireland's address entitled "The Mission of Catholics in America," delivered at the centennial celebration of the American hierarchy (1889). He declared that the work of the church during the next century was "to make America Catholic, and to solve for the Church the all-absorbing problems with which religion is confronted in the present age."

To accomplish this, the laity had to be in the forefront of intellectual, scientific, and social movements, thereby demonstrating the compatibility of the church with the age, while investing those currents with religion. Under the guidance of the Holy Spirit, Catholic laypeople were to live by the motto "'Dare and Do.'" "Layman need not wait for priest, nor priest for bishop, nor bishop for pope," declared Ireland. "Priests are officers, laymen are soldiers. . . . The soldier is not always near the officer, and he must be ready to act without waiting for the word of command. Laymen . . . must think, work, organize, read, speak, act, as circumstances demand."[13] Such a Spirit-filled laity, acting when necessary without the guidance of the hierarchy, clearly ran counter to O'Connell's understanding of how the church was to operate.

Ireland considered America's conversion of paramount importance because the country was "a providential nation." In this regard, he adopted the millenarianism of his contemporary non-Catholic countrymen, who believed that America was the redeemer nation. For them, to be Protestant and American was to be the best the world had to offer and bore with it the divinely imposed duty of uplifting less fortunate peoples by bringing to them pure, that is, Protestant, Christianity and the American way of life.[14]

For Ireland, to be Catholic and American was to be the best the church had to offer. America had a divine mission to bring two of its cherished values, democracy and the separation of church and state, to the Catholic world. The nation's aspirations and sense of liberty had cast their "spell across seas and oceans," thus preparing "distant continents for the implanting of American ideas and institutions." "Ours is essentially the age of democracy," declared Ireland. "The days of princes and of feudal lords are gone. Woe to religion where this fact is not understood! He who holds the masses, reigns."[15]

While the church must woo the common citizen, it could ignore governments. Because the U.S. Constitution precluded any state interest in religion, the Americanists viewed the separation of church and state as ideal. There could be no concordat between Washington and Rome whereby the church bartered concessions to the government in return for favored status. In the United States, the church remained free to be itself, sacrificing nothing. What was good for the American church was good for the church universal. So believed Ireland and the other Americanists.[16]

Their belief, however, ran counter to then official Catholic teaching, which opposed the notion that the church and state could or should be separated. Ironically, early ultramontanists had also espoused the separation of church and state, an ideal not formally embraced by Catholicism until the Second Vatican Council (1962–1965).[17]

A final element of the Americanist program was assimilation. Although Ireland upheld that the American church must be "as Catholic as in Jerusalem or Rome," its "garments may be colored to suit the environment." "Americans have no longing for a Church with a foreign aspect," he said, "they will not submit to its influence." This meant two things: the church must adapt to society if it hoped to convert the nation, and immigrant Catholics must adapt to the American church.[18]

The movement received quiet but strong support from the Sulpician community in the United States, especially from Alphonse Magnien, rector of St. Mary's Seminary in Baltimore. The Sulpicians found the tenets of Americanism an appealing substitute for their traditional Gallicanism, i.e., the defense of the rights of the local French church against the those of the Vatican, eclipsed in 1870 by the definition of papal infallibility. The movement also enjoyed the support of the Paulist Fathers, an American religious community founded by the convert Isaac Hecker, whose thought on the church influenced the Americanism of both Ireland and Keane.[19] Although Rome initially took a benign view of the movement, a series of Americanist accommodations involving ethnicity, parochial schools, and labor, turned the Vatican cautious.

While the Americanists sensed harmony between the principles of the church and those of the nation, Archbishop Michael Corrigan of New York experienced uneasiness. Destined to become the leader of the conservatives, he was a man on the horns of a dilemma—"which first: Roman or American?"—an issue he never satisfactorily resolved.[20] Certainly, the church always adapted to local customs, but this meant something different to him from what it meant to the Americanists. Rather than conform to America and thereby lead the world into a new age, the church was to safeguard the nation's future by acting as a brake against the excesses of democracy. In effect, Corrigan implicitly denied concord between the assumptions of America and those of the church.[21]

As early as 1870 Thomas Scott Preston, later Corrigan's vicar general, articulated the heart of the issue: "Here in New York we are loyal Catholics. We are devoted to the Holy See, we do not believe in the great folly and absurdity of Americanizing the Catholic Church. We propose to Catholicize America."[22] Supporters of Corrigan included Charles McDonnell, his secretary and later bishop of Brooklyn, Bishop Bernard McQuaid of Rochester, and Archbishop Frederick Katzer of Milwaukee. It should be noted that while conservatives like Corrigan and McQuaid upheld papal authority (as did the Americanists), they could be critical of and cynical about it,[23] unlike O'Connell whose excessive ultramontanism made him practically unique in the hierarchy.

While in Rome during the winter of 1887, the Americanists began to implement their program, sparking a division in the upper echelon of American Catholicism described by historian R. Emmett Curran as "the War of the Prelates."[24] They received the warm support of James Gibbons, archbishop of Baltimore, recently named a cardinal and in Rome to receive the red hat. On the advice of Denis O'Connell, he took possession of his titular church with a panegyric to liberty and the American separation of church and state.[25]

The Americanists then aided the Vatican in confronting three problems facing the American church. First, Gibbons forestalled an attempt by German-American Catholics, who felt subjugated to Irish-American bishops, to have German vicars general appointed in dioceses with large Teutonic populations.[26] Because a vicar general was a priest named by a local bishop usually to exercise the same authority as the bishop himself, the proposal seemed to the Americanists as an attempt to establish a German national church within the American church, something that offended their accommodative sensibilities. Gibbons then prevented the Vatican from condemning the Knights of Labor, an early union, in part on the ground that the future belonged to the people, whom the church must not alienate.[27]

Finally, he intervened to keep off the index of forbidden books

Henry George's *Progress and Poverty*, which proposed to cure destitution by replacing all taxes with a single one levied against the rent accruing to property owners who benefitted from the unearned income they received from renters paying ever-increasing sums as property values rose. The single-tax theory had the support of Father Edward McGlynn, a freethinking priest in the archdiocese of New York. Dedicated to social reform, opposed to parochial schools, and committed to an American Catholicism that had to be different from what it was in the Old World, McGlynn was considered a radical by Corrigan. Gibbons argued that condemnation was unnecessary because the "practicable" people of the United States would consign George's "bizarre and impractical" theory to the trash heap.[28] Corrigan interpreted the new cardinal's prevention of the condemnation of George's idea as support of McGlynn.

The issue that most bitterly divided Americanists and conservatives was the school question. Both sides recognized the need for religious education but differed over the means of attainment. Arguing that the state had only a limited right to educate and viewing public schools as hostile to Catholicism, conservatives sought to keep Catholic children in parochial institutions. Conceding the state's role in schooling and taking a benign view of public education, Americanists devised ways to turn it to Catholic advantage. In 1890, Ireland told the National Education Association that public schools should be the only ones in the land. He proposed two plans for making Catholic schools public. The first was to allow Protestantism to be taught in state schools, provided that the state paid for the secular education of children in parochial ones. The second called for leasing church schools to the state system. In the latter plan, such "public" schools were to be open to all children, but the teachers were to be qualified Catholics, and religion was to be taught before or after class hours.[29]

The speech raised the hackles of conservative Irish and German prelates. The Germans were especially disturbed because Ireland's concession of the state's right to educate seemed an endorsement of Wisconsin's Bennett Law mandating compulsory attendance at a school within the district (preventing children from obtaining a parochial education if that meant crossing district lines) and making English the language of instruction in all schools, both public and private. The German bishops in the state hotly contested the legislation as a threat to Catholic schools, especially German-language ones.[30]

Ireland fueled the controversy by leasing the parochial schools in Faribault and Stillwater, Minnesota, to the local boards of education, thereby touching off an angry debate. In spring 1892, the Vatican declared that the Faribault-Stillwater system could be tolerated, but the decision settled nothing. The Americanists considered it a complete vindication of Ireland's position; the conservatives interpreted it as sanctioning a particular exception to the norm that children should attend parish schools. In the fall, Leo XIII sent Archbishop Francesco Satolli to speak to the American archbishops about the school question. He laid before them fourteen points written by Denis O'Connell, which encouraged religious instruction for children in public institutions, upheld the Faribault-Stillwater plan, and declared that the Holy See desired "the joint action of civil and ecclesiastical authorities" in the promotion of public schools. Although the American archbishops refused to endorse the propositions, Satolli sent them to the pope for approval. When it became clear that the majority of the hierarchy objected to them, Leo issued a letter which, while upholding the points, declared that they did not abrogate the fact that each parish ought to have a parochial school.[31]

Tactically, the school fight was a draw. Strategically, it was a defeat for the Americanists because Ireland had managed to alienate most of his episcopal colleagues. Moreover, Leo had used Satolli's visit as the opportunity to appoint him apostolic delegate to the hierarchy of the United States, thus extending the ultramontane hand into American church affairs.

By early 1895, the Roman tide had ebbed from the Americanists. In January, Leo sent the letter *Longinqua Oceani* (*The Vast Expanse of Ocean*) to the United States. Intended to ease tensions in the hierarchy, it was decidedly conservative. The pope expressed caution about issues dear to the Americanists. After praising the separation of church and state embodied in the U.S. Constitution, he warned that "it would be very erroneous to draw the conclusion that in America is to be sought the type of the most desirable status of the Church, or that it would be universally lawful or expedient for State and Church to be, as in America, dissevered and divorced." The pontiff went on to urge Catholics to hold themselves apart from American society. "Unless forced by necessity to do otherwise," said Leo, "Catholics ought to prefer to associate with Catholics, a course which will be very conducive to the safeguarding of their faith." This admonition dealt a blow to the accommodativeness of the Americanists.[32]

It should be noted that, although the letter took aim at cherished Americanist values with the obvious intention of restraining their implementation, it was not a condemnation of them. The ideas of the Americanists were decades ahead of their time. Seventy years after *Longinqua Oceani*, the Second Vatican Council (1962–1965) advocated that a spirit-filled laity engage with the world, the very concept promoted by the Americanists. Moreover, the council endorsed the separation of church and state and described the benefits to be enjoyed by the church from such a separation in terms almost identical to those uttered by Archbishop Ireland.[33]

Given the ultramontane bent of William O'Connell's ecclesiology, his attitude toward the Americanist controversy of the late 1890s readily followed. Recalling the conflict some thirty-five years after it occurred, he saw it as a regrettable tragedy that might have been avoided by discretion on both sides. His sympathies, however, clearly lay with the conservatives. The leader of that bloc, Archbishop Corrigan, "had had the advantage of schooling and training in Rome" and so "knew his books and his place." He also knew from his European experience that when churchmen meddled in politics, it often led to a weakening of ecclesiastical liberties. Corrigan wanted his clergy to tend to their own business, to stick to their parishes and care for souls. "This was certainly sound doctrine and sound Catholic practice which, if more widely understood and more generally practiced by the ecclesiastics of the time, would have spared the Church in America many disagreeable and even dangerous incidents."[34]

The Americanists, though "excellent prelates of high character," were men of a different temperament. "They were distinctly public men," who thought that an enthusiastic show of Americanism would lessen much of the prejudice against the church. They lacked, however, the "erudition or innate Roman and Catholic sense and feeling" of the conservatives.[35] Though sincere and conscientious in purpose, they trusted too much in politics. "Their point of view, whether of doctrine or administration, was very much colored by too close proximity to Washington and to the methods and measures proper enough in Washington, but not quite in place in an Episcopal See." For a short time the apostolic delegate, Archbishop Satolli, O'Connell's former mentor, had fallen under their sway. "Once he had freed himself from [their] biased advice he was big enough to recognize his mistaken judgment and to make magnanimous amends for it."[36] He befriended the conservatives and worked against the Americanists.

These reflections on the Americanist controversy, however, were the thoughts of a septuagenarian, colored by a sense of detachment that comes with distance and age. In fact, O'Connell's rise to power owed directly to the Americanist conflict and the use he could make of it. It was the sacking of Denis O'Connell as rector of the American College that opened the way for the ascendancy of William O'Connell. As will be seen, the latter would use his anti-Americanist views as the fulcrum to lift himself onto the archiepiscopal chair of Boston over those with a more legitimate claim to it.

CHAPTER 2

Roman Son Rising

IN 1895, FATHER WILLIAM O'CONNELL, assistant pastor of St. Joseph's parish in Boston's West End, got the chance to return to the Eternal City. The war of the prelates was in full swing, and the Vatican, initially friendly to the Americanists, had begun a shift toward their opponents. The first casualty of the change in attitude was Denis J. O'Connell, rector of the North American College. An Americanist partisan, he incurred the disfavor of Archbishop Michael Corrigan who collected a dossier against him and sent it to Rome. Acting on the information, Pope Leo XIII demanded O'Connell's resignation.[1]

In October, the Board of Governors of the American College drafted a *terna* (a recommendation of three names in order of preference) to fill the vacancy. Those nominated were the Reverends Thomas Kennedy of Philadelphia, Nathan Mooney of Chicago, and William O'Connell of Boston, in that order. Dissatisfied with the *terna*, which seemed a scheme by the Americanists to promote Kennedy, Archbishop Corrigan and Bishop Charles McDonnell of Brooklyn urged Rome to compromise by selecting a neutral candidate. The Vatican chose O'Connell. Although sources, both published and unpublished, have claimed that Francesco Satolli, the Bostonian's former professor who was then apostolic delegate to the United States, was responsible for his appointment, Satolli himself declared that he was unfamiliar with O'Connell, and so recommended Kennedy for the post. Once in office, O'Connell pursued a policy of strict neutrality on Americanism.[2]

Had Americanism remained a conflict internal to the Catholic church in the United States, it may have attracted no further attention from the Vatican. Unfortunately, the movement became internationalized in two distinct ways: the first was a French translation of the biography of Father Isaac Hecker, and the second was the Spanish-American War. Hecker founded the Congregation of St. Paul, commonly called the Paulists, a community established to win Protestant

Americans to Catholicism. Three years after his death in 1888, one of his disciples published a biography of the founder that unintentionally did injustice to Hecker's spiritual teaching, leaving it vulnerable to charges of error regarding such matters as the nature of virtues and the guidance of the Holy Spirit. Archbishop John Ireland wrote the introduction to the book, praising Hecker as the flower of the American priesthood. In 1897, the biography, which carried an *imprimatur* by Corrigan, appeared in translation in Europe, touching off a violent reaction by conservative Catholics in France who denounced Hecker's teaching as heretical. They viewed the book as yet another weapon used by their liberal Catholic countrymen to pressure them into reconciliation with the French Republic on the ground that the church had fared so well under the American republic.[3]

Simultaneously, the United States was drawing closer to conflict with Spain over the revolution in Cuba, which threatened American business interests on that island. The Cuban question became interlocked with American expansionism in the Far East by virtue of Spain's possession of the Philippine Islands and America's need of a foothold in that region to protect its interests in Chinese markets. The seizure of the Philippines was an integral part of the United States' war plan in the event of hostilities with Spain. In early 1898, conflict seemed certain, pitting the Old World against the New, Catholic Spain versus Protestant America, with Americanism in the balance. The queen regent asked her ambassador at the Vatican, Rafael Merry del Val, to urge the pope to intervene to prevent war. The Vatican called on Archbishop Ireland to intercede with President William McKinley to forestall a rupture between the two countries. Through intense negotiations, Ireland was able to secure belated concessions from Spain, but the desire for war by McKinley and the American public was too strong to be denied. On 25 April 1898, Congress obliged by declaring that hostilities had existed since the start of that month. Ireland's failure further lowered his prestige and the Americanist cause at the Vatican. Though nativists in the United States alleged that American Catholics would support Spain in the fight, Americanists and anti-Americanists united in patriotic support of the war.[4] As will be seen, however, O'Connell's patriotism would later be called into question.

In February 1899, Pope Leo XIII attempted to quiet the controversy then raging in France over the biography of Hecker by condemning the distorted view of his spirituality with the letter *Testem Benevolentiae* (*A Witness of Good Will*). The pontiff was careful to avoid stating that anyone in the United States actually subscribed to the condemned doctrines. Indeed, the principal promoters of the Americanist movement —Ireland, Cardinal James Gibbons, and Archbishop John Keane— assured him that the erroneous teachings had never existed in America and that it was unfortunate that the term "Americanism" had become associated with them. With the papal condemnation, O'Connell abandoned his neutral stance toward the controversy and sided openly with Corrigan and the Vatican.[5]

Like other national colleges in Rome, the American College was essentially a residence for seminarians from various dioceses in the United States who attended one of the Vatican universities. Functioning more like a dean of students than a college president, the rector was nonetheless the chief American cleric at the Vatican. During his five years as rector, O'Connell cultivated a network of potent friends, including the two Merry del Vals, the father Rafael, Spanish ambassador to the Vatican, and his English-born son Monsignor Raphael, one of four private secretaries of the pope and special papal envoy to Canada (1897); Monsignor Sante Tampieri, a functionary in Propaganda; Monsignor Antonio Savelli-Spinola, a consultor in Propaganda; and Satolli who in 1896 was named a cardinal and returned to Rome. O'Connell also circulated in the wealthy American colony there, where he befriended a number of influential people, including Francis Mac-Nutt, a man of independent means who had held minor posts in American diplomatic delegations and whom Leo XIII had recently pressed into Vatican service. He soon became an ardent promoter of the rector's advancement. As the ranking American ecclesiastic at the Vatican, O'Connell entertained wealthy visitors from the United States and arranged papal audiences for them. One visitor in particular would play a role later in O'Connell's life: Benjamin Franklin Keith, who made his fortune in vaudeville and befriended the rector. This relationship would prove to be a financial boon. One that was destined to become an albatross was O'Connell's friendship with Dr. William Dunn, a former parishioner at St. Joseph's in the West End and a notorious homosexual in an age when such notoriety was far from common. Late in O'Connell's rectorship, Dunn went to Europe to join his friend on a walking tour of Switzerland and Bavaria.[6]

O'Connell was an able administrator of the college. During his tenure he doubled the enrollment, enhanced the financial base, purchased a new summer villa, and procured benefactions from his philanthropic acquaintances in the American colony.[7] For these reasons, a rumor published in the *St. Louis Review* that he intended to resign the rectorship came as a complete surprise to his friend Cardinal Satolli. The latter confessed reluctance to believe the story because the Vatican was well satisfied with O'Connell's administration and because the rector himself knew the bright advantages of tending the college's helm. "Therefore," concluded Satolli, "except for a promotion to a higher dignity, I repeat I cannot believe that the news is true." To set his mind at rest, he asked O'Connell to let him know the facts.[8] Whatever may have been the response, a higher dignity, one that Satolli had a hand in gaining, removed O'Connell from the college and sent him back to New England.

In 1900, the see of Portland, Maine, fell vacant. The consultors of the diocese drafted a *terna* of candidates, and the bishops of the ecclesiastical province of Boston drafted another, each group naming the same three men, but not in the same order. O'Connell's name was not among them, nor was Michael O'Brien's, the administrator of the diocese. Backed by restive French-Canadian Catholics whose candidate he became, O'Brien advised Rome that the consultors' *terna* was void because their terms of office had expired, and he put forward his own nomination.[9]

In January 1901, Satolli presented the case to Propaganda, which decided to defer the appointment and seek additional information from the apostolic delegate, Archbishop Sebastiano Martinelli, O.S.A. The latter reported that there were serious questions about the worthiness of some of the candidates, including O'Brien. When Satolli laid this new intelligence before Propaganda, its members, including Cardinal Antonio Agliardi (another of O'Connell's former Roman professors), set aside the proposed candidates and elected the rector of the American College to the see of Portland.[10] On taking possession of the diocese, O'Connell "solemnly" promised that he would spend all his energy "to forge a tighter and stronger link of union and attachment to the Holy See."[11]

Romanism was one hallmark of his administration; another derived from his years as rector of the American College. O'Connell's connection with the high society of the American colony gave him what one biographer describes as a "veneer of aristocratic self-importance, a quality which eventually became an integral part of his personality."[12] O'Connell possessed a rich baritone voice and cultivated a cultured, upper-class style of speech. As bishop of Portland, he combined a cosmopolitan image with an aggressive, public style of leadership that signaled to Yankee Brahmins the arrival of Catholics. While Americanists and their sympathizers, like Ireland, Gibbons, and even Archbishop John Williams of Boston, preferred an accommodative approach toward society, O'Connell's attitude was militant: the time had come for Catholics to claim the place in society to which their numbers and the social standing of their elite rightfully entitled them. In part, this meant that the local bishop must maintain a high profile in the press and consort with those of equal station in the political and social realms.[13] If this was true for a small see like Portland, it would be even more so for the archdiocese of Boston.

Initially the forging of a tighter link with Rome meant securing a cardinal's hat for Archbishop Corrigan, the leader of the conservatives in the Americanist controversy. O'Connell and MacNutt worked together to this end, but their efforts came to grief because of Corrigan's unwillingness to advance his own cause. His untimely death in 1902 ended the campaign.[14]

Although Corrigan never received the honor some felt he deserved, O'Connell seemed destined for greatness, at least in the eyes of his Roman friends. Tampieri believed that the American church needed bishops and cardinals who, without prejudice to national characteristics, knew "how to make the life of papal Rome live." He hoped that Providence would soon smile on O'Connell and make him a cardinal.[15] Father Giuseppe Marucchi, a member of Satolli's household, considered O'Connell "one of the most precious pearls of the American episcopate" and predicted that "the day will not be long distant on which . . . [he would] ascend even higher in the Catholic hierarchy."[16] Indeed, within two years Roman fortune smiled on O'Connell.

In the spring of 1903, the Vatican considered him for a promotion. As part of the treaty that concluded the Spanish-American War (America's venture into imperialism), the United States acquired the Philippine Islands, so Rome wanted American replacements for the Spanish bishops there. President Theodore Roosevelt asked Cardinal Gibbons to have the Vatican appoint Father Thomas Hendrick, a priest of Rochester, New York, as archbishop of Manila. Gibbons obliged, but Rome had other ideas. It offered the archdiocese to O'Connell, and the apostolic delegate, Archbishop Diomede Falconio, summoned him to Washington, D.C., to inform him of the news. After discussing the matter with the delegate, O'Connell declined the post.[17]

He explained his refusal in a letter to the pontiff. Though "greatly touched" by the offer, he felt compelled to decline it for two reasons. First, whoever might be named as archbishop, he wrote, "must be a person acceptable to the American Government and in favor of its politics in those islands." Here was the rub. "In this regard," continued O'Connell, "my nomination to Manila would, without doubt, give way to stern comments, cause problems, and would upset the civil authorities who know very well my ideas on the war between Spain and America, so that sooner or later this would cause great difficulties because I never kept my sympathy for Spain a secret, openly stating that the war was unjust and ill-omened; consequently I was widely criticized for not being patriotic."[18] This reason was at once a candid and disingenuous admission. Candid because during the war O'Connell was in Rome as rector of the American College and, as will be seen, had taken the Spanish side. Disingenuous because it is doubtful that few, if any, in the United States knew then or at the time of his writing about his feelings regarding the war. There is no evidence that he was ever criticized for lack of loyalty prior to the offer of Manila. Perhaps, however, that offer sparked interest in the matter of his patriotism, which would soon be called into question.

O'Connell's second motive for declining Manila was closer to home and, in his estimation, "more important than the first, and also much more delicate and difficult to explain." Recently, Williams had announced that he would be asking Rome to appoint a coadjutor archbishop with right of succession to assist him. O'Connell stated that "Williams had indirectly, if not directly, let people understand that he would nominate me, whom he considers most suitable." As will be seen, the matter was otherwise. "He has many times made it plain," continued O'Connell, "that he has great confidence in me and holds me in high esteem, asking my opinion about how to solve important problems and adopting my stance instead of that of other Bishops. In fact, Your Holiness well knows that none of them has been educated in Rome and therefore they are not well informed on how to deal with the Holy See or with the various Congregations."[19] Here was O'Connell in his first tentative effort at playing the Roman card. He would soon become a bold practitioner.

When the letter of refusal reached Rome, MacNutt reported on the impression it made. "Your first reason," he told O'Connell, "was excellent and sufficient and has not been misunderstood as far as I can see. I have explained, what they seemed already to grasp, that there was a very numerous and important element in our country which had always opposed expansion, annexations and imperialism generally." In fact, a prominent, if eclectic, group of Americans had formed an anti-imperialist league, though O'Connell was not a member nor had he openly opposed the war to subdue the Philippine insurrection against American rule that lasted from 1899 to 1902. With regard to O'Connell's second reason for refusing Manila, MacNutt chided him for stating that he "might be wanted as coadjutor in Boston," especially since Williams had yet to submit a request for one. "I have not at all discovered," he hastened to add, "that this has been taken amiss. . . . You did very well to refuse Manila and both Savelli[-Spinola] & Merry [del Val] are of this opinion." He assured O'Connell that if his name was on the *terna* for coadjutor of Boston, there was "little doubt but that it will be chosen."[20]

Several months later O'Connell's Roman stock rose. Pope Leo died, and his successor Pius X chose Archbishop Merry del Val for secretary of state. When the new secretary received the red hat in November, O'Connell had two cardinal patrons in Rome: Satolli and the power-fully placed Merry del Val. The latter, moreover, had been a classmate with MacNutt at the Academy for Noble Ecclesiastics where the pair had studied for the priesthood until the American decided that he lacked a vocation. The two were friends, and the new cardinal took the layman into his confidence. With this happy turn of events, MacNutt informed O'Connell that if his name was on the *terna* for Boston, "it will not be my fault if you are not named to the desired place. If your name is *not* on it, then I hope all the names that are will be poor ones."[21]

In September 1903, Archbishop Williams finally submitted the long-awaited request for a coadjutor archbishop. A month later, Prop-aganda approved and asked for nominations. Williams quietly let it be known to his suffragans that O'Connell was not to be a choice.[22]

The bishop of Portland's Vatican friends weighed in on the situa-tion. Satolli worried that factions were forming in New England that might hinder "a healthy election." Tampieri feared a repeat of the Americanist controversy and warned O'Connell that "there is a very great need among you for bishops animated by the spirit of Rome. . . . I always hear you talked about here in this sense, that is, that you are pointed out and represented as more Roman than American. *Et hoc est bonum* [and this is good], in view of the burning question of so-called Americanism and the so-called Americanizers, [who are] anything but disappearing from the field." He promised to work on behalf of O'Con-nell and the church in America.[23]

Then in February 1904, with his hope for the coadjutorship of Boston in the balance, O'Connell's patriotism during the Spanish-American War came into public question. The New York *World* reported that during the conflict, O'Connell had given then Monsignor Merry del Val 1,000 *lire* to outfit a Spanish battleship, a charge that amounted to treason. The Portland prelate denied the account and had politicians send ringing endorsements of his patriotism to the apostolic delegate, who may have been confused by the fact that just a year earlier O'Connell had refused Manila because of his open sympathy for Spain during the late war. O'Connell then began tracking down the perpetrator of the rumor. He suspected Denis O'Connell, who at the time was rector of The Catholic University of America. William O'Connell believed that the story rested on an incident that had occurred after the American victory at Santiago de Cuba in July 1898. When his students rejoiced over the outcome of the battle during classes at the Urban College, he admonished them. One went to Denis O'Connell, then vicar of Cardinal Gibbons's titular church Santa Maria in Trastevere, and complained that William O'Connell had forbidden displays of patriotism and had himself declined to celebrate the victory. The rector later denied the student's accusation and urged Denis O'Connell to confirm that this incident was the foundation of the charge of disloyalty.[24] The latter never responded.

William O'Connell had the right man but the wrong episode. Denis O'Connell had learned from Cardinal Serafino Vannutelli that the rector had given Ambassador Merry del Val, the monsignor's father, a contribution for a Spanish hospital ship, perhaps in the amount of $200, a sum with purchasing power of about $6,300 in 2006. The cardinal said that the elder Merry del Val showed him the check with the declaration: "There is a real American." After the Spanish defeat at Manila, William O'Connell sent the Merry del Vals a letter of sympathy and a bouquet of flowers. On various occasions throughout the war he gave similar proofs of his devotion to the family and Spain. These were the incidents that caused Denis O'Connell to believe that William O'Connell put Roman friendship above patriotism.[25] Denis's silence in response to William's queries allowed the item to die. With no controversy, there was no news.

On 4 April 1904, the consultors and permanent rectors of the archdiocese of Boston drafted their *terna* for coadjutor. In order of preference they listed Bishop Matthew Harkins of Providence, Bishop John Brady, auxiliary of Boston, and Monsignor William Byrne, vicar general of the archdiocese. Three days later the bishops of the Boston province, with

O'Connell acting as secretary, drew up their *terna*. When Archbishop Williams declared he had no preference, the suffragans nominated Harkins, Father W. P. McQuaid, and Father Richard Neagle, a former chancellor of the archdiocese. O'Connell recorded that he himself "for good and legitimate reasons took no action in the election."[26]

A native of Boston born to Irish immigrant parents, Harkins had attended Holy Cross College in Worcester. He then studied for the priesthood at Douai University in Belgium and St. Sulpice Seminary in Paris. On his return to Boston, he developed a lifelong friendship with Archbishop Williams. Harkins became bishop of Providence in 1887 and distinguished himself there because of his solicitude for immigrants, orphans, the infirm, and the elderly.[27]

Two weeks after the suffragans met, Williams wrote to the apostolic delegate, Archbishop Falconio, in support of Harkins's selection for the post. Nine other archbishops around the country did the same.[28] Obviously, Harkins was the overwhelming choice of those whose ranks he had been nominated to join.

Piqued at being passed over, O'Connell took counteraction and framed the issue in ideological terms: Americanism versus ultramontanism. To Cardinal Merry del Val, he wrote, "The one frank and avowed motive actuating these men was to keep off the *terna* at all costs any name which stood for Rome, for Roman views and for Roman sympathies. . . . Boston is at this moment in the balance between Rome and her enemies." He offered to go to the Vatican to prove the charge.[29] O'Connell apparently made the same allegations to his friend Savelli-Spinola, who responded that his letter "only confirms all of our fears." The Vatican priest recommended against O'Connell's coming to Rome because it "could be unjustly interpreted." Rather, he informed O'Connell that Satolli was on his way to visit America. "Therefore it is better not to move," said the priest, "but to tell *everything* to Card. Satolli, who *is so well disposed* toward the Bishop of Portland."[30]

Tampieri read the news about the proposed candidates "with a sense of true disgust, even regret." He commiserated with O'Connell for what he must be suffering on account of the hostility directed at him because of his Romanism, something "that should not even be considered possible." Tampieri told his friend that he should regard it "an honor and a consolation" to be "fought against, charged with what constitutes your praise, and which more and more recommends you to the esteem and consideration of Propaganda and of the Holy See." He advised O'Connell to "be at peace, because you have here in Rome a great appreciation at the highest levels."[31]

On 18 May 1904, Falconio requested an explanation for O'Connell's refusal to speak or vote at the meeting of the suffragans.[32] The bishop responded that prior to the meeting of permanent rectors and consultors, a group led by William Byrne had agreed upon the conditions for candidacy and had drafted a tentative slate of nominees. Only men who promised to continue the status quo in the archdiocese were to be proposed. Because O'Connell had indignantly refused to make such a promise, his name was stricken from the list. He could support none of the men on the bishops' *terna* because their views, health, or age made them unsuitable for the office.[33]

O'Connell made his case directly to Propaganda in a document that commented on the worthiness of each of those nominated, tarring the principal contenders with the brush of Americanism. He believed that Harkins was unsafe because of "his open sympathy . . . with what is called the Americanistic feeling and sentiment, which has clearly defined itself as nationalistic in spirit, and is openly, if not antipathetic, certainly apathetic to everything emanating from Rome, other than an article of Faith." O'Connell said that his own name did not appear on the *terna* because both Byrne and Neagle had lobbied at the priests' meeting for candidates who would "'keep Rome out.'" According to O'Connell, Byrne then asked him to wield influence at the Vatican to secure the coadjutorship for him, with the promise that he would later return the favor. O'Connell refused. So Byrne entered into such an agreement with Harkins.[34]

As for Neagle, he was "rabidly inimical to everything Roman." At the priests' conference, he publicly urged that they keep O'Connell off the *terna* and avowed privately to some that "'this time they would choose the bishop—not Rome.'" Neagle's hatred of the American College and its alumni was well known, wrote O'Connell. He found it horrifying to think that such a man might be appointed archbishop of Boston, a position that would make him an ex officio trustee of the college. As for the other nominees, they were either too old, too feeble, or too ordinary to be considered for the post. O'Connell urged Propaganda to take time in deciding and suggested that it delay any decision until Cardinal Satolli returned from visiting the United States.[35]

O'Connell's allegations about the Americanism of the candidates are hardly credible. Historians have never associated Harkins with the Americanist movement. As for Byrne, he was O'Connell's former pastor at St. Joseph's in the West End. The worst O'Connell ever said publicly about him was that he was an intellectual who bored his curates at table with monologues about the most recent books he had read. It is unlikely, if not preposterous, that a seventy-two year old man, who, if O'Connell is to be believed, opposed Roman intervention in America, would have sought the assistance of the Vatican's son to gain a position that he would use to subvert papal power. With regard to Neagle, a former chancellor of the archdiocese, little is known or can be verified. But if what O'Connell said of Harkins and Byrne is suspect, the same can be inferred about the information regarding Neagle.[36]

O'Connell's supporters, some of them his former students at the American College, also complained to the delegate and Rome. Father Patrick Daly of St. Francis de Sales parish cautioned Falconio that there was an episcopal plot afoot. Stung by O'Connell's appointment to Portland, five suffragans had met in Vermont in the summer of 1903, said Daly, and decided on a plan to keep him out of Boston. They swore to "have 'home rule,' not 'Rome rule.'" Within weeks, Daly argued the same case to Cardinals Satolli, Merry del Val, and Girolamo Gotti, Prefect of Propaganda.[37]

Father Patrick Supple, curate of St. Peter's church, corroborated O'Connell's story that a clique of powerful pastors, known more for their business than their spiritual acumen, intended a continuation of the status quo to the detriment of archdiocesan interests. St. John's Seminary in Brighton, run by the Suplician priests, was "notoriously infected with the views of higher [biblical] criticism," leaving the students more versed in Protestantism than Catholicism; numerous

Italian immigrants lacked pastors or a bishop who cared about them; laypersons, mainly second-generation Irish who had achieved a degree of social standing, wanted a prelate who could command the dignity and respect for Catholics warranted by their station. None of the men on either *terna* was capable of meeting Boston's needs. Words, moreover, failed Supple in describing the depth of "Americanism which has penetrated here," the chief offender being Harkins. "'Keep Rome out' has been the cry," said the priest, and was the determining criterion in the formation of both *ternae*.[38]

Like Supple, Father John Cummins of Sacred Heart parish suggested that the Americanist controversy was not dead. Arguing that Archbishop Ireland was interfering with the election, Cummins asked Merry del Val if the church had two popes, one in Rome and the other in St. Paul.[39] Laymen, too, protested the omission of O'Connell from the *terna* and pleaded for a more vigorous style of leadership.[40]

To be sure, neither Williams nor his suffragans wanted O'Connell as the next archbishop of Boston. The aged Williams had put that word out through Harkins. Daly's allegation that the five suffragans (there were only five at the time, not counting O'Connell) had met in Vermont to plot against O'Connell, lacks substance. If true, Harkins would have to have been a participant, but he was abroad throughout the summer. Certainly, the old Americanist warhorse Archbishop Ireland was interested in the Boston succession, as was the Americanist sympathizer Archbishop Patrick Riordan of San Francisco. That the issue was Americanism, at least in the sense condemned by Pope Leo (a theological distortion of the movement), is unlikely. Rather, it seems that the prelates resented O'Connell's self-aggrandizement, his overweening attentiveness to Rome, and his preferential treatment by the Vatican without regard to the American hierarchy. In August 1904, Bishop-elect John Delany of Manchester, New Hampshire, who supported O'Connell, verified that the latter's desire to carry out Rome's "least behest" had moved the suffragans to "unreasonable animosity in his regard."[41]

Viewing the situation in broad terms, O'Connell's most recent biographer, James O'Toole, considers the Boston succession as a renewal of the liberal-conservative conflict that racked the church in the late nineteenth century. Both Ireland and Gibbons continued to promote certain cherished Americanist values like the harmony of Catholicism with democracy and the separation of church and state. Corrigan's death had left the conservatives without a captain. O'Connell stepped forward to fill that role by upholding a clearly articulated philosophy of papalism supported by Rome.[42] Moreover, there was a further concern, namely, whether to continue the laissez-faire, low-profile administration of Williams, a style described by Robert O'Leary, another of O'Connell biographers, as "an ecclesiastical throwback to the first half of the nineteenth century" and uncharacteristic of the centralization and forceful leadership taking shape in other large dioceses.[43]

O'Toole does not gloss over the fact that O'Connell's drive for Boston was first and foremost a naked grasp for power. "He had mastered the intricacies of church politics in a way no American before him ever had," he writes. "His long years in Rome had taught him the rules of the game. He accepted those rules on their own terms, and he played the game to win. The constant contacts with Vatican officials, the readiness to be seen as obedient to Rome's slightest wish, . . . and the denigration of his enemies—all displayed his willingness to use methods whose principal justification was that they were likely to succeed."[44]

Apparently, the accusations of O'Connell and his supporters had their effect. MacNutt informed him that even though the slate of nominees had not yet reached Rome, "the actual *terna* is considered *nil* here and the very least that can happen will be its rejection." The apostolic delegate, Falconio, who was bearing the document, was to arrive at Rome in early June. MacNutt predicted that depending on the delegate's report, Propaganda would either ask for a new slate or set the *terna* aside and make the appointment on its own. Satolli, he reported, was very active on O'Connell's behalf. Both MacNutt and Savelli-Spinola related that Cardinal Gotti, prefect of Propaganda and protector of the American College, described by conservative contemporaries as "a good man beyond parties," was intensely interested in the Boston succession. He wanted a man with both the Roman spirit and an interest in the college.[45]

Not leaving anything to chance, O'Connell smoothed his path in a variety of ways. He had sent a generous gift of money to Satolli. On the feast of the pope's namesake St. Pius V, O'Connell offered greetings to the holy father from one who had been "educated and ordained a priest in the Eternal City and for years rector of the Pontifical American College of Rome, consecrated in the cathedral of the bishop of Rome, and from that sacred place returning as bishop to this see of Portland, my heart, educated and reared more and more in an ardent devotion to the Holy See and to its great pontiff." He also sent, hand delivered by Falconio, a Peter's Pence collection of $3,000 ($61,700 in 2006 terms) to support papal causes, for which Pius rendered deep thanks. Through the good offices of Cardinal Gibbons, O'Connell had the pope make MacNutt a monsignor and appoint him one of four ranking papal chamberlains.[46]

In June 1904, Cardinal Satolli came to the United States as Pius X's envoy to the World Fair in St. Louis. From there, he journeyed to St. Paul for a visit with Archbishop Ireland and thence to Portland, via Newport, Rhode Island, to see O'Connell. Because Archbishop Williams was on vacation in New York, Satolli received no invitation to Boston. In mid-July, Ireland wired Byrne: "You make fatal mistake. He resents not being invited. Meanwhile others are working against Boston."[47] When Byrne belatedly sent the cardinal an invitation, it had to be forwarded to O'Connell's chancery office "so that it would intercept him in Portland." The invitation either went astray or was itself intercepted. Byrne waited in vain for a response. Meanwhile, O'Connell hosted a luncheon for Satolli, attended by several distinguished citizens and clergymen, and had his long awaited chance to discuss the Boston succession with his friend.[48]

On 27 July, Satolli departed Portland for Albany. Boston was "doomed to disappointment," reported the city's *Journal*, because he would not be coming to town, "due . . . to the fact that he had not received an official invitation from the Catholic authorities . . . which neglect, on their part, was keenly felt by his eminence." Byrne detected "a spice of malice" in the column. In the meantime, he sent a second invitation for delivery to Satolli through the chancery office in Albany. The cardinal replied that it was the first such communication he had received from Byrne. Unfortunately, he could not rearrange his engagements to accommodate a stop in Boston. Even though he subsequently extended his stay in the states an additional week, he failed to go there.[49]

Shortly before Satolli left America, Monsignor Thomas Kennedy, rector of the American College in Rome, informed Byrne that Propaganda intended to appoint Harkins coadjutor. Byrne put little stock in the news. In reporting on Satolli's itinerary, the *Boston Journal* said that "it has been given out officially that the appointment of a coadjutor will not be made until the return of Satolli to Rome."[50] This information proved to be correct. On 22 August 1904, while the cardinal was still at sea, Propaganda decided to defer a decision on the Boston succession. A month after returning to Rome, Satolli informed O'Connell that in his opinion the *terna* was dead and that rather than appoint a coadjutor, Propaganda would probably wait for Williams's demise.[51] Before news of the deferral reached New England, O'Connell departed on his routine visit to report to the Vatican on the state of his diocese, a trip he turned into a six-month sojourn in Rome. During this stay, MacNutt later recalled, "his nomination became as certain as anything could be in a world of uncertainties."[52]

Meanwhile, on 13 December 1904, Williams, Harkins, and several other suffragans urged the pope to take decisive action in the appointment of a coadjutor. Three days later the aged archbishop received notification of Propaganda's decision to defer settlement of the succession. The following day, Williams and his suffragans again petitioned the pontiff that if the *terna* was unsatisfactory, another be requested. In January 1905 Merry del Val notified them that their petition had been forwarded to Propaganda. There the matter lay for more than a year.[53]

In August 1905, the Holy See again singled out O'Connell for honors. Pius X appointed him papal envoy to Japan to report on the condition of the church there and to explore the possibility of opening diplomatic relations between Tokyo and the Vatican. The bishop departed in September with Fathers Patrick Supple and Charles Collins, and the three arrived in Japan the following month where they remained through November. After carrying out the mission, they headed for Rome via Indonesia, India, and the Suez Canal.[54]

With O'Connell out of the country, Williams and his suffragans begged Propaganda to name a coadjutor. According to accounts later related to Bishop Louis Walsh by those in Rome at the time of the appointment, Cardinal Gotti who presided over Propaganda made known to Williams his "intention . . . to follow the Terna" and elect Harkins as coadjutor archbishop. Gotti, however, fell ill, allegedly near death. At the same time O'Connell arrived in the Vatican fresh from his Japanese mission. He met several times with his old friend Cardinal Merry del Val and visited other strategically placed cardinals, including Serafino Vannutelli, Sebastiano Martinelli, Francesco Satolli, and Antonio Agliardi. Agliardi "spoke very plainly of [the] need of recompense" for O'Connell's services in Japan. Cardinal Vincenzo Vannutelli, Serafino's brother, later told Walsh that O'Connell had gone about proclaiming that he was the only Roman in America and that he alone understood the Vatican and could represent it in the United States. Said Vannutelli, O'Connell knew that that was the way to act. "It was an evil business."[55]

On 22 January 1906, in the absence of the ailing Gotti, Cardinal Martinelli, seconded by Agliardi and Satolli, nominated O'Connell for the coadjutorship of Boston, and Propaganda elected him. That evening, Merry del Val sent O'Connell word of his election, and the troika from Boston fell into rejoicing. Bishop Thomas Beaven of Springfield, Massachusetts, reported that a number of Vatican officials were astonished by the appointment, and rumors were circulating that it was the work of Merry del Val. Vincenzo Vannutelli, Father Alexis Orban, S.S., and Father Giovanni Genocchi later claimed that Satolli had maneuvered the appointment. Genocchi visited Pius X sometime after the fact, and the pontiff had told him, "It was against my wish, but Satolli pushed and I yielded." The acerbic Ella B. Edes, a longtime American correspondent at the Vatican and opponent of Americanism, reported to Bishop Bernard McQuaid of Rochester, New York: "I have no doubt that Pomposity [O'Connell] paid well, Falconio, Merry del Val, and especially, Satolli, and that they seized the moment when Cardinal Gotti is lying at point of death, to carry out their design." She thought that the bishops of New England ought to protest the appointment. In retrospect, the recovered Gotti thought it difficult, if not impossible, to know all the circumstances of the affair. Although he regretted the situaton, "it was a fact and irrevocable" and had to be accepted as such.[56]

News of the election made a painful impression on the hierarchy and Catholics of the Northeast. Bishop William Stang of Fall River told Falconio: "The consternation over Bp. O'Connell's appointment is great and dangerous here in New England. It is regarded as an affliction 'sans pareil [without equal].'" A priest of the "'orthodox'" segment of the Boston clergy wrote to Stang to urge that the bishops of the province petition the Vatican to rescind the appointment, gained as it was by the "'arbitrary & treacherous overturning of the established system of nominating Bishops in the United States.'" Perhaps over dramatically, Stang concluded: "The prestige of the Holy See is gone in New England. Yesterday I heard an eminent Catholic Lawyer talk of the affair as he would talk of *corrupt* politics."[57]

The appointment was especially painful to Archbishop Williams. Stang related that the aged prelate was "greatly disappointed & depressed by the news" and had declared to Harkins, "I did not think that Rome would treat me thus; I fully believed that I would be asked for *my* opinion before an appointment would be made."[58] Although prepared to receive anyone assigned by Rome, Williams had learned that the pope had been told that O'Connell's appointment would be pleasing to him. The archbishop was ready to sign a memorial to the contrary.[59]

In the end, Williams did no such thing. Ever the gentleman, he set personal feelings aside and gave his new coadjutor a warm reception. O'Connell arrived back in America in early March and went directly to see Williams. "I found him standing at his door awaiting me, with both hands outstretched towards me," he told Falconio, "and when he took them he pressed warmly and said much moved—'You are very welcome!'" The two agreed that O'Connell should remain as administrator of Portland until the *terna* for his successor was prepared.[60]

A movement was soon underway to petition the archbishops of the country to protest O'Connell's appointment. When Archbishop Riordan counseled against such action, a plan was formed to have the Boston suffragans do it. Monsignor Byrne turned to Stang for help, but the latter refused on the ground that Williams should take the initiative. When Williams failed to act, Stang sent Pius X a memorial "in the name of all the suffragans of the province (except the Bishop of Manchester [Delany]) and with many Archbishops and Bishops of North America in agreement," urging that in the future if Propaganda deemed "it prudent to pass over the names presented by the Bishops and priests, no new names, on which the Bishops have had no opportunity of expressing their opinion, should be presented to Your Holiness for election." Stang argued that such a course accorded with the norms established by the Second Plenary Council of Baltimore. He informed Falconio that he had made known the contents of this memorial to Cardinal Gibbons and Archbishops Williams, Riordan, John Farley of New York, and John Ryan of Philadelphia. Stang asked the delegate to endorse the norms of the council and urge both Gotti and the pope to follow them.[61]

O'Connell's triumph was a signal and successful instance of personal ambition. Using the condemnation of Americanism as a fulcrum, he lifted himself to power on the lever of *Romanità* (Romanness). Through a network of powerful Roman friends, he never ceased to stress his absolute deference to the Holy See, while accusing his rivals of being Americanists. Yet their Americanism was not of the condemned variety. They held for absolute unity with Rome in matters of doctrine but for latitude in the local or national expression of the non-essentials of religion. O'Connell's excessive ultramontanism and his rise through independent channels alienated him from most of the bishops of the province. This estrangement was to deepen as O'Connell sought to impose his views on the New England church.

His departure from Portland occasioned the first recorded allegation that the new coadjutor archbishop was wanting in spirituality. It arose from the very segment of the population that had made it possible for him to become bishop of that see in the first place: the French-Canadians. In 1900, they had complained about the nominees for bishop, thus providing the opening for Propaganda to take independent action and appoint O'Connell. In 1906 they did so again.

Like other immigrant groups, the French-Canadians believed that the survival of their culture, customs, and religion depended on the survival of their language. Having come from a country where the Catholic church enjoyed financial support from the state, French-Canadians found the American church system somewhat mercenary, charging fees for sacraments and pew rent while simultaneously taking up collections.

Certainly, there were ethnic tensions between them and their departing bishop. The Irish resented the maintenance of the French tongue, and O'Connell proved no exception. He had ordered all French-Canadian nuns to learn English, something that was no doubt meant to have a repercussion in the classrooms of French-Canadian parish schools. One French-Canadian paper accused him of trying to eradicate the French language in Maine. It further claimed that O'Connell was delaying his departure from Portland simply to collect the tax levied for the bishop's salary, a large portion of which, argued the paper, ought to be returned because he had been absent from the diocese for six months. In fact, O'Connell did collect the salary of $4,925 (equivalent to $121,000 in 2006 terms). Moreover, during his brief stay as administrator, he engaged in creative bookkeeping, as will be seen in chapter four.[62]

The diocesan council met in late March to draw up a *terna*. The council consisted of four Irish priests and three French-Canadians. The French-Canadian community believed that because it comprised two-thirds of the church in Maine, the next bishop ought to be one of their countrymen. The council recommended Fathers Michael Walsh, Edward Hurley, and Michael McDonough in that order. Both Walsh and Hurley had been on the *terna* rejected by Propaganda in 1901, when the Vatican selected O'Connell. The French-Canadian members of the council protested to Archbishop Williams because all three candidates had voted for themselves, and two of the three had been elected without an absolute majority.[63]

Casting O'Connell as the negative model against which to compare the current slate of equally unworthy candidates, Father Adolphe Lacroix of Skowhegan, a priest who had early run afoul of the departing prelate over financial procedures, told Gotti: "It is painful to acknowledge that this bishop has gained here the sad reputation as a man of the world. . . . Unfortunately, all that is said on his account is only too true, and all the truth is still not known. The people are weary of this unworthy and even scandalous conduct, and if it must be, by misfortune, that there arrives after him on the episcopal throne of Portland a worldly bishop similarly devoid of piety, it will be all over for religion among a very great number. The people have a right to expect piety and virtue in their principal pastor."[64] No doubt, Lacroix's low opinion of O'Connell owed in part to his public style of office-holding, namely, maintaining a high profile in society and in the press. Yet, as will be seen, there was a darker side. Allegations of worldliness and impiety would surface in Boston on a grander scale than in Portland.

The French-speakers of Maine were promoting Father Narcisse Charland of Waterville as their candidate to succeed O'Connell and had won a delay in the appointment process. Lacroix seems to have interpreted the willingness of Propaganda to defer the decision as a sign of O'Connell's weakening influence in Rome. Word from the Vatican convinced him that with Stang's backing, Charland would be appointed bishop. Lacroix tried to enlist Stang's support. "The triumph of our cause is the nearly certain fall of Monsignor O'Connell and the premature end of his reign," he told Stang. "His star is beginning to fade in Rome and it is in the interest of religion in New England that his influence in the eternal city disappear completely."[65] Lacroix was mistaken. O'Connell's star was nowhere near eclipse at the Vatican. As for Charland, he was passed over in favor of Louis Sebastian Walsh, a priest of the archdiocese of Boston who as bishop would eventually go head-to-head with the French-Canadians himself. Walsh was to become an implacable foe of his predecessor.

CHAPTER 3

Romanization and Alienation

WITH THE DEATH OF JOHN WILLIAMS in August 1907, William O'Connell became archbishop of Boston and set out to bring Roman discipline to the ecclesiastical province of New England. He began with his own seminary, St. John's in Brighton, which educated many of the clergy of the province. This effort alienated him from the Sulpician Fathers who had run the seminary since its foundation in 1884. By contract, they had been given perpetual charge of the institution, which was "to be governed in the temporal and in the spiritual according to the rules and habits of St. Sulpice." Their system involved a regimen of prayer, spiritual conferences, study, and recreation in which both students and faculty participated, thus forming one homogeneous community. Professors doubled as spiritual directors and confessors. According to the contract, the treasurer was subject to the rector, who in turn was subject to the archbishop alone.[1]

Having spent the first years of college with the Sulpicians in Maryland, O'Connell developed a distaste for their system. Some of the Sulpicians attributed his attitude to his difficulties with other students. Yet, there were other more substantial matters. In the first place it was French, not Roman. His time as a student and later as rector at the American College had given him the Roman perspective which he wanted to impart to his seminary. In his view, the Sulpician system over emphasized external minutiae, enforced through espionage. The mingling of students and professors in a common life was wrong. O'Connell also connected Sulpicianism with the "Gallican" or "national" spirit prevalent in his province. He loathed the memory of Alphonse Magnien, S.S., the late rector of St. Mary's Seminary in Baltimore and éminence grise of the Americanists, because the priests trained under him had made untold trouble for church authorities. "The conflict between O'Connell and the Sulpicians," aptly remarks historian Christopher Kauffman, "was rooted in conflicting ecclesiologies: ultramontanism versus moderate transplanted Gallicanism, that is, Americanism."[2]

Moreover, certain members of the Sulpicians, like Francis Gigot of St. Joseph's Seminary in Dunwoodie, New York, and Joseph Bruneau and the late John B. Hogan of St. John's in Brighton, were involved in the Modernist movement, which applied historical and literary criticism to scripture and dogma and used a post-Kantian notion of immanence (that is, the presence of, or the need for, the divine implanted within humankind) to balance the exaggerated transcendentalism of neo-scholasticism. Although most expressions of Modernism were legitimate and sound, to the conventional mind they appeared disconcerting or dangerous. In some instances they were dangerous, verging on heresy or bare humanism. "What lay behind these variously radical statements," observes historian Roger Aubert, "was a common desire . . . to concede what seemingly had to be conceded to the modern world in order that Catholicism, shorn of its superannuated contingent elements, might keep in step with it." To be sure, the American Sulpicians who were involved in the movement were Modernists of moderate hue, unlike some practitioners of the movement in Europe. In the month after O'Connell became archbishop, Pius X condemned Modernism in the encyclical *Pascendi dominici gregis* (*Feeding the Lord's flock*).[3]

From the start O'Connell intended to show the Sulpicians that he would control the seminary. Late in 1907, he removed from their hands the administration of the canonical examination required of candidates for the priesthood and entrusted it to a board of diocesan clerics. In accord with the mind of Rome, he demanded that henceforth courses be taught in Latin. No longer was the seminary treasurer to report to the rector. He was subject to the archbishop alone, even though this violated both the contract with the Sulpicians and a decree on seminaries issued by the Vatican's Congregation of Bishops and Religious in January 1908. This violation was one of those instances in which O'Connell showed his own flexibility about obedience to Rome. While ignoring the decree in his own regard, he noted that it forbade professors to function as spiritual directors or confessors for the seminarians and demanded to know if the Sulpicians intended to change their system accordingly.[4] In the face of this relentless badgering, the

Sulpicians came to believe that the archbishop was trying to make life so miserable for them that they would choose to leave the seminary.[5] On the contrary, he would have to force them out.

In early 1909, the orthodoxy of Bruneau came into question, an issue that would lead O'Connell to dismiss him from the seminary. The Sulpician procurator general, Father Marie-François-Xavier Hertzog, undertook Bruneau's defense at the Vatican. In March, he reported that the situation seemed in hand. He noted, however, that O'Connell was then in Naples and was soon to arrive in the Eternal City. "The prelate [O'Connell] is clever," he wrote; "he has many friends here; he is ready to take up the interests of Roman systems and methods; he patronizes the men come from Rome." Two months later, he added, "The position of Msgr. O'Connell in Rome is certainly good because of his generosities."[6] Hertzog warned that the Vatican attached great importance to the security of doctrine and advised that "our professors ought to be very exact in their teaching."[7] Within months of his return to Boston, O'Connell ordered the Sulpicians to remove Bruneau and Father Jules Baisnée from St. John's Seminary, the former because of his Modernist tendencies which "might involve His Grace [O'Connell] in trouble at Rome," the latter because he was too young for seminary work. Sometime later, the archbishop demanded that the retired Father Henri Chapon be dismissed from the seminary because he was "not earning his salt."[8]

As early as January 1910, O'Connell was laying plans to take complete control of the seminary. He wrote to one of the diocesan faculty members on sick leave in Rome to ask him to find a man to fill the scripture chair at St. John's, a position already occupied by a fully qualified Sulpician.[9] At some time during that year, the seminary rector, Father Francis Havey, S.S., received a "private 'tip'" that the archbishop did not intend to keep the Sulpicians at the seminary indefinitely.[10]

In September 1910, O'Connell made his move. Father Henri Garriguet, superior general of the Sulpicians, and Hertzog attended the Eucharistic Congress in Montreal, Canada. There they met O'Connell who invited them to Boston to discuss the seminary. Prior to the conference, which took place at the end of the month, the diocesan priests on the faculty grew apprehensive "because of what one of them called 'the preparations' of His Grace." Although these words puzzled Havey, their meaning soon became clear.[11]

On 29 September, Garriguet, Hertzog, and Havey visited the archbishop at his residence in Boston. Present were his nephew-secretary, Father James P. E. O'Connell, and the chancellor, Monsignor Michael Splaine. The elder O'Connell told Garriguet that the contract with the Sulpicians was void for two reasons. First, according to Cardinals Raphael Merry del Val and Girolamo Gotti, the perpetuity clause was inadmissable; second, according to the pope, the bishop was to have complete charge of the seminary. When Garriguet acquiesced, the elder O'Connell agreed to retain the Sulpicians at St. John's, but by his good will, not by contract. He promised that if at some future date he thought it best that the Sulpicians leave, he would give them at least two and perhaps three years' notice.[12] The meeting left Havey with a bad impression. "It struck me," he later commented, "as the springing of a trap. . . . The interview seemed to me like a 'hold up.'"[13]

Three weeks later, O'Connell ordered Garriguet to withdraw his men at the end of the academic year. In an apparent attempt to forestall recriminations, the archbishop advised that in communicating the decision to the faculty, the superior general should remind his subjects to obey it without public comment so as not to prejudice the good order of the seminary or archdiocese. "I take this occasion," added O'Connell, "to thank you from the heart for your candid behavior with me."[14]

The same could not be said for the archbishop, a fact not lost on Garriguet, who replied that the Sulpicians would withdraw without complaint but not without regret. "Permit me to add this remark," he continued, "when you told me your absolute will to break the contract concluded by your predecessor, you spontaneously took the initiative to say that if we must leave, we would be given two years' notice. Your letter coming twenty days later must cause me sorrowful surprise. You have the kindness to render testimony to my candidness and my straightforwardness in the settlement of this matter. I await from God testimony for my confreres that they were good servants of the Church, and that they remain worthy to be employed in other fields of work that his Providence will be able to assign them."[15]

Meanwhile, O'Connell commissioned Father John Peterson, a diocesan professor at the seminary who was soon to be appointed rector, to develop a new curriculum modeled on a program established by the Vatican for seminaries in Italy. Peterson complied. The new program differed remarkably from the existing system. Instead of offering different courses in each grade, all students took the same classes simultaneously; the courses themselves rotated from year to year. Symbolic of the change was the addition of a class in Italian. The new program was implemented the following academic year.[16]

On 16 May 1911, O'Connell announced to the clergy that because of the growth and development of the church in Boston, it was time for the archdiocese to take over the education of its own priests. No one, he said, realized this better than the Sulpicians themselves, whom he thanked for their years of service.[17] His explanation was protested by the Sulpician vicar-general, Father Edward Dyer. "I did not wish to believe," he wrote to O'Connell, "that Your Grace would be responsible for a statement which you knew to be untrue, and, by alleging that the Sulpicians were fully of your own mind about the change in your Seminary, would seek to shelter yourself behind men upon whom you were inflicting grievous hardship."[18] O'Connell never retracted.

His method of removing the Sulpicians from St. John's, his holding them to a Roman standard while exempting himself from the same, his duplicity in his negotiations with them, his issuance of a false statement about their understanding the necessity of their departure, all reveal another aspect of O'Connell's personality: his arrogance. "Like many who had risen to high places from unpromising beginnings," remarks his biographer James O'Toole, "he came tacitly to believe that the rules of behavior he unhesitatingly enjoined on the community did not apply to himself, simply by virtue of who and what he was. Morality was for others."[19] Sadly, the events recounted in ensuing chapters will bear ample testimony to the truth of this statement.

While O'Connell worked to Romanize his seminary, he sought to do the same with the Boston province, something that increased the conflict with his suffragans. The archbishop intended to fill vacant dioceses with men of like mind. Two opportunities presented themselves in 1908. In spring of that year, John Michaud, bishop of Burlington, Vermont, who was rallying from a series of strokes, received permission for a coadjutor with right of succession, that is, an assistant bishop who would automatically replace him at death. O'Connell informed the chancellor of the diocese, Father Joseph Gillis, that the archbishop of Boston would preside over the convocation of diocesan consultors and permanent rectors when they met to select a *terna*. Fearing that the news would give Michaud another stroke, Gillis told Bishop Thomas Beaven of Springfield, Massachusetts, about O'Connell's intention. To the apostolic delegate, Beaven protested this "'ukase' from Boston" contravening the statutes of the Third Plenary Council of Baltimore regarding the nomination of bishops. The delegate, Archbishop Diomede Falconio, ordered O'Connell to stay in Boston, and the priests met without him on 19 May.[20]

Their choice was Father D. J. O'Sullivan, a man totally unacceptable to the archbishop. O'Connell wrote to Cardinals Raphael Merry del Val, Francesco Satolli, and Sebastiano Martinelli that the candidate was a poor administrator, an insubordinate clergyman, and "an Americanist who would inevitably create trouble but just for those reasons [was] popular with his kind." If the Vatican expected "a renewal of the Catholic spirit here and an elimination of certain tendencies which in the late past have been dangerously obvious," said O'Connell, "then I emphatically assert, as Metropolitan of the province, that O'Sullivan ought to be excluded."[21] On 20 August, the suffragans of Boston drafted their own *terna* for Burlington. They nominated the chancellor, Gillis, whose candidacy also displeased O'Connell.[22]

In October 1908, Bishop Michael Tierney of Hartford died, giving O'Connell another chance to secure a favorable appointment. The priests of the diocese proposed three names, with James Donovan first and John Duggan last. The suffragans reversed the order. O'Connell urged Donovan's candidacy. He was the only one worthy of consideration because of his talent and zeal. He was also "the only one of the three educated in Rome." O'Connell considered Duggan "local in every sense of the word," like "some of the bishops of the province who are also local in experience and sentiment." For that reason, the interests of Hartford, of the province, and especially of the Holy See would best be served by the selection of Donovan who "will bring a larger and truly more Catholic [i.e., Roman] spirit."[23]

In February 1909, O'Connell made his first visit to Rome as archbishop to report on the status of Boston. While there, he made personal interventions regarding the *ternae* for both Hartford and Burlington. In March, the Consistorial Congregation, which assumed jurisdiction over the American church in June 1908, requested a new *terna* for Burlington and sought explanations for the change made by the bishops in the one for Hartford. With O'Connell still in Rome, the suffragans drafted a new *terna* for Burlington with their minds "very nearly agreed upon all important matters and names."[24] Even so, appointments to the two sees were not forthcoming. During the summer, O'Connell accused Sulpician Procurator General Hertzog of meddling in the selections. In fact, some priests of Hartford had written to Hertzog about the nomination, but the latter wisely had declined to respond.[25]

In the fall of 1909, Bishop Louis Sebastian Walsh, O'Connell's successor in Portland, took an interest in the Burlington and Hartford successions. Although he was only a year older than O'Connell and had been a priest of the archdiocese of Boston, the paths of the two had rarely crossed. Walsh had studied for the priesthood under the Sulpicians at the Grand Seminary in Montreal and at St. Sulpice Seminary in Paris. Completing his preparation at the Apollinaris and Minerva in Rome, he was ordained there in 1882. After a brief stint of pastoral work at St. Joseph's parish in Boston's West End, where O'Connell later followed him, Walsh became a faculty member with the Sulpicians at St. John's Seminary and taught history and canon law. In 1897, Archbishop Williams appointed him supervisor of Catholic schools in the archdiocese, a post he held until his appointment to Portland.[26] Walsh was to become the most ardent foe of O'Connell.

During his routine visit to report to Rome on his diocese, Walsh tried to discover what was happening regarding the vacancies in Burlington and Hartford. Definitive information was difficult to obtain because the "*Secretum*" (the oath of secrecy about the selection of bishops) lurked like "a real lion at all the doors." The city, however, was alive with rumors, many of them contradictory. Father Salvatore Brandi, S.J., claimed that Duggan had virtually been decided on for Hartford when O'Connell vetoed the selection. Bishop Thomas Kennedy, rector of the American College, held otherwise. Hartford, he told Walsh, had never been near a decision, and a new a *terna* would be requested. O'Connell, it was said, wanted only American-College men for bishops, and yet the story was out that he had proposed Bishop Philip Garrigan of Sioux City, Iowa, an alumnus of St. Joseph's Seminary in Troy, New York, as a compromise candidate for Hartford.[27]

One thing was certain. Walsh heard both from Cardinal Gaetano De Lai, secretary of the Consistorial Congregation, and also from Monsignor Sante Tampieri, O'Connell's old friend then in the Secretariat of State, that conflicting reports from America had flooded the Vatican. Consequently Rome was seeking a candidate who would please all parties. Walsh tried to convince De Lai that peace, harmony, and unity had prevailed in New England until the accession of O'Connell. He pressed the secretary to trust the New England hierarchy and declared that Williams's last words to him were "Rome should have confidence in the Bishops." To his fellow suffragans, Walsh wrote that if the Hartford *terna* was rejected, he favored re-nominating Duggan with two new candidates.[28]

Not until winter of 1910 did Rome settle the affairs of Burlington and Hartford. Joseph Rice was appointed to the former and John Nilan to the latter. Rice soon sided with his fellow suffragans. Nilan was more of a compromise candidate. A cleric of the archdiocese of Boston, he had the confidence of O'Connell, who in 1907 assigned him to give canonical examinations to the candidates for priesthood. On the other hand, he was known to be friendly to the suffragans. His appointment pleased O'Connell because, as an alumnus of the Troy seminary, Nilan had not been educated by the Sulpicians. "Anything," wrote O'Connell to Merry del Val, "which breaks that blighting tyranny [of Sulpicianism] in this Province is a thing to be grateful to God for. It was true— further propagation of it meant a speedy misfortune to the Church here in its relations with Rome. . . . It will not be so easy now to manage and manipulate the *ternae*—hitherto that was a very easy and simple matter."[29] O'Connell was too sanguine. An outsider to the diocese of Hartford, Nilan chose Duggan as his vicar general and relied heavily on him. This he did, it was reported, at the urging of the other suffragans.[30]

In order to circumvent O'Connell's further interference in episcopal appointments, the suffragans decided in 1914 that it would be best for the aging Matthew Harkins of Providence to ask for an auxiliary bishop (an assistant without right of succession), rather than a coadjutor. While he alone had the authority to propose candidates for the position of auxiliary, the prelates of the province had the right to propose nominees for the position of coadjutor. As a courtesy, the Vatican allowed O'Connell to comment on Harkins's candidates. He adversely criticized them and warned that the procedure was simply a trick to secure auxiliaries as successors. Rome ignored him.[31]

In 1918, after two auxiliaries died tragically early deaths, Harkins finally asked for "either an auxiliary or a coadjutor 'with right of succession,'" as it pleased the pope. The bishop recommended three names: Peter Blessing, already passed over once as successor of the first auxiliary; Thomas Duggan, a prime candidate for Hartford back in 1908 but rejected by O'Connell; and William Hickey.[32] Rome appointed the last named as coadjutor. Hickey shared the other suffragans' distaste for their archbishop.

In October 1911, Pius X elevated two American archbishops to the cardinalate: O'Connell and John Farley of New York. The festivities in Rome surrounding the bestowal of the red hat on these new princes of the church received volumes of press coverage in Boston. There was little celebrating in certain quarters of the American hierarchy. On hearing the news of O'Connell's selection, Cardinal James Gibbons of Baltimore wept. His Americanist colleague, Archbishop Patrick Riordan of San Francisco, reported that news of the Boston prelate's elevation met with universal disfavor. Bishop Walsh commented in his diary: "Boston has reached the goal he set for himself in Rome in 1900 and . . . if the whole truth were known or could be told the story is a more remarkable 'Drama' than any page of our American Church history up to the present. History will perhaps tell the truth and vindicate honesty and right ecclesiastical procedure against intrigue and other brutal methods. Veritas praevalebit [truth will prevail]."[33]

Visible proof of the gap between O'Connell and the bishops of both New England and elsewhere came when the two new cardinals returned home. Their celebrations were starkly different. To Farley's came Cardinal Gibbons, Archbishop Edmond Prendergast of Philadelphia, and twenty other bishops, including some of the Boston suffragans. O'Connell's boasted only three bishops, Nilan, George Guertin of Manchester, and Joseph Anderson, the new cardinal's auxiliary. The contrast was striking and apparent to all.[34]

O'Connell returned the insult in the speech delivered at a banquet given in his honor on 5 February 1912 by the clergy of the archdiocese. He declared that his elevation to the cardinalate was "a supreme indication" that his "heart and mind [were] set toward the right direction." The red hat had come to him because of his absolute unity with the Vatican. "I have," said O'Connell, "never feared misunderstanding or criticism on the part of those who felt less than I did the urgent necessity, especially in this new country, of this perfect accord and entente between Pope and Bishop." He held that a contrary spirit infected some prelates. That any bishop "should assume a merely parochial, or provincial, or national attitude," he considered "a most glaring contradiction of terms." A bishop who dared to toy with the cord that bound each see to Rome, he dubbed "a renegade and a traitor to his office."[35] Many priests who heard the address interpreted it as an assault on the suffragans in particular and on the American hierarchy in general. The speech was widely publicized and read by O'Connell's episcopal colleagues.[36]

In mid-February 1912, Archbishop John Ireland of St. Paul and his long-time friend and supporter, Bishop Thomas O'Gorman of Sioux Falls, South Dakota, went to Washington to speak with Monsignor Bonaventura Cerretti, who was in charge of the apostolic delegation until the arrival of the new delegate. A thoroughly disgusted Ireland considered O'Connell's address a direct assault on the loyalty of the American hierarchy as a whole. Cerretti tried to calm him by pointing out that no names were mentioned and that the speech itself could be interpreted as rather theoretical. Ireland would have none of it. Five days later, Harkins and Walsh came to complain as well. At the end of the month Cardinal Gibbons, too, visited Cerretti to say that O'Connell's remarks were inopportune.[37] The blood between the prelate of Boston and his brother bishops was bad and getting worse.

In March, he heaped fuel on the fire with more inflammatory references, this time directed against the Sulpicians. At an event held in his honor by Boston College where he had completed his degree after leaving the Sulpicians at St. Charles' College, O'Connell delivered a speech contrasting the systems of the two institutions. Boston College, he declared, fostered a "manly spirit of honorable competition," and its "very air . . . breathed liberty." St. Charles', which the cardinal said he "was fortunate enough to escape," produced persons who were "petty . . . not bearing defeat like men . . . but cherishing the peevishness against their rivals." Its spirit was "more Puritanic and Jansenistic than Catholic." Boston College, on the other hand, had genuine Catholicity. "The squeamish, fretful scrupulosity of the mere pietist was unknown here," O'Connell told the students. "Be straight and frank,— Uriah Heaps belong elsewhere. Boston College never produced one."[38] This contrast between the two institutions was far more acerbic than the more genial one expressed in his *Recollections*, noted in the Prologue of this volume.

Cerretti reported to Rome that the address caused quite a stir among the bishops and priests of the country because a sizeable number of them, including four of the Boston suffragans, had been educated by the Sulpicians.[39] The Sulpician vicar-general, Father Dyer, wrote a stinging protest to the Boston *Pilot*, the archdiocesan newspaper, which had published the speech. He hinted that O'Connell had left St. Charles', not because of strict discipline, but because of difficulties he had experienced with other students. Dyer held that on taking over the Boston seminary, the cardinal imposed a more rigorous discipline than that demanded by the Sulpicians. Furthermore, it was unfair to compare Boston College with St. Charles', especially when the commentator was O'Connell. "Why," asked Dyer, "should the discipline in a Sulpician ecclesiastical college be contrasted with an exaggerated presentation of the freedom in a day college for secular students, qualified by opprobrious epithets and judged by the standards of a disgruntled boy?"[40]

The *Pilot* made no retraction nor did it publish Dyer's protest.

Father William Starr, pastor of Corpus Christi Parish in Baltimore, condoled with Father Thomas Gasson, S.J., president of Boston College, over the new cardinal's misuse of the institution's hospitality. "I do not stop to characterize, as should be, the cowardice of his act, contrasting as it did with all his cheap bluster about manliness etc. That a man whose high station in the Church, and that alone, protects him against public protest and recrimination should take advantage of the immunity from attack which his purple [i.e., his rank] affords him, and from that vantage ground perpetrate so beastly an outrage upon a body of men who . . . are inclined to turn the other cheek to the smiter, is a spectacle to fill all the manly and generous souls with unspeakable disgust." In Starr's view, O'Connell's behavior on an occasion designed to honor him, and his compelling of his hosts "to be the reluctant witnesses of his brutality should for the rest of his days put him outside the pale of decent society."[41]

Several months later, Cardinal Gibbons used his address to the graduates of St. Charles' College to counter the insult and praise the Sulpicians. He reminded his listeners that the first bishop of the United States, John Carroll, had brought the Sulpicians to America to train men for the priesthood. "What Bishop Carroll has been to the hierarchy of the United States," said Gibbons, "the Sulpician Fathers have been to the clergy; he has been the model of the American episcopate, they have been the model of the clergy. . . . No stain has ever sullied their bright escutcheon." Gibbons was pleased to note that when Pius X issued instructions several years earlier about the rule and discipline to be observed in seminaries, these new regulations were no different from those that "have always been observed in institutions under Sulpician control." He thanked the Sulpicians for the kind but strong discipline that helped him develop his moral character under their tutelage.[42]

In April 1912, O'Connell, who for two months had handed out insults, found himself on the receiving end. Bishop Harkins was to celebrate his episcopal silver jubilee on the fifteenth. Ten days later, he was to consecrate one of his priests, Father Austin Dowling, as bishop of Des Moines, Iowa. Dowling had studied for the priesthood at St. John's

Seminary in Brighton and later served on the faculty with the Sulpicians. At the time of his selection for Des Moines, he was rector of the cathedral in Providence. Neither Dowling nor Harkins invited O'Connell to their celebrations, so the cardinal dispatched two of his priests, Fathers Joseph Coppinger and Edward Moriarty, to visit Cerretti at the apostolic delegation. Informing him of the lack of invitations, they said it was rumored that the Sulpicians and suffragans planned to use the occasions to get back at the cardinal for his Boston College address. "It would be a question," alleged Coppinger, "of an anti-Roman demonstration." The two emissaries urged Cerretti to see that the cardinal be on the guest lists.[43]

Cerretti summoned Harkins to hear his side of the story. When told what the Boston envoys had said, the bishop replied that nothing could be further from the truth. Harkins had not invited the cardinal because the jubilee was to be a small gathering of intimate friends. No one from Boston was invited. While Harkins admitted that he and O'Connell had once been close, at present their relationship was confined to that of an inferior with his superior. No demonstration or counterattack against the cardinal was planned for the celebration. As regarded Dowling's consecration, the final preparations were yet to be made. Harkins assured Cerretti that he would urge the appropriateness of inviting the cardinal.[44]

On 15 April, O'Connell came to Washington for the annual meeting of the archbishops. Cerretti explained the situation regarding Harkins, and the cardinal seemed reassured. O'Connell then conversed for an hour about his relations with his suffragans. "The situation," he concluded, "has become intolerable; it is now time to know whether I am to be metropolitan or not. The manner of acting of those bishops in my regard is a scandal to the faithful and something must be done about it." Cerretti suggested that O'Connell take the matter up with the new apostolic delegate when he arrived. "Let these bishops tell me," insisted the cardinal, "where and when I have offended them; let them tell me what they want of me, I am ready to do everything, so that this state of affairs will come to an end."[45]

O'Connell's remarks bespoke the depth of the rift separating him from his suffragans. They also indicated his inability to grasp his own role in bringing about the alienation, which in his view seemingly had no basis. Without excusing the behavior of the suffragans, the fault was not entirely theirs.

Three days later, Cerretti sent Harkins a letter urging him to have Dowling invite O'Connell to his consecration. Because Dowling was out of town on a spiritual retreat in preparation for his elevation to the episcopate, Harkins was unable to reach him immediately. By the time he did, Cerretti had telegraphed Dowling directly to ask if he had invited the cardinal. The response to both men was the same: no.[46]

The new cardinal suffered insult in a less public forum. Poems lampooning him circulated among the clergy. To be sure, some Boston Catholics, who for more than a half century had been on the bottom of the city's totem, gloried vicariously in the attention and fame that accrued to their chief, but others of the priests and laity found the publicity difficult to take. Even Governor Eugene Foss, disgruntled by his own sudden demotion in status, absented himself from a St. Patrick's Day celebration when it became evident that political etiquette demanded that O'Connell, as royalty (a prince of the church), speak second at the event after President William Taft, shunting his excellency the governor to third place.[47]

Father Hugh Roe O'Donnell wrote a satire that took O'Connell to task for his high-profile, public style of office-holding which won immense press coverage, especially during his accession to the cardinalate. He was careful to include a reference to Foss's demotion in the verse *How History is Made, 1911–1912*.

The journals produced illustrations
        Of red hats and garments galore;
And this most democratic of nations
        Saw princes, in print, by the score.

The supplement sheets issued photos
        Of churches and palace hotels,
With His Eminence riding in autos,
        The prince of American swells. . . .

There were views of the Vatican, showing
 The great consistorial hall,
With the Pope in the act of bestowing
 The hat on the prince of them all. . . .

We were told in a way that convinces,
 How blue blood now flows in his veins;
How ranking with royalty's princes,
 This prince over governors reigns.

There were hints that an honor awaits him,
 Exchanging a crown for his hat
And surely the world estimates him
 As worthy, in time, to get that.

In fine, it is hardly surprising
 That people exclaim,—quite aghast—
"For lime light and big advertising,
 Old Barnam is nailed the mast!"[48]

Picking up on O'Donnell's reference to exchanging a cardinal's hat for a crown (the papal tiara), another wag took aim at the cardinal for his ambition and reliance on Vatican patrons for advancement.

It is said that one Cardinal hopes
Through his knowledge of Rome and the ropes,
 That, when good Pius dies,
 Boston's prelate will rise
The first of American Popes.

The world knows that Merry del Val
Arranges the sha'n't and the shall
 So cease all misgiving;
 No Cardinal living
Has chances like Raphael's pal.

The tiara will sit on him well,
For he is no end of a swell;
   And if his use of the keys
   Should not happen to please,
He can send all creation to H—.[49]

Verses like these, and others which will be cited later, indicate the depth of feeling that existed toward O'Connell. Ridicule, however, is an instrument that cuts two ways: one incisively lays bare the interior of the adversary; the other exposes the weakness of the antagonist, who feels powerless to do aught but belittle.

O'Connell's banishing the Sulpicians from St. John's Seminary, his attempting to control the selection of bishops to ensure that men of like stripe reached the episcopate, and his questioning of the loyalty of his fellow prelates to the pope, all served to alienate him from his suffragans, some of his priests, and the episcopacy at large. His estrangement from them would increase with suspicion of his malfeasance in office and the discovery of the tactic he used to place himself on the archiepiscopal throne.

CHAPTER 4

Malfeasance

THE DISTANCE BETWEEN Cardinal William O'Connell and his suffragans was deepened by a mounting suspicion of his misuse of office. He had left the finances of Portland in shambles. For more than two years, his successor Bishop Louis Walsh had been puzzled by certain aspects of the diocesan accounts. In 1909, he gave them careful study and then confronted the chancellor, Monsignor Charles Collins, whose answers ranged "all the way from evasive to insolent." Following a second fruitless meeting, Walsh told Collins that he had until noon the next day to come clean or face removal from office. The chancellor then confessed that the records were doctored copies made by O'Connell during the month prior to his installation as coadjutor of Boston. When he left for the new post, he took the original books with him. Walsh found the investigation of his predecessor's administration difficult and painful, "for evidently the *personal* and *official* obligations had been too much confused." O'Connell had left the cathedral parish, the orphan asylum, the diocesan cemetery, and the diocesan trust funds deeply in debt.[1]

Word of the inquiry reached O'Connell, who summoned Walsh to Boston in October 1909, shortly before the latter was to depart on a visit to Rome to report on the state of his diocese. The archbishop promised to make everything right and to pay whatever amount could be surely proven, a condition almost impossible to satisfy because he had since burned the original financial records. In June of the following year, Walsh again confronted O'Connell in a stormy meeting. Getting no satisfaction, he sent the archbishop a statement of diocesan finances. It showed that the fluid assets of Portland, amounting to $20,562 ($429,000 in 2006 dollars), had been used to meet the most pressing debts incurred by O'Connell, and still the bishopric remained $25,578 ($531,000) in the red. Although the archbishop made good his obligation with a check for that amount—a tacit admission of guilt—the incident turned Walsh permanently against him.[2]

The festivities surrounding O'Connell's reception of the red hat served to focus attention on his love of money. Two nights after the banquet given him by the clergy at which he cast aspersions on the loyalty of other bishops to Rome, laymen hosted another at the Hotel Somerset.[3] The chancery planned the affair and invited six hundred to attend at $5 per plate and $100 per capita for a gift to the new cardinal. In effect, the night generated between $50,000 and $60,000 (sums with a purchasing power between $1 and $1.2 million in 2006). O'Connell gave an address praising the laity who supported him and excoriating the complacency, conceit, and pusillanimity of the layman who failed to do so, branded a "Judas" and "Pharisee."[4] The event was satirized in *The Charge of the Gold Brigade*, a parody on Alfred Tennyson's poem, which went in part:

Half a leg, half a leg,
Half a leg onward!
Into the Somerset
Strode the six hundred. . . .

"Forward the Gold Brigade!"
Was there a man dismayed?
No! For they all had paid
Five and one hundred. . . .

"Judas and Pharisee"!
That's what you're said to be,
If cursed with poverty
And minus the hundred.

But incense and blessings rare
Fell on the heroes there.
Though they swore,—paying the fare,
Five and one hundred. . . .

This verse, running ten stanzas, was written by M. J. Dwyer, assistant district attorney of Boston, and was read publicly at the Ladies' Night of the Clover Club, a satirical society in the Hub. The *Boston Globe* published a like-minded poem about O'Connell, *Lord Dollars-and-Cents*, penned by Thomas F. Porter, former mayor of Lynn, Massachusetts.[5] This was the underside of the festivities. O'Connell's opponents inside and outside the church ridiculed him in poetry, some public, some private, the majority of it dealing with money.[6]

Allegations of bribery surrounded O'Connell's election to the cardinalate. One came in the form of a limerick in Italian written by an anonymous New Englander (no doubt a priest):

A Roma, si dice, la cassa
Riceve danaro in massa,
La banca pertanto
Rialza, in quanto
"Il Cardinalato s'abbassa"

Freely translated: In Rome they say that the cashier's window/ takes in money in great quantities/ for this reason, the bank rises in the measure/ that the Cardinalate sinks.[7]

A Boston clergyman told the apostolic delegate, Archbishop Giovanni Bonzano, that O'Connell's reputation was "so vile that he has become a stench in the nostrils of Catholics," everyone of whom believed him "to be a simonist [one who had purchased an ecclesiastical position] (how else, they say, could he have been named to Boston and the Cardinalate if he did not buy—excuse the word—his office; we must conclude that Rome regards the bishops of the U.S. as untruthful, for surely they protested against the naming of this man devoid of faith and morals." Another anonymous clergyman wrote directly to O'Connell to tell him that he was "clad in royal, but bought purple; lolling in luxury, like a sow on a cushion; feared by every decent bishop and priest; despised and ridiculed by the people! A very Nero in shape and in character."[8]

According to Archbishop John Ireland, the Italian press published a letter in 1914 written by Cardinal Benedetto Lorenzelli to Cardinal Mariano Rampolla just after the 1912 consistory that elevated the Boston prelate. In it, Lorenzelli declared: "The College of Cardinals has fallen low through the accession of O'Connell. It is a clear case of Simony."[9] During a visit to the Vatican in 1914, Walsh had been told that Pius X had not wanted to make O'Connell a cardinal, but the secretary of state, Cardinal Raphael Merry del Val had insisted. Archbishop Bonaventura Cerretti informed Walsh that the pontiff, three days prior to his death, had described O'Connell as "*la più grossa spina del mio cuore* [the biggest thorn in my heart]." According to Walsh's Roman notes, O'Connell had allegedly paid $60,000 for the cardinalate during the first four years in Boston and another $100,000 at the time of receiving the honor, a sum equivalent in purchasing power to more than $3 million in 2006.[10]

Whether or not O'Connell had engaged in bribery in the strict sense of the term may never be known. It is certain, however, that he funneled vast sums of money to the Vatican through legitimate means. He raised funds from his parishes to assist victims of an earthquake in Italy. He contributed regularly to an orphanage founded by his friend Cardinal Merry del Val. Finally, he sought to ingratiate himself with the pope through the Peter's Pence collection. Under Archbishop John Williams, the archdiocese routinely raised about $10,000 a year for the pontiff. In O'Connell's first year as archbishop, he pressured pastors to raise a spectacular Peter's Pence collection. The amount offered to Rome in 1908 was $40,000, four times the usual size. For the next three years, the sums amounted to $20,000 annually, bringing the total to $100,000 for the four years prior to O'Connell's elevation to the cardinalate, or about $2 million in 2006 terms.[11] It appears that O'Connell had risen to the honor in large measure on the backs of his people.

Questions about the Boston finances surfaced at this time. Both the Portland and the Vatican archives contain a typed, unsigned letter addressed to "Reverend and dear Father." An anonymous informant sent a copy of it to Bonzano with the comment that the letter had initially been delivered to several priests, but was then in wide circulation among the clergy and prominent laity. Written by a layperson in Boston, it urged that some priest "with the prophet's zeal and courage" step forward and speak to O'Connell "the necessary warning" about the painful impression caused by his administration. While the writer considered it "preposterous" that the cardinal actually made as much money from his office as people claimed, the author was less concerned about the facts than the appearance.[12]

The unsigned letter averred that comments about the cardinal "which a few years ago would scarcely be made by careless Catholics above a whisper, have now become public and everyday talk of family-circle and street, of club and barroom." The open recitation of the *Charge of the Gold Brigade* at the Clover Club was a case in point. Good Catholics, moreover, were gravely alarmed by the "cardinal's public inveighing against his brother bishops" and the apparent advantage he took of his high office "to acquire vast sums of money for private use."[13]

The allegations in the unsigned letter were later echoed by Father John Mullen, a confirmed opponent of O'Connell. Several years younger than the cardinal, Mullen had studied at St. Sulpice Seminary in Paris and then at the Canisianum in Innsbruck. After ordination, he earned a doctorate in canon law at Rome. On returning to Boston, he became an assistant at the Cathedral of Holy Cross and within a few years was appointed to the marriage tribunal as defender of the bond. In 1905, he became rector of the cathedral, though his tenure lasted little more than two years. Shortly after O'Connell succeeded Williams, he exiled Mullen to St. Michael's parish in Hudson at the outskirt of the archdiocese and refused to allow him to take vacations. O'Connell's reasons for doing so were several. Mullen had belonged to the group of priests who had sought to prevent him from becoming coadjutor. A celebrated teetotaler, the priest also refused to serve the new archbishop wine at dinner. "The real reason," Mullen told the apostolic delegate, "was that I did not accept the new Archbishop's invitation to 'work in with the administration,' which meant to do things unworthy of my priesthood, close my eyes to abuses, offer flattery and gifts to the Archbishop."[14]

The author of the unsigned letter and Mullen cataloged the ways in which O'Connell used his office for gain. In 1909 he had raised the cathedraticum, his official salary which also funded the central operation of the archdiocese, to 4 percent of all pew rent. "If only half the people [450,000 out of 900,000] attend Mass on Sunday and give ten cents for their seats," reckoned the anonymous author, "—surely not an excessive average for most Boston churches—four per cent of the resulting income would be a round hundred thousand dollars yearly for the Cardinal from this single source," or $2 million in 2006 terms. That amount was eight times the cathedraticum of New York, an arch-diocese with a Catholic population one-quarter larger than Boston's. In 1919, Mullen claimed that the cathedraticum, by then reduced to 3 percent, certainly had to generate over $50,000 per year.[15]

In addition to the cathedraticum, the cardinal derived income from two parishes. After exiling Mullen, he appointed himself rector of the cathedral and several years later made himself pastor of St. Cecilia's church in fashionable Back Bay. The archdiocese operated on the benefice system whereby a pastor had the right to the Christmas and Easter collections, weekly offertory collections, sacramental fees, and a wage of $600. Out of these sources was to come the board and salary of his assistant priests, but the residue belonged personally to him. Combined, the Christmas and Easter collections of O'Connell's two churches alone brought him at least $12,000 per year ($237,000 in 2006 terms), the equivalent of the New York cathedraticum. Moreover, the revenue of St. Cecilia's consistently outstripped expenses by a margin of three to one.[16]

Furthermore, Mullen alleged that when pastors died, the cardinal appointed administrators to replace them so that the parish technically remained vacant and, according to the benefice system, collections reverted to the archbishop. In fact, *The Official Catholic Directory* shows that the number of churches continuously under an administrator after the pastor's death rose from two in 1910 to forty-two in 1920. At the very least, this was a serious violation of canon law which required that vacancies be filled within six months. Mullen also learned from pastors in Newton, South Boston, and Waltham—two of them priests in favor with O'Connell—that during the period of vacancy prior to their appointments, the cardinal had taken out mortgages on the churches and diverted the money from parish use.[17]

Too, there were suspicions that O'Connell was making money off church insurance. During the administration of Williams, various companies recognized the chancery office as an agency and granted it the commissions for all the policies it issued. Williams divided the proceeds, assigning half to diocesan projects and returning half to the contracting church. Parishes, however, remained free to deal directly with any company they wished. In 1909, O'Connell demanded that all insurance be taken out through the chancery and stopped the refunds. Where and how he used the commissions, estimated to be over $50,000 annually, no one knew, not even the diocesan consultors.[18] In 1909, that sum had purchasing power equivalent to $1 million in 2006 terms.

The *Pilot* was another cause of concern. In his memoirs, O'Connell stated that he had purchased the failing paper for a small sum of personal money and turned it into the archdiocesan organ. He used the paper not only to convey official views, but also as a vehicle to promote his public image by the carefully managed reporting of his every movement. Mullen underscored for the apostolic delegate that the paper belonged personally to the cardinal. With mixed success, O'Connell attempted to suppress parish papers and require the faithful to subscribe to the *Pilot*. Some pastors simply paid for subscriptions out of parish revenues in order to avoid friction with the chancery office. To be sure, other bishops sought to make the diocesan organ their official voice, but few, if any, were the owners of the paper. In little more than a year after its acquisition, the *Pilot* was turning a profit, estimated at $50,000 annually in 1912, equal to nearly $1 million in 2006. In 1919, Mullen estimated that the *Pilot* generated between $20,000 and $50,000, sums then equivalent to $229,000 and $573,000, respectively, in 2006 dollars, down from the 1912 figures because of the recession that struck in the wake of World War I.[19]

Both the anonymous letter writer and Mullen estimated that the cardinal made $150,000 to $200,000 per year, sums that in 1912 had a purchasing power equivalent to nearly $3 and $4 million, respectively, in present-day dollars.[20]

The anonymous clergyman, who alleged that O'Connell bought his election to the cardinalate, had scathing words about his archbishop for the apostolic delegate. "Everybody knows him to be a sacrilegious thief," he told Bonzano, "(he robbed the diocese of Portland of its pious funds, destroyed the records, substituting false records to cover his crime; this was common knowledge all over the country prior to his appointment to the Archbishopric; it is reported that Bishop Walsh forced him to restitution. . . .)" The priest enclosed a copy of the *Charge of the Gold Brigade*, which he said was now in the hands of most of the Boston clergy and prominent laymen. The poem ridiculed O'Connell "and the GOD he serves: *money*." Throughout Boston, said the anonymous priest, people speculated that if the cardinal were not a man of the cloth, "he would be committed to the STATE-PRISON." The clergyman claimed that many had left the church because they contended that "unless Rome shared in the plunder Rome would unfrock him [O'Connell] and send him to a monastery for the remainder of his life."[21]

The facts about the finances of the *Pilot* and church insurance will probably never be known. It is certain, however, that the Christmas and Easter collections from the cardinal's two parishes alone gave him an income equal to that of Cardinal John Farley in New York. If only one-sixth of Boston's Catholics paid ten cents in pew rent per Sunday— a highly underrated scenario—O'Connell would have received more than double Farley's cathedraticum. What accrued to him from the dozens of parishes left under administrators is a mystery. These allegations became the stock in trade of his detractors, who, though they had no way of proving the amounts of money involved, believed that the prima facie evidence of corruption was overwhelming, as indeed it was.

By 1919, O'Connell held a considerable amount of property. As coadjutor, he had purchased for his residence a house on Union Park Street near the cathedral, a property he retained when he became archbishop. Soon after Williams's death, a committee of priests organized a subscription for the purpose of buying O'Connell a new residence so that he would not have to live in the archiepiscopal apartment in the cathedral rectory. According to Mullen, these clergymen did so at O'Connell's command, and the latter had already selected a house at 25 Granby Street on the banks of the Charles River in the Back Bay. The building served as both home and chancery office. Within two years, this residence was expanded at a cost of $50,000 (equivalent to $1.04 million in 2006). In 1916, O'Connell purchased a new home for himself on Rawson Road in Brookline.[22]

In addition to these residences, O'Connell held property under the name of his nephew, Monsignor James P. E. O'Connell, chancellor of the archdiocese. The cardinal owned the home in which the nephew's parents lived. He also purchased two apartment buildings in Brookline as income properties. In 1918, these three pieces of real estate were valued at $100,000, or $1.3 million in 2006 terms.[23]

Finally, according to Mullen, by 1919 O'Connell also owned six summer homes, in Gloucester, Waverley, Centre Harbor, Duxbury, Nantasket, and Swampscott. Priests who were permitted to visit them reported that "the furnishings are of the costliest kind." Mullen added that the cardinal "has the name among dealers at stopping at no expense when purchasing articles for himself."[24]

In 1918, O'Connell's personal fortune stood to increase considerably when A. Paul Keith died, leaving the cardinal half the residue of his estate. O'Connell had become acquainted with Keith's parents while he was rector of the American College. The family had made its fortune in vaudeville. Keith's mother was a Catholic devoted to charitable work. A bachelor with little interest in religion, the son wished to continue his mother's legacy. Keith split the residue of his estate between the President and Fellows of Harvard College, a corporation; and "His Eminence William O'Connell of Boston, Massachusetts, a Cardinal of the Holy Roman Catholic Church."[25] Keith carefully avoided referring to the cardinal as the Roman Catholic archbishop of Boston, a corporation sole, because that would have meant that the money went to the archdiocese. As a corporation sole, the archbishop and the archdiocese were legally interchangeable, one and the same. This deft wording of the will left the money to O'Connell personally, although it stipulated that he use the proceeds at his discretion for charitable purposes. Mullen detected the cardinal's hand in the manner of the bequest. He complained that because the money was left to O'Connell rather than the nonprofit archdiocese, "hundreds of thousands of dollars have been lost on unnecessary taxes." Furthermore, Mullen was convinced that the cardinal simply "wished to misuse the funds."[26]

He was not alone in his irritation over this matter. In December 1923, George F. A. McDougall, a Catholic layman in Dorchester (by some accounts a non-practicing one), had a bill introduced into the Massachusetts legislature revoking the corporation sole and entrusting all church property in the archdiocese to a board of trustees consisting of clergymen and laypersons, chaired by O'Connell. The bill further required that the corporation sole "immediately give an accounting to the new board of trustees of all church funds and property." Though nothing came of the measure, it received countrywide attention. Arthur Preuss, doughty editor of the *Fortnightly Review,* a national Catholic magazine published in St. Louis, considered the bill "a plain symptom of dissatisfaction, not to say distrust, on the part of the Catholic laity in the Archdiocese of Boston, inspired largely, we believe, by the famous Keith bequest." Like Mullen, Preuss lamented the loss of money for charitable purposes because O'Connell would have to pay not only an inheritance tax of 12 percent but also annual state and federal income taxes on the proceeds. "And who is to know how the rest of the money is to be used?" he asked.[27]

While there is no doubt that O'Connell benefitted personally from the bequest, he did not mismanage it. When the estate was finally settled in 1923, his share was appraised at $1.892 million, though its actual value was closer to $2.5 million, a sum with a purchasing power equal to $29.5 million in 2006. Most of his portion was in commercial property in several states, some of which produced a handsome income in rent. He sold some of the less productive pieces immediately and the rest by 1928, retaining for himself a house in Marblehead, Massachusetts. Using proceeds from the sales, he built an Italianate *palazzo* near the seminary in Brighton to serve as the archiepiscopal residence, another symbol of the social arrival of Boston Catholics. He immediately used a portion of the liquidation for charity. The greater part, however, he invested in equities whose dividends were used to support his own activities and those of the archdiocese. The stocks performed quite well, even during the Great Depression. In 1936, the aging O'Connell used money from the bequest to fund a massive archdiocesan building campaign. The Keith estate was finally liquidated in 1941, three years before the cardinal's death.[28]

On O'Connell's behalf, it should be noted that he was generous with his earnings and inheritance. In 1914, for instance, he used a $25,000 gift (nearly a half million in 2006 dollars) given by Boston bankers on his reception of the red hat to save his titular church, San Clemente in Rome, from subterranean flooding.[29] Still, there can be little doubt that he used his position to amass a fortune in personal funds that were eventually blended into archdiocesan accounts.

More disturbing to some than the finances of the archdiocese was the discovery of the tactic O'Connell used to succeed Williams. In 1914, Bishop Walsh was appalled to find in the Portland archives the document written by his predecessor at the time of the Boston succession denouncing Bishop Matthew Harkins and other candidates as Americanists. He sent it to Bonzano with the comment that it was "so false and calumnious in so many important points that it really constitutes a 'Libel.'"[30] Bonzano agreed, but there was little to be done about it. "The libel, as your excellency has rightly described it," he replied, "shows to what extremes passion can drive a man. I do not believe that the author of the libel is able to enjoy peacefully the honors acquired at such a dear and shameful price. And God may not wish that he have to experiment with the concept of an eye for an eye and a tooth for a tooth!"[31]

In September 1912, O'Connell tried to mend fences with the two suffragans he had offended most: Harkins and Walsh. While on retreat at St. John's Seminary, the cardinal wrote to each and asked them "to let byegones be byegones [sic]." To Harkins he declared that "false friends have perhaps more than any personal act of ours severed relations which once were cordial, and on my side deeply reverential toward you as an older minister of God." This last sentence is hard to believe, coming from a man who during the campaign for Boston had accused Harkins of Americanism. In reply, Harkins declared that he bore O'Connell no resentment, so there was no need of offering forgiveness.[32]

With Walsh, the cardinal was more reserved, stating that he would do what was in his "power to avoid future misunderstandings." Walsh refused to reply until he had received a second letter in which the cardinal suggested that tale-bearers had poisoned their relationship. The Portland bishop fired back that he held no truck with gossips. "But let me see," he continued, "is there not in the official organ of the Boston Archdiocese [the *Pilot*] some time last spring a record of a speech given by Your E[minence]. at some banquet and containing an almost unparalleled vicious attack upon Bishops—I suppose this is not gossip simply but a real historical fact." Walsh likewise brought up the Boston College speech, which he considered "a most cowardly assault and calumny upon every Seminary, and student of the Sulpician Fathers." Rather than extend the olive branch, he suggested that the cardinal might be mentally abnormal and accused him of being the cause of friction in the New England hierarchy since 1901.[33] Walsh remained an unreconciled, implacable foe of O'Connell. Disturbing as were the Boston finances and the documents detailing how O'Connell had slurred with the charge of Americanism the nominees for the archbishopric, what gave the suffragans their opportunity to move against the cardinal was a very real and palpable scandal that touched his very household and family.

CHAPTER 5

A Married Clergy

LITTLE MORE THAN A YEAR after William O'Connell's elevation to the cardinalate, a calamity of monumental proportion was underway. In order to understand the depth of outrage and shock caused by the events described below, it is necessary to set aside present-day assumptions. In the wake of Vatican II, it has become commonplace for priests to leave the ministry in order to marry. Such was not the case in the decades prior to Vatican II. The expectation of lifelong celibacy was hard and fast. The rare occurrence of a priest's departure from the ministry, which meant his exit from the church, was a cause of notoriety and grave scandal. What made such departures even more damaging was their occurrence in the face of a Protestant majority with a long tradition of anti-Catholicism, an element of which was belief that Catholic priests were lascivious, allegedly preying on women in the confessional and nuns in convents that secretly doubled as brothels for the sexual pleasure of clerics.[1]

To be sure, sexual transgressions by priests did occur, but they were usually kept under wraps and seldom made it into the local press. One paper that delighted in airing them was the *Menace*, a national, anti-Catholic weekly published out of Aurora, Missouri. Founded in 1911, the *Menace* was but one manifestation of a new episode of this prejudice. With a circulation of more than a million and a half in 1914, the paper had reporters in most major cities throughout the country to keep tabs on the doings of Catholics, especially allegations of clerical dalliances. Between June 1913 and June 1914, its columns contained two stories about young women being seduced by their pastors, a court case in which a Catholic clergyman was sued for alienation of affection, another story of a priest shot by a relative of two women in whom the clergyman was taking an "undue interest," an allegation of a priest eloping with a girl, and an uncorroborated tale about an escaped nun, gang-raped by priests in a New Jersey convent.[2]

A most sensational case, however, did make it into the general press and rocked the Catholic community. An immigrant priest in New York had conducted a two-year affair with a young domestic servant, who insisted that he wed her. He did so in a ceremony conducted by himself, acting the part of both clergyman and groom. Unwilling to leave the ministry and the church, and equally unwilling to live apart from his wife, he murdered her in bed, dismembered her body, and tossed the parts from a ferry into the Hudson River. When apprehended by the police, he openly confessed to the crime. The priest's defense attorney argued that his client was insane. "It will be noted," concluded the editor of the *Menace*, "nobody had ever doubted his sanity until after he was caught with the goods." The *Menace* never reported, however, that the man had been suspended from the ministry for fraud by two German dioceses, after which he migrated to America with falsified papers attesting to his worthiness as a priest. In fact, a court in Munich had found him insane. The man came from a family with a history of mental instability and had entered the priesthood against his will to please his mother.[3] These horrendous happenings stunned an American Catholic community unused to such notorious behavior on the part of its clergy.

Even as the scandal in New York was unfolding, there was another situation brewing in Boston with the potential of a similarly disastrous consequence for the Catholic church. Living with Cardinal O'Connell in his Back Bay mansion at 25 Granby Street were his nephew, Father James P. E. O'Connell, chancellor of the archdiocese, and Father David J. Toomey, editor of the *Pilot* and personal chaplain of the uncle. The two priests had become friends as students at the American College in Rome. The nephew had been studying there for his uncle's diocese of Portland until he was expelled in 1903 for carrying on a morally suspect correspondence. He then continued studies at the Grand Seminary in Montreal. He completed his education at the Canisianum in Innsbruck, where he gained a reputation for spending money impulsively. The uncle was quite fond of his nephew and bore the expense of his education both in Italy and Canada.[4]

On 8 September 1906, the elder O'Connell, then coadjutor of

Boston, ordained his nephew privately in their hometown of Lowell. The new priest, twenty-two years old, was two years shy of the canonical age requirement and without a dispensation. He later asserted that he entered the ministry against his will and only for the "business end." His first assignment was as his uncle's personal secretary, a post he held until becoming chancellor in 1912. In both positions, he oversaw all the finances of the archdiocese and did so with a very careful eye. There was something of the worldling about him. Prior to being named a monsignor in 1914, the nephew preferred lay dress to clerical attire and was especially fond of "brown-striped suits with turned-up trousers and short jackets." He was chauffeured about Boston in his expensive automobile.[5]

In April 1912, the Sulpician vicar-general, Father Edward Dyer, informed both Bishops Matthew Harkins and Louis Walsh that a former domestic in the cardinal's personal household was living in St. Peter's parish in New Brunswick, New Jersey, where he talked "freely about the happenings on Granby Street, and that to say that it is not edifying is putting it mildly."[6] By 1913, rumors were abroad in Boston that the younger O'Connell and Toomey were frequently seen wining and dining at hotels and cafes "with women of all kinds of character and no character at all."[7]

In fact, the two were the core members of a group known as *Il Circolo* (The Circle), a cadre of younger clergymen known for their wild times together. On one occasion in 1916, the circle gathered for a dinner reported to have cost over $500 ($9,100 in 2006 terms) or $35 per head. The menu, printed specially for the occasion, was so risqué that the printer would not allow the women in his shop to see it. The event boasted a seventy-six-year-old vintage Madeira wine.[8] A Boston cabby recounted that on a Good Friday evening, he picked up at Granby Street the younger O'Connell, Toomey, and some women— all of them inebriated—and delivered them to the opera. Good Friday is among the holiest days in the Catholic calendar, to be devoted to fasting, prayer, and reflection on the sufferings of Jesus.[9]

In March 1913, the *Boston Globe* carried a back-page notice that Toomey was being sued for $20,000 ($400,000 in 2006 terms) by Alice

Leary, who alleged breach of promise to marry. Such a suit normally implied cohabitation, and there were reports that Leary had borne a child. Although the item failed to identify Toomey as a priest, both Bishop Thomas Beaven and Father John Mullen noted that the suit and Toomey's clerical identity were public knowledge before the paper went to press. Henry V. Cunningham, the cardinal's attorney and a longtime friend of Mullen, represented Toomey. When Mullen learned that Cunningham was inclined to doubt Toomey's guilt, the priest informed the lawyer of the stories abroad concerning Toomey and urged him to investigate them before deciding to contest the issue in open court. Soon thereafter Cunningham settled the suit privately, paying Leary the $20,000.[10] Still, Toomey remained at Granby Street and continued at his post.

All of the suffragans were made aware of the situation because an anonymous informant sent each of them the item in the *Boston Globe*. One of the bishops also received a letter from an unidentified writer asking how "a man might be elected [cardinal] who could make such a choice for a private chaplain?" He urged the bishop to "look into it and see if Granby Street has a moral tone." The occupants had money for vacations, dinners in hotels, and season tickets to the opera. "Can it go forever?" wondered the writer. "$20,000 paid by Lawyer Cunningham and all publicity hushed, and the three bulls still at large."[11]

Even though Monsignor Bonaventura Cerretti, then in charge of the apostolic delegation in Washington, was abreast of these happenings, Beaven felt compelled to express himself directly to Rome. Dramatizing the situation, he forwarded the *Globe* clipping to Cardinal Diomede Falconio, the former apostolic delegate to the United States, and described the reaction in the Hub:

> His eminence of Boston is en route to Rome "to supervise the drainage of San Clemente [his titular church]." An excellent purpose. He goes at a time when his Metropolitan City is abashed with shame and stirred "ab imis" [from the depths] by the notoriety of a scandalous happening. It is sad beyond measure that the

sensibilities of the respectable Catholic should be exposed to the ridicule of the Protestant public and the Church besmirched in the eyes of a cynical populace.... The public now accepts the Cardinalitial [*sic*] activities of Boston as a "mise en scene" full of pomp and show, well staged and full of the glamour of insincerity. Right into the midst of this public mentality, is thrown a petard of scandal affecting intimately his own household of Granby Street and arousing the general public with the startling query—"In God's name, where are we drifting?"[12]

In December 1913, the *Menace* went public with the story of the Toomey-Leary affair, gleaned from court records. It identified the defendant as "Reverend, or Father, David J. Toomey, who lives in the same house with Cardinal O'Connell" and who was being represented by the cardinal's attorney. It also noted that the priest was the editor of the *Pilot*, which frequently referred to the *Menace* as a "filthy sheet." The irony of the epithet was not lost on the Missouri editor, who said that all the Boston dailies knew that the man named in the suit was a sullied priest, but none had gone to press with the story. A reporter for one of the biggest Boston papers informed the *Menace* that when he had asked his editor for permission to publish the item, he was told: "Nothing doing. Do you think we can afford to touch that, in a Catholic city like Boston?"[13] Though the papers of that city kept the story quiet, the *Menace* gave it a national, if limited, airing.

A drive was soon underway for the cardinal's ouster. During the winter of 1914, Bishops Beaven, Walsh, Joseph Rice of Burlington, and Daniel Feehan of Fall River went to the Vatican for this purpose. Harkins was soon to follow. The first group spoke to nine cardinals. "In every case, except Del Val [*sic*]," reported Walsh, "the Boston tragedy and comedy was the chief topic." With regard to O'Connell's removal, the only answer available was "Cui bono? Qui [*sic*] lo sa? [For what purpose? Who knows?]" Summarizing the situation, Walsh told Harkins: "I assure you that there is and can be no longer either ignorantia or bona fides [ignorance or good faith]. By the time you get here the climax ought to be clear and easy, but the remedy nobody seems willing to propose or to push, except Falconio, who is certainly speaking and hitting out."[14]

Some old Americanists and anti-Americanists sided with the suffragans. During this campaign for O'Connell's removal, Archbishop John Ireland of St. Paul described Harkins variously as "my ideal type of a bishop," "our leader," and "a valiant fighter in the present war." He informed Walsh that Archbishop Sebastian Messmer of Milwaukee, an anti-Americanist lately reconciled with his former opponents, was one with the New England bishops. Before going to Rome in the spring of 1914, Messmer told Archbishop John Keane of Dubuque, "On my knees I will beg the Pope to remove O'Connell from America."[15] Nothing came of the drive and the cardinal remained in Boston. But even conservative churchmen in Europe were sizing him up negatively. As the pope's health failed, anti-modernists (integralists, as they were known in Catholicism) inventoried the college of cardinals. Their assessment of O'Connell was unflattering: "Childhood friend of Merry del Val, made himself indispensable to the latter, plays the Roman, represents Romanism in America, very shady, an ambitious man who forced his way to the top through money."[16]

It may be that events saved O'Connell. In August 1914, Pius X died and was succeeded by Cardinal Giacomo della Chiesa, archbishop of Bologna, who took the name Benedict XV. In the very month of Pius's death, World War I broke out. During the next four years, travel between America and Europe was hampered. While the disruption of communication and the change in papal administration may have spared O'Connell, the accession of Benedict XV signaled a marked decline in the Boston cardinal's influence. The new pontiff was a disciple of Cardinal Mariano Rampolla, Leo XIII's conciliatory secretary of state, and was opposed to Pius X's repressive measures against Modernism. The new pope and Cardinal Raphael Merry del Val were in opposite camps. When the latter perfunctorily resigned as secretary of state, Benedict replaced him with the progressive Cardinal Pietro Gasparri.[17] O'Connell's Roman star was on the wane.

Meanwhile a more serious tragedy was unfolding. A year prior to Toomey's dalliance with Leary, the cardinal's nephew-chancellor had met a young married woman, Frankie Johnson Wort, at a party in New York City. They fell in love. James P. E. O'Connell was forthright, telling her who and what he was. She took up residence in South Dakota for six months to avail herself of the state's liberal policy toward divorce. On 7 April 1913, Wort sundered the union with her husband and two days later married O'Connell at Crown Point, Indiana, under his real name. Throughout the summer the couple traveled Europe with Toomey. O'Connell and his wife assumed the surname Roe, and Toomey took the alias Fossa. On their return, the three were detained by U.S. Customs officers for failing to declare items. An agent became suspicious when he saw a small gathering loudly admiring Frankie Roe's pearl necklace. Upon inspecting the luggage, agents found undeclared purchases, including cuff buttons, shirt studs, a silver cigarette case, and a number of obscene pictures valued at $25 ($500 in 2006 terms). The pictures were confiscated and destroyed.[18]

The newlyweds took up residence on Long Island for the first year or so of their marriage and then moved to an apartment in New York City on West End Avenue. Their lifestyle was high-class. The apartment cost $300 a month ($6,000 in 2006 terms), and the Roes had a butler and servants. James had given Frankie a necklace valued at $20,000 ($400,000 in 2006 dollars), perhaps the pearls that were so admired on the dock. Leaving for New York on Wednesdays, Mister Roe spent half the week with his wife. Back in Boston, he was Monsignor James O'Connell, chancellor of the archdiocese. With regard to priestliness, he had told his wife that he had "nothing to do with that end of it." His was simply a business function.[19]

To support his new lifestyle, he no doubt turned to embezzling archdiocesan funds, which he oversaw. Within about four years, the cardinal may have suspected as much. In 1917, he requested that henceforth checks from parishes—for the cathedraticum and parish collections—be made out to him personally rather than in the name of the nephew.[20] Still, the uncle kept his young kinsman at his post.

In June 1914, the Roes introduced Toomey/Fossa to a twenty-one-year-old Catholic girl, Florence Marlow. Telling her he was a federal secret agent with business between New York and Boston, Toomey/Fossa quickly enticed her into marriage before a justice of the peace in Hempstead, Long Island. The next month the conscience-stricken bride begged to have the nuptials validated by her pastor at Corpus Christi parish in New York City. Toomey/Fossa agreed. Lacking proof of baptism under that alias, the errant priest was conditionally re-baptized before the ratification of the marriage. Like the Roes, the Fossas took an apartment in New York where the husband spent several days each week. In the course of their union, Florence came to know the true identities of both her husband and James O'Connell/Roe.[21] Thus, two of Cardinal O'Connell's closest associates, men with whom he lived, were leading double lives.

Nor were they careful about their situation. On one occasion when the uncle was away, the two brought their wives to Granby Street, and the nephew allowed his spouse to sleep in the cardinal's bed. According to Mullen, the staff at the Granby Street house was in collusion to keep the uncle in the dark about what was going on. Someone, however, let the uncle in on the secret. Florence Marlow Fossa later testified that in 1915 her husband Toomey/Fossa received a late-night call from O'Connell/Roe telling him "to come at once by the midnight train to Boston because the Cardinal had learned about them." When O'Connell confronted the pair with the allegation that they were married, they told him that "the information must have originated with some old crank."[22]

In that same year or the year following, the district attorney of Boston, Joseph Pelletier, a prominent Knight of Columbus who, at O'Connell's request, was made a Knight of St. Gregory by Pope Benedict XV, informed the cardinal that people were making remarks about the chancellor "affecting his character, by reason of his association with women in Hotels, not precisely about deeds of moral turpitude, but rather touching his moral reputation in general." Although the cardinal pursued these matters no further, Pelletier began to have the nephew watched.[23]

The deception unravelled in the fall of 1918. During that year,

Toomey/Fossa took a mistress, Catherine O'Leary, a secretary on the staff of the *Pilot*. Thereafter, he began to visit his wife less and less frequently until he finally ceased visiting her altogether. Florence went to Boston and hired detectives, who discovered that he was living with O'Leary across the Charles River in Cambridge. On 19 October, Florence surprised her husband and his mistress in their love nest on Williams Street and was arrested for disturbing the peace. Toomey/Fossa abandoned priesthood and wife and fled to New York. It was said that a review of the *Pilot*'s financial records revealed that he had misappropriated more than $30,000 of the paper's funds ($394,000 in 2006 terms). After posting bail, Florence was advised to see Cardinal O'Connell. She informed him of both Toomey/Fossa's and the nephew's marriages. O'Connell promised to pay her bond if she would fail to appear in court. When she asked him why he kept "his skunk" of a nephew as chancellor, the uncle replied that it was "for his mother's sake." Florence later testified that after the interview, the cardinal's attorney, Cunningham, opened negotiations with her "to purchase my silence" about the younger O'Connell. Mullen went to see his friend Cunningham and "spoke to him of the common rumors about the marriage of Mgr. O'Connell, and he gave every sign of believing the story." In Mullen's view, "If he [Cunningham] knew, the Cardinal knew also." Ultimately, Cunningham gave Mrs. Fossa $7,200 ($94,500 in 2006 terms) in cash and property; he also took care of her lawyer's fee, another $1,000 ($13,000). Though the press never got wind of the story—or at least never ran it—word of Toomey's doings quickly spread through the clergy.[24]

Before Florence Fossa had taken the hush money, a Catholic policeman, who learned of her arrest, "took a sympathetic interest" in the twenty-six-year-old and brought her for advice to Father Michael Doody, pastor of St. Mary of the Annunciation parish in Cambridge. Doody had been chancellor under Archbishop John Williams and, according to Mullen, was universally esteemed by the laity and "treated with great regard by the Cardinal himself." Prior to meeting Florence, Doody was, in Mullen's words, "not inclined to believe the reports about the immoral life of the Chancellor and Toomey." The priest advised her to send for her father, Michael Marlow, in New York so that he could support her during her difficulties. When Marlow arrived, he and his daughter told Doody about the marriages of both Toomey/Fossa and O'Connell/Roe. Doody contacted Mullen, and the two priests put the father and daughter in touch with the apostolic delegate, Archbishop Giovanni Bonzano.[25]

Informed of the younger O'Connell's marriage, Bonzano asked the New York chancery office to begin an investigation. The chancellor, Father John Dunn, hired two detectives to verify that James Roe and James P. E. O'Connell were indeed the same man. At the time O'Connell/Roe was living with his wife and her mother in a house at 102 E. 36th Street, a property valued at $36,000 ($413,000 in 2006 dollars). The couple had obviously scaled down from their apartment on West End. In early April, the detectives followed O'Connell/Roe on a walk. He went into Ovington's department store where he remained for some time. When he emerged, he kept glancing over his shoulder as if to see if he was being followed. The detectives then set up surveillance on his residence. They in turn were being observed by agents of a private firm that provided security to the neighborhood. These agents let O'Connell/Roe know that he was being watched, and they reported the chancery's men to the police. All four—the two chancery detectives and the two security men—were taken to the local precinct house, where the assistant district attorney of New York, Alfred J. Talley, intervened. He warned the security agents to cease and desist their interference with the chancery's detectives because they were obstructing justice. Even so, Dunn pulled his people off the case lest their activity confirm O'Connell/Roe's suspicion that he was being tailed.[26]

At this point, Talley used police detectives to hunt O'Connell/Roe to ground. They noted that several pieces of mail had come from 25 Granby Street in Boston to the house on 36th Street in New York. On Friday, 11 April 1919, O'Connell/Roe himself arrived at the residence. The following afternoon he took a long walk with his wife, and that evening they attended a performance of *Carmen* at the Metropolitan Opera, where one of the detectives approached within five feet of the husband and got a very good look at him. The next afternoon the couple went to the Eltinge Theater on 42nd Street to see *Up in Mabel's Room*, a comedy described by Dunn as "a lascivious production." On Wednesday, 16 April, a detective followed O'Connell/Roe from New York to Boston. He boarded a train in the former city, traveled in a private compartment, and stepped off at Bay Station in Boston wearing a Roman collar, with his coat collar turned up. He was met by a friend, Vincent Garo, an attorney with an unsavory reputation. After a brief stop at Granby Street, the two went to dinner at Pollesippo's Italian restaurant on Richmond Street in a then rough area of Boston's North End.[27]

At this establishment, Dunn's and Pelletier's investigations came together literally by accident. While the New York detective was inside observing O'Connell/Roe, Inspector Cavangaro of the Boston police, who was also tailing the nephew, approached the latter and Garo. The attorney introduced his friend as James O'Connell. After dinner at about 10:00 P.M., Garo and O'Connell abruptly rose, left the premises, jumped into a taxi, and sped away. In his haste to pursue them, the New York detective collided with another automobile, and "the quarry was lost." Already at the scene of the accident, Cavagnaro discovered that one of the drivers was a policeman also tailing O'Connell/Roe. The two officers exchanged information, including that Garo's dinner companion was James O'Connell.[28]

Apprised of the New York investigation, Pelletier went to the cardinal on Easter Sunday, 20 April 1919, to tell him that detectives had reason to believe his nephew was married. Dismissing the allegation as the invention of enemies who had made the same accusations several years before, O'Connell assured Pelletier there was nothing to fear. Not satisfied with this explanation, Pelletier went to New York to check with officials there, who told him everything. Hoping to save the church from scandal, he returned to Boston and laid the facts before the cardinal, namely, that investigators had positively identified his nephew as James Roe, a New York businessman married to Frankie Johnson Wort, a divorcée, and that David Toomey, former editor of the *Pilot*, was also married and living in that city. The cardinal denied all. When Pelletier offered to supply information and witnesses to prove the allegations, O'Connell refused to see them. His enemies, he declared, were conspiring to ruin the young chancellor, "a poor slandered boy, who spends his life between the office and home in order to surround his sainted mother with attention." Pelletier asked the cardinal to give him the names of the enemies, and he would use every means to investigate and vindicate the nephew. O'Connell declined the offer, stating "that after the example of our Lord we ought to put up with persecutions and slanders." The cardinal's refusal to allow an investigation convinced Pelletier of the nephew's guilt and the uncle's knowledge of it.[29]

Immediately after Pelletier's visit, O'Connell attempted to secure his position. He began summoning priests to inquire if they had heard any talk about Toomey. When they answered affirmatively, he told them to keep quiet because the gossip was nothing but false rumors.[30]

In late spring, Bonzano sought information about the situation in Boston from Father James A. Walsh, superior of the Catholic Foreign Mission Society of America, popularly known as Maryknoll because of the location of its headquarters. Walsh had been ordained for the archdiocese of Boston in 1892 and had served as diocesan director of the Society for the Propagation of the Faith. He had spent his last seven years in Boston at the cathedral under both Archbishops John Williams and O'Connell. In 1911, Walsh had gone to the Vatican to secure approval for the establishment of Maryknoll. Bonzano apparently considered him an impartial observer and wanted his read on conditions in the archdiocese. Walsh replied that during his time under O'Connell, he found the latter "courteous and cordial." He stated, however, that he had recently seen evidence of the tactic that the cardinal had used to become archbishop of Boston, material that revealed "plotting such as never before stained the clean pages of ecclesiastical history of New England." The incriminating proof was Father Patrick Supple's letter to Cardinal Girolamo Gotti at the time of the Boston succession, accusing Bishop Matthew Harkins of Americanism, a charge Walsh considered false and "ridiculous." "The 'anti-Roman' idea seems to have been played rather skillfully," he told Bonazano.[31]

Walsh thought that if upon succeeding Williams, O'Connell "had surrounded himself with a group of worthy priests, he could have overcome to a considerable extent the bad effect made upon the public mind . . . by the idea—new for Boston—that a bishopric could be secured by political trickery." Instead, he had gathered about himself "relatives and personal friends" without regard to their standing. "Those favored by the Ordinary [O'Connell]," continued Walsh, "have practically paid to him the tribute of money. . . . Even honest and unsuspecting priests have been approached and urged by intimate friends of the Ordinary to send him on certain occasions, e.g., his birth-day, gifts of money." With regard to the finances of Boston, Walsh remarked, "Certainly, every possible source of income has been developed so that to-day the Archbishop of Boston is often spoken of as 'money-mad.'" Walsh said "that keen and experienced pastors reckon his personal income as between $100,000 and $150,000 a year from known sources of revenue [$1.14 and $1.79 million respectively in 2006 dollars]." He added that there were many among the clergy who suspected that the cardinal's position "as Corporation Sole" gave him the power "to transfer vast sums of money to his personal account." In order to deflect such criticism, said Walsh, O'Connell at times privately "declares that everything in his name belongs to the Archdiocese, but nobody takes the statement seriously."[32]

Walsh referred to the tragedies in the curia only in passing, stating that Bonzano already had "certain knowledge of the scandalous career of the Archbishop's nephew, and of Dr. Toomey." He noted that "common gossip" held that another priest close to the cardinal was also leading a double life. Walsh said that he had often been asked why the priests of the archdiocese had not risen to express their feelings. His answer: "The traditions of Boston were utterly against such action. Rome had spoken and that was enough even if it brought sadness." The clergy of Boston loved Pius X, "and they knew he had been deceived." Concerted clerical action against O'Connell was impossible, wrote Walsh, because "critical remarks reached headquarters through unknown agents; and individual priests felt helpless against the cleverness that had enabled an American curate to boldly push his way, through high and responsible positions, into the College of Cardinals." Quoting from Supple's letter to Gotti and turning it against O'Connell, Walsh concluded: ". . . '[T]here is a universal cry for change'; and that 'the change so ardently desired by hundreds of priests and thousands of laymen must come from Rome.'"[33]

In July 1919, Archbishop Bonzano sailed to Italy and presented the initial dossier on the younger O'Connell to Pope Benedict XV. Basically, it included the testimony and evidence gathered thus far about the chancellor's marriage, but lacked a crucial piece: the wedding license. Without success, detectives had tried to locate the place of the marriage.[34]

Perhaps acting on Bonzano's evidence, Cardinal Gaetano De Lai, secretary of the Consistorial Congregation and a supporter of O'Connell, sent Father Giuseppe Schwarz, procurator general of the Redemptorists, to make discreet inquiries about affairs in Boston. Schwarz filed a favorable report indicating that all accusations against the cardinal were "*calumnies*" instigated by Supple, who had once been close to O'Connell, but had lately broken with him. De Lai forwarded the report to Bonzano, who had since returned to America. Bonzano replied that the majority of the charges brought against O'Connell had come "from priests not at all friendly to Supple, and even before the break." The report convinced Bonzano that Schwarz had taken no sworn depositions but had simply "contented himself with news and information, indirect and gathered in conversations with persons who did not suspect the purpose of his visit. . . . That would also explain why the visitor seems not to have had an inkling of the scandals given by the Rev. David Toomey and by the nephew chancellor which indeed are in the public domain." Schwarz's approach, said Bonzano, was doomed to failure. People would never casually speak of the scandalous behavior of the two for fear of reprisal from the cardinal. The only way to get the truth was "to ask it under oath, assuring the informants that their names would not be revealed." Bonzano recommended that if Schwarz was still in New England, he should take sworn testimony from Father Doody and Bishops Rice and Feehan.[35] Apparently, the visitor had already left.

Feeling like a scapegoat for the cardinal's troubles, Toomey invited Doody to New York to hear his side of the story. In November 1919, Doody went to see him in company with Mullen. Toomey, who had been the cardinal's personal chaplain, averred that the uncle had no faith: he never said mass, never went to confession, and never recited the breviary. Moreover, the nephew had stolen perhaps a million dollars from the archdiocese, while the cardinal had misappropriated thousands from diocesan collections. The two kinsmen quarreled frequently and violently, even to threats of shooting. On one occasion, the uncle had tried to get rid of his nephew, who replied, "You go to hell; I'll leave when I damn please." The younger O'Connell could not be dismissed, said Toomey, because he had proof that the cardinal had stolen church funds. More significant, the nephew "had manuscript love letters and love poems written by the Cardinal to four men who were intimate with him." Toomey named names. Though the men will remain nameless in this volume, one was an administrator at St. Elizabeth's Hospital, another was a lieutenant in the Brookline Fire Department, the third was a dentist, and the last was a non-Catholic. Toomey then delivered a crucial nugget of evidence: the general location of the younger O'Connell's marriage. Without knowing the exact spot, he assured Doody and Mullen that the nephew had married somewhere along the rail line between Chicago and Hammond, Indiana, at a place that was a virtual "Gretna Green."[36]

Given this information, Pelletier went to work. Within three weeks his detectives found both O'Connell's marriage license and the wife's decree of divorce, the former in Lake County, Indiana, and the latter in Sioux Falls, South Dakota. Mullen made photostat copies and sent them to Bonzano in January 1920. The delegate held them for three months because of reluctance to involve himself "in such disagreeable matters." On Easter Sunday, 4 April 1920, O'Connell gave his flock short notice that he was going to Rome for a routine visit to report on the archdiocese. When he sailed two days later, Bonzano decided to act, sending the documents to Cardinal Pietro Gasparri, Vatican secretary of state.[37]

At the same time, Mullen posted a report to Archbishop Bonaventura Cerretti, secretary of the Congregation for Extraordinary Ecclesiastical Affairs, a branch of the Vatican Secretariat of State. It offered a complete reconstruction of the Toomey and O'Connell marriages so that "from these two cases the irreligious spirit and the deplorable condition of Cardinal O'Connell's regime in Boston may be judged." Painstakingly, Mullen showed that the cardinal knew of and tolerated the scandalous behavior of his two intimates. Piece by piece, he rehearsed the evidence, beginning with Toomey's liaison with Alice Leary in 1913.[38]

Mullen also attacked the uncle's spiritual life, as the reason why the cardinal, whose duty it was to take swift action against the transgressions of Toomey and the nephew, had failed to do anything. The elder O'Connell seldom presided at mass in public, and when he did, the ceremony was always truncated. It was widely believed that he never said mass in private, an allegation corroborated by Toomey, who had stated that the cardinal in fact had no faith. Finally, noted Mullen, O'Connell was a longtime, intimate friend, and sometime traveling companion of the late Dr. William Dunn, who had gained a reputation for homosexuality in an age when that was a dark secret. Dunn's will had been contested by relatives because the bulk of the estate went to an unnamed male friend. The incriminating documents were not admitted into evidence and were subsequently destroyed by O'Connell's attorney, Cunningham. Mullen learned from Pelletier that the letters showed "immorality on the part of Dr. Dunn and C[ardinal]. O'C[onnell]."[39]

The implication of Mullen's argument was clear. O'Connell could not have been expected to act against the nephew and Toomey because he was as corrupt as they were. Indeed, in Mullen's view, he was the source of corruption. "There is a mortal disease in the Boston diocese that Rome alone can cure," concluded the priest. "To remove the Chancellor and the other unpriestly officials of the curia is only to paint the wound. Others coming in their place will be ruined as long as the Cardinal is alloed [sic] to stay in Boston. . . . [He] is radically unfit to remain here. If he were 'promoted' to be a Cardinal in thc [Vatican] curia he would be saved from harming the Church. . . . The Bishops of the country look forward with horror to the thought of such a man being spokesman for the American Church in case Cardinal [James] Gibbons should die."[40] This last sentence was true of the Boston suffragans and many bishops around the nation. With regard to the suggested "promotion," neighboring dioceses buzzed with rumors that Rome intended to do it.[41] Unfortunately, they were wrong.

On 2 May 1920, Cardinal O'Connell had a private audience with Benedict XV. To convey his disgust at the crimes of the Boston curia, the pope received the American in a cold, informal manner. When confronted with the story of the nephew's marriage, O'Connell denied it. In proof, Benedict produced the copy of the marriage license. The cardinal dropped to his knees and begged for mercy. Infuriated by his disclaimers, the pontiff warned him of his bad position for tolerating the nephew. Although Benedict seriously considered removing O'Connell from his see, dealing with the chancellor came first.[42] The pope struck the nephew from the list of monsignors and gave the uncle a month to remove him from office. By attempting marriage, moreover, James O'Connell had incurred automatic excommunication and was to be defrocked if he failed to amend.[43] According to the teaching of the church, the sacrament of ordination made it invalid for a priest to marry because it constituted an impediment to any union, hence the term "attempting marriage."

Once back home, O'Connell angrily denounced the pope and the Roman cardinals to his auxiliary bishop, Joseph Anderson, as God-damned sons of bitches. He then brazenly mounted a defense of his nephew and in July sent a preliminary brief to Benedict. Although it failed to win a dismissal of the charges, it gained a stay of execution. Granting a continuance until 30 October to enable a complete presentation of the case, the pope allowed the nephew to remain in office until that date; Benedict himself would render final judgment.[44]

No doubt aware that Mullen was one of the nephew's principal accusers, O'Connell summoned him to the chancery office in August. He asked the priest if he had seen a certified copy of James O'Connell's wedding license. Mullen admitted that he had. The cardinal told him it was a forgery. The priest replied that he had no reason to believe that it was. All the evidence he had seen corroborated its genuineness. O'Connell simply stated, "It is not true."[45]

On 18 September, the uncle submitted a thorough argument to Rome. Basically, he attacked the credibility of the witnesses by alleging that the New York detectives had falsified their report about the nephew and that Florence Fossa was a compromised woman with a jail record (her arrest for disturbing the peace). Toomey was a man without honor for fleeing his post under criminal accusation. Moreover, he and his wife had attempted to extort money from the uncle and nephew in return for keeping silent. When the two kinsmen refused to be blackmailed, Toomey sold his testimony to "those [Doody and Mullen] nourishing a vendetta against the chancellor . . . because he has done his duty without respect of persons." Positively, the cardinal asserted that his nephew had never set foot in Frankie Roe's home in New York and had never been in Indiana. It was impossible that James O'Connell had married Frankie Johnson Wort on 9 April 1913, because on that date she and her mother were visiting friends, and the nephew was working at the chancery office, as two curia officials, Monsignor Richard J. Haberlin and Father Charles J. Sullivan, swore under oath. Supporting documents were attached.[46]

While O'Connell made a last ditch effort to save his nephew, others were attempting to unseat the uncle himself. In May, Bishops Feehan and Rice had followed him to Rome, where the pope informed them of all that had occurred in the interview with O'Connell. Returning home two months later, the two met at Springfield, Massachusetts, with Bishops Beaven and Walsh. "We all four," noted the latter, "made up our minds on what course it was our sacred duty to take, now that the Holy See had spoken and we agreed upon all points."[47] Their plan was to ask the pontiff for O'Connell's removal, which they did on 31 July 1920. The quartet was supported by Harkins, his coadjutor bishop, William Hickey, and Bishop John Nilan of Hartford. The only suffragan who refused to sign the petition was Bishop George Guertin of Manchester. The request was brief. It began, "The facts, based on definite testimony, concerning the most grave affair in Boston are already well known to Your Holiness." Impelled in conscience by their sacred office as bishops, the undersigned declared that the "salvation of the church—of course, humanly speaking—and for that reason honor, reverence, and confidence toward the Holy See" throughout New England if not all North America, "intensely urges that the present cardinal archbishop be removed immediately from the archiepiscopal see of Boston."[48]

Their petition drew a request from Cerretti for additional evidence of the serious consequences that would result from leaving O'Connell in office. Walsh drafted a response complaining that he did not know what more "tangible proofs" Rome could want. The Vatican already possessed all the details and overwhelming testimony. He warned that the scandals were becoming known in the Catholic community and might eventually become public. "It will be a calamity and catastrophe," he wrote, "if the responsibility for the conditions of the last ten or more years in the Boston Curia is not placed where it belongs, on His Em[inence]., who gave almost 'carte blanche' to the Chancellor and Editor and their coterie." The suffragans cared little about the "opprobrium" that would befall Toomey and the two O'Connells when the marriages became public. They were concerned for the reputation of the pope because the cardinal had consistently portrayed himself as "the special representative of the Holy See . . . and quasi mouthpiece of the Holy See, not only in his own Diocese, but for the country at large." Pressured by work, Walsh set this draft aside for more than a month.[49]

When he returned to it in December 1920, he let the first part of the letter stand, but now took an assertive approach about the repercussions on the pope. Walsh said that the scandal would certainly become public. When it did, "the surprise and the indignation" would be "crystallized" in the simple sentence: "Concubinage among officials of the Boston curia was approved by the archbishop and tolerated by the Holy See." That would be "the intelligent public verdict." If people asked why the suffragans permitted this behavior, they would truthfully say that they had informed the apostolic delegate and the Vatican and had begged for the removal of the cardinal. Walsh told Cerretti that he was "free to use this letter with the Holy Father."[50]

As Walsh indicated, the affair was becoming known. Mullen's classmate, Bishop Michael Gallagher of Detroit, told him that Archbishop Daniel Mannix of Melbourne, Australia, who was visiting in the states, refused an invitation to Boston because of the scandals in the curia there. In a conversation with Mullen, Joseph O'Neil, a Catholic banker, made no secret of the nephew's marriage or the papal order to remove him. The layman wondered why the cardinal had not carried out the pope's command. All he could figure was that "Jimmy must have something on the Big Fellow." According to Mullen, the *Menace* knew the details of both Toomey's and O'Connell's marriages, but lacked sufficient proof to make it legally safe to take the scandals to press.[51] Several years later, he averred that the *Boston Herald* too was aware of the unfitness of both O'Connells, uncle and nephew, but because "of the overwhelming strength of Catholic influence" in Boston, the journal did "not dare to open up publicity."[52] Although the *Herald* might have been willing to defer to Catholic sensibility, it is probable that if the *Menace* had the requisite documentation to prove its story, it would have taken the item public, despite the well-financed legal defense O'Connell might have mounted.

While Cerretti sought more evidence, his superior, Cardinal Gasparri, sent O'Connell's defense of the nephew to Bonzano for examination and verification. At the same time, he told the latter that since the nephew no longer enjoyed the reputation necessary for the office of chancellor, Benedict ordered him to be removed no later than the end of November.[53] On the eighth of that month, James O'Connell submitted his resignation, effective the twenty-seventh. Claiming the strain of duty, he asked for a year's leave of absence to rest and reminded his uncle of a promise to reserve "a parochial appointment commensurate as a just reward for the work I have done, with the merits my years of special service have earned me." Apparently, the two were putting an official veneer on a seamy tale. Mullen informed Bonzano that the *Boston Herald* had reported the younger O'Connell's request for a leave and announced that in the meantime, Monsignor Haberlin, the cardinal's secretary, would act as chancellor. The brief notice was buried with the shipping news on page sixteen. Never a word appeared in the *Pilot*, the cardinal's newspaper. After the nephew's departure, it was learned from sources originating among New York banks that he had taken with him $750,000 in archdiocesan funds, a sum that would run to almost $8.25 million in present-day terms.[54]

Bonzano mailed the cardinal's defense of the nephew to Mullen. In late December, the latter returned a lengthy commentary refuting most arguments and casting doubt on the rest. Essentially, he showed that the cardinal's affidavits hammered at ancillary points, while avoiding the marriage altogether, thus creating a smoke screen. The only document to the contrary was Haberlin and Sullivan's testimony that the chancellor had worked in the office on the wedding day. Mullen marveled at how lightly they swore "that they knew just where they were on an ordinary day in April over seven years before!" He believed the cardinal had put them up to the falsehood. Both were the nephew's friends, and the notary public who sealed their testimony was Garo, the chancellor's "boon companion" and "his friend in their carousals."[55]

With this information, Bonzano replied to Gasparri. In addition to the points made by Mullen, Bonzano noted that the detectives on the case were working for the district attorneys of Boston and New York, and their report simply confirmed proven facts. Mrs. Fossa had indeed been in jail for one night, but that had been for making a scene when she surprised her husband, Toomey/Fossa, with another woman. Far from vengeance, Doody and Mullen's sole motive was "to save the diocese and the cardinal himself from public scandal." Moreover, a forensic handwriting expert had determined that the nephew's signature was identical to the one on the wedding license.[56]

During the winter of 1921, Pope Benedict studied the evidence and defense. Not satisfied with his own reading of the documents, he sought advice from someone "as expert in the English language as he [was] learned and experienced in dealing with similar cases."[57] The cardinal's rebuttal, as Cerretti later told Walsh, "was riddled by shot and shell from the special consultor."[58] Both the advisor and Benedict reached the same conclusion as Bonzano and Mullen, that is, James O'Connell was guilty as charged.[59]

On 22 April 1921, Gasparri sent the uncle a thorough rebuttal of his arguments. He reminded O'Connell that the Vatican possessed "an authentic copy of the civil marriage contract entered into by Mrs. Frankie Johnson with James O'Connell at Crown Point, 9 April 1913." A handwriting expert confirmed that the signatures of the nephew and the O'Connell on the wedding license were the same. "The sworn declarations given by the priests Haberlin and Sullivan to create an *alibi* in favor of Rev. James P. E. O'Connell," wrote Gasparri, were worthless because, as friends of the accused, "their testimony appears somewhat biased and at the very least suspect." Echoing Mullen, he found it hard to believe that they could remember the nephew was in the office on a day so distant in time because it was "a fact that . . . has nothing of the extraordinary about it." If the chancellor had been in the office the day of the marriage, it would have been easy "to present some incontrovertible proof." Gasparri noted that "if the accused were really conscious of his innocence, he ought to have denied openly and without evasions that he had contracted the marriage he is accused of instead of either proposing doubts that were easily shown to be baseless or hurling reproaches against his supposed enemies." Nor did the young monsignor invite his wife "to make a formal declaration that she is not married to him and instead bring forward the real husband, James O'Connell." Gasparri reminded the cardinal "that such proof could be produced without difficulty." Therefore, the pontiff carried out the sentence against the nephew, who was defrocked and excommunicated. Gasparri urged O'Connell, "as ordinary of the unfortunate priest and with that affection that you have always demonstrated toward him, to invite and persuade him to look seriously and with solicitude to his own conscience."[60]

James O'Connell lived out his life with his wife in New York. The couple retained the surname Roe, and the husband maintained a low profile as a businessman. In 1948, he died of a heart ailment at the age of sixty-three. His wife followed him to the grave twenty-one years later.[61] According to Dorothy Wayman, a newspaper reporter and biographer of Cardinal O'Connell, in the 1950s Richard Cushing, Boston's second cardinal, found the elderly and infirm Toomey. Cushing placed him in a Catholic hospital and helped him make peace with the church before his death.[62]

Why Cardinal O'Connell retained his nephew may never be known for certain. Reasons there were aplenty, most given by the participants, but often conflicting. The cardinal, for instance, had told Florence Fossa that he kept James O'Connell for the sake of the young man's mother, a tacit admission that uncle knew what was going on. Yet the nephew hinted at another reason for his being retained. In the summer of 1918, he had tried to resign the chancellorship, but the cardinal refused to allow it. In a subsequent letter to Cunningham, the nephew explained that he felt overworked from bearing the burden of office alone; the cardinal considered him essential and entrusted tasks to no one else. Yet James O'Connell confided that he was "indispensable only inasmuch as he [his uncle] believes so."[63] Certainly, the uncle was attached to his nephew; he had paid for the lad's clerical training in both Rome and Canada, and fostered his career.

Toomey, on the other hand, alleged that the chancellor remained because he held so much of the cardinal's money and had proof of his sexual preference for men. The cardinal had indeed kept property in the nephew's name. In accord with Toomey's picture, Mullen noted that for more than twenty years Dunn, the homosexual, was the cardinal's longtime, intimate friend—the implication being that a man was to be judged by the company he kept, circumstantial evidence to be sure. Perhaps Toomey and Mullen were right, the nephew held property and knowledge of sexual preference as blackmail against his uncle.[64] It is possible that all these reasons played a part. Human relations are complex and at times messy. A combination of attachment, dependency, family loyalty, and blackmail might best explain why the Boston prelate stood by his nephew to the bitter end.

If O'Connell's attempts to Romanize the New England province and his arrogant use of his office for personal gain had estranged him from his suffragans, the scandals of Toomey and the nephew positively alienated them from him. Though Rome had failed as of yet to take action against the cardinal, the bishops of New England remained committed to his removal at all hazard. They would carry the fight to the American hierarchy at large, something that would have near disastrous consequences for the fledgling National Catholic Welfare Council (NCWC), an organization barely two years old and one for which O'Connell had very little use.

CHAPTER 6

To Bring Down Dagon

ESTABLISHED IN 1919, the National Catholic Welfare Council (NCWC) was an outgrowth of what was called the "new lobbying." In the nineteenth century, political lobbying had been done behind closed doors by powerful business interests. With the Progressive movement of the early twentieth century, the new lobbying occurred in the open and was conducted by public advocacy groups. In 1901, the Catholic laity formed the American Federation of Catholic Societies (AFCS), a national organization dedicated to grounding the nation on Catholic principles. Gradually, the AFCS began lobbying to protect church rights and to apply Catholic principles to social issues. When it prepared to enroll every layperson in a local chapter, Cardinal William O'Connell urged that the hierarchy "systematically control [the AFCS] and thus guide it along safe channels instead of risking an outbreak of irresponsible people," a course of action in keeping with his belief that laypeople should take no public stands except under the guidance of a bishop. In 1917, the American Board of Archbishops established an episcopal committee under O'Connell to govern and direct the AFCS.[1]

The First World War gave added impetus to the new lobbying. Like other Americans, Catholics united behind the war effort by forming the National Catholic War Council, a nationwide organization to coordinate the church's mobilization. The wartime lobbying of organizations like the Anti-Saloon League and the National Education Association, which attempted to capitalize on the crisis to enact reforms that the Catholic church perceived as detrimental to its interests, convinced the hierarchy that it needed its own postwar lobby. Rome gave the notion indirect blessing and encouragement. In February 1919, Archbishop Bonaventura Cerretti, secretary of the Vatican Congregation of Extraordinary Ecclesiastical Affairs, told those gathered in Washington to celebrate Cardinal James Gibbons's fiftieth anniversary as a bishop that the pope wanted the United States to show the way in postwar reconstruction. "Rome," declared Cerretti, "now looks to America to be the leader in all things Catholic and to set the example to other nations"—a statement that would have warmed the hearts of the Americanists. Though the pope wanted The Catholic University of America to take the point, the bishops had other ideas.[2]

They decided to establish the NCWC, a voluntary association of the American hierarchy meeting annually to serve as the voice of Catholic America. It was also a lobby to represent the interests of the Catholic church before the federal government and to offset the political influence of the Protestant Federal Council of Churches and the National Education Association. The decisions of the hierarchy were implemented by an administrative committee of seven bishops, which operated through a secretariat with five departments, each headed by a member of the committee. Possessing both a women's and a men's branch (the National Councils of Catholic Women and Men), the NCWC quickly supplanted the AFCS.[3] In effect, the bishops established informal collegial government for the church in America.

Located in Washington, D.C., the secretariat was under the supervision of a general secretary. By extension, the name Welfare Council applied to the entire organization: hierarchy, committee, and secretariat. The NCWC's voluntary nature was underscored by the fact that decisions of the hierarchy were non-binding on members. This resulted in the anomalous situation that while the NCWC might set a national policy, an individual bishop remained free to take independent action. The organization was funded by proportional assessments against each diocese based on its size and circumstances, the total budget amounting to $200,000, a sum equivalent to $2,292,000 in 2006 dollars.[4]

O'Connell had never been friendly to the organization. His ecclesiology had no place for a collegial body of bishops managing the public affairs of the church through a secretariat run by priests and laypeople. Moreover, the NCWC was the brainchild of Sulpician-trained Bishop William Russell of Charleston and his friend the Sulpician provincial, Father Edward Dyer. At the NCWC's foundational meeting, O'Connell told the hierarchy: "We are already organized, divinely organized, and what we need is not more mere mechanical union but unity of plan. We can assemble annually, discuss a few leading questions and pass on them. . . . Better go slowly." In his view, the church was hierarchically arranged by God with each in his proper place, cardinals being situated just below the pontiff. It was one thing for bishops to gather and talk, but another for them to organize into a body, to deputize a few to act in their names, and to establish departments conducted by priests and laity. That was too democratic. It was undivine.[5]

Nor did it help matters that four of the seven bishops elected to the administrative committee—Russell, Austin Dowling of St. Paul (who had earlier snubbed O'Connell), Peter Muldoon of Rockford, and Joseph Schrembs of Toledo—had been educated by the Sulpicians, something that further jaundiced O'Connell toward the NCWC. By 1921, Cardinal Dennis Dougherty of Philadelphia, an early supporter of the NCWC, had come to agree with his colleague in Boston. As cardinals, both men were ready to assert control over the hierarchy and redefine the NCWC as simply the administrative committee and secretariat.[6]

For the first two years of the NCWC's existence, the aged Cardinal James Gibbons of Baltimore presided over the annual meetings of the hierarchy by virtue of an 1858 Vatican decree that gave the archbishop of that city prerogative of place because of his position as incumbent of the first diocese erected in the United States. Prerogative of place meant that the archbishop of Baltimore had the right to preside at any meeting or assembly. In addition to prerogative of place, Gibbons was the senior cardinal in the American church, which gave him precedence of place among all other prelates in the country according to canon law. In fact, he had functioned for decades as the de facto primate (official head) of the American church.[7]

At the 1920 convention of the hierarchy, when it was clear that Gibbons might not survive until the meeting of the following year and that the see of Baltimore might then be vacant, Archbishop Edward Hanna, chairman of the administrative committee, introduced a resolution proposing that in the absence of the archbishop of that city, the chairman of the administrative committee should preside at the annual meeting of the bishops. Although it seemed that the resolution carried, the secretary of the convention garbled the minutes, leaving the matter open to question. When Gibbons died in March 1921, the administrative committee discovered the error, which left a peaceful succession up in the air.[8]

The matter of the succession would be greatly complicated by the New England suffragans. In February 1921, when it was clear that Gibbons would soon pass away, Bishop Louis Walsh conferred with the apostolic delegate, Archbishop Giovanni Bonzano, about the chairmanship of the convention. Walsh was obviously concerned that the death of Gibbons would leave O'Connell as the senior cardinal and therefore dean of the hierarchy. In that capacity, he might attempt to assume the chair of the annual convention in 1921. Walsh asked the delegate if the hierarchy was free to elect its president. Bonzano replied that because the meeting was a conference without canonical status, the bishops could choose whomever they wished for their leader. Neither church law nor the concession to the ordinary of Baltimore applied to the chairmanship.[9]

This advice was incorrect because prerogative of place applied to all meetings or assemblies of any kind—canonical or otherwise. Still, coming as this opinion did from Bonzano, Walsh accepted it. Obviously, the New Englander was maneuvering to keep his metropolitan out of the chairmanship.

On 21 April 1921, the New England bishops met with O'Connell at the Boston chancery office for a routine biennial meeting to surface names of men worthy to be nominated for the episcopacy. After conducting this official business, the meeting turned confrontational. As senior suffragan, Walsh proposed a frank discussion of the effects of the Boston scandals, news of which "was spreading rapidly all over New England, and to a lesser extent into various other parts of the U.S.A." He then recounted the facts of the Toomey and O'Connell marriages and the lifestyle of the two priests over the past several years, immoral behavior that had been countenanced by the cardinal. It was time, said Walsh, for the suffragans to take action to repair the damage. O'Connell replied that he would listen to what the others had to say before making any remarks.[10]

First to speak was Bishop George Guertin of Manchester, who wanted his colleagues to maintain a charitable silence about the situation because it would soon be forgotten and things would resume their normal course, an opinion that prompted Bishop Daniel Feehan of Fall River to reply that such a course would be "little less than criminal." Feehan said that the proximity of Boston to his see city "made these scandals a topic of common discussion, and it was freely said that if the Bishops of the Province did their duty and acquainted the Holy Father of conditions here, he would quickly suppress the cause of these evils." O'Connell took exception to bringing the pope into this discussion and demanded that he be left out of it. Feehan shot back that Benedict XV could not be left out. The pontiff, Feehan said, had informed him that he had a copy of the nephew's wedding license and had confronted the cardinal with it. The pope had even told Feehan to let other bishops know of his repudiation of the crimes of O'Connell's curia.[11]

Bishop Joseph Rice of Burlington recounted that Boston Catholics on vacation in Vermont spoke openly about the Toomey-O'Connell scandals to the great detriment of his flock. Worse, a prominent Protestant had told him, "Judged by the Cardinal of Boston, the morality of Cardinals must be of a low order." For the good of religion, Rice urged O'Connell to resign from Boston and place himself at the disposal of the pope. Bishop John Nilan of Hartford remarked of the scandals that "he had heard the facts rehearsed oftener outside the diocese of Boston than in it." They were known beyond New England and even the United States. "No one finds a way to absolve Your Eminence . . . from responsibility," he told the cardinal. Like the others, Bishop William Hickey, administrator of Providence, said that his people were aware of the scandals and that the latter had rendered difficult "the management of young priests of wayward inclinations." He noted that the misdeeds of David Toomey and James P. E. O'Connell were common coin among the American bishops. Even a certain anti-Catholic paper—no doubt the *Menace*—had the story but was keeping it suppressed for the time being, "supposedly for a price."[12] The accuracy of this last comment is unlikely. The *Menace* relished too much exposing Catholic sexual wrongdoing to have its silence purchased.

Ignoring the earlier exchange with Feehan, the cardinal thanked his suffragans for their information but denied responsibility. True, his nephew had been accused of being married, but no one had brought forth proof of the crime, so O'Connell dismissed the allegation as owing to "jealousy and enmity." Rice asked the cardinal about the large sum of money his attorney paid Alice Leary in 1913 to protect Toomey from prosecution. O'Connell denied any knowledge of it. Aware that Joseph Pelletier had informed the cardinal of the nephew's marriage some time ago, Hickey asked O'Connell if the Boston district attorney had not apprised him of the facts. The cardinal again denied it. With regard to the entire confrontation, Hickey remarked: "He did not manifest any indignation over the charges. He seemed rather to be most abjectly afraid of the whole affair. His denials did not bear any resemblance to those of an innocent man."[13]

Shortly after this confrontation, Walsh departed for Rome where he arrived on 8 May. The following day he saw Archbishop Cerretti, who arranged an audience with the pope for Thursday, the twelfth. Walsh gave Benedict XV a blow by blow account of how the suffragans had confronted O'Connell and then recounted for the pope O'Connell's crimes of the past fifteen years. Pleading the salvation of the people and the honor of both the cardinalate and Holy See, he argued that Boston's prelate "must get out or be put out." The pope seemed to agree and even suggested the means. Unwilling to institute formal proceedings against O'Connell, he said that he would not be opposed to withdrawing the cardinal to Rome if the bishops would manifest such a desire or act in such a way that would necessitate his spontaneous removal. The pontiff thought that perhaps the absolute refusal of the American bishops to attend any meetings presided over by O'Connell would provide sufficient warrant. Thus, the affair would, in the words of Walsh, "be clinched without any canonical process and with very sure success." However, the pope wanted time to ponder the matter and asked the bishop to return the following week.[14]

The canonical process the pope hoped to avoid was an ecclesiastical trial (canon 1933), which would be initiated by the filing of formal charges. If authorities deemed the allegations credible, a special investigator would be selected to conduct an inquest. Should authorities have reason to believe that O'Connell might attempt to bribe or intimidate witnesses, they had the right to command him to take up residence in a location of their choosing during the investigation. In such a circumstance, a temporary replacement would be appointed to fill his vacant office until the matter was adjudicated. With compelling results from the inquest, authorities would then send the case to trial.[15] Perhaps, the pontiff wanted to avoid this formal process because of the possibility of its becoming public, especially if it was necessary to suspend O'Connell and distance him from Boston.

During the days between his audiences with Benedict, Walsh visited several cardinals, including Gaetano De Lai, secretary of the Consistorial Congregation; Pietro Gasparri, Vatican secretary of state; Donato Sbarretti, prefect of the Congregation of the Council; Michele Lega; and Vincenzo Vannutelli. He informed each of them about the scandals and of the April meeting in Boston. All were amazed by the suffragans' courage and "the big man's cowardice." Concluding that "he was put out of commission," they agreed to speak with the pope. Gasparri in particular was convinced that the time had come for O'Connell's removal. The question was how to do it. Like the pontiff, he recommended that the suffragans balk at attending any meeting chaired by O'Connell and then petition the Vatican to sanction their action. The Holy See would use the situation as a pretext for bringing the cardinal to Rome.[16] Thus, a plan was beginning to form: the repudiation of Boston's leadership.

Before Walsh's second papal audience, he received an affidavit from Rice. It was a sworn deposition by Boston District Attorney Joseph Pelletier recounting his two interviews with O'Connell during the Easter season of 1919 when he informed the cardinal of the nephew's marriage.[17] Walsh translated the document into French and presented it to Benedict XV on 21 May. It convinced the pope that O'Connell had lied wholesale. Walsh agreed, contending that the cardinal had deceived Rome from the beginning, that is, 1901. He told how he had discovered O'Connell's "financial crookedness" in Portland, how Archbishop John Williams of Boston had sized up his coadjutor, and finally how "our strong, beautiful, united and unsurpassed Province of Boston in 1900 had been torpedoed and was now in danger of ruin from the words, and deeds and maladministration [*sic*] of the present Metropolitan."[18]

Still committed to the idea of removal, Benedict commissioned Walsh to secure fifteen or more bishops on whom he could count to refuse to recognize O'Connell as dean of the hierarchy and presiding officer of the annual meeting of the NCWC. Walsh assured him that the majority of them would reject the cardinal's leadership. Victory seemed certain. "It is now clearly understood," he wrote to Rice, "that His Bigness will be brought to Rome as soon as conditions can be adjusted and the sooner the better." Three days later Walsh met with Gasparri and Cerretti to hammer out the details, namely, that fifteen bishops should refuse to attend a conference chaired by O'Connell and should petition the pope to approve their action.[19]

On 1 July 1921, Walsh returned to New York where Feehan and Rice met him. Rome's plan delighted them. The next day, Walsh explained it to Archbishop Patrick Hayes of New York, who agreed to support the New England bishops in repudiating O'Connell. Walsh then made the rounds of his fellow suffragans; all were of one mind except Guertin, who wished to follow his own conscience.[20]

At the end of the month, Walsh traveled to Atlantic City where Bonzano was vacationing with his friend, Archbishop George Mundelein of Chicago. Learning of the pontiff's decision, both were eager to help. Bonzano insisted that the episcopate had the right to select the chairman of the annual meeting. Like Hayes, Mundelein favored ousting O'Connell and promised to propose the election of the presiding officer of the annual convention. Despite present smooth sailing, the New England suffragans felt "it would be desirable, if not necessary," to have the support of written instructions from Rome that could be used as proof that Walsh had been commissioned to carry out the contemplated plan. On 1 August, Walsh informed Gasparri of the steps taken thus far and asked for documentation of his instructions for the sake of the Boston suffragans and the archbishops of the country.[21]

Soon thereafter, Walsh learned that Bishop Michael Curley of St. Augustine, Florida, had been named to succeed the late Gibbons in Baltimore. He wrote to the new archbishop-elect to inquire if he would assert the right of prerogative of place to preside at the annual meeting of the hierarchy in September. Curley replied that since he would not yet be installed in Baltimore, he did not believe that he would have a right to do so. "In any case," he continued, "how about a young, ignorant and inexperienced Archbishop [himself] presiding at any meeting where there are present two red-robed Princes of the Church? All this will have to be settled by someone else." Regarding the scandalous behavior in Boston, he considered it "a fearfully delicate situation." "I dread a public break with its terrible publicity," he told Walsh, although Feehan of Fall River seemed to think that "just that will come some day."[22]

With it unlikely that Curley would be able or willing to assert his right to the presidency of the convention, Walsh gathered more backing. He visited Bishops Thomas Hickey of Rochester, William Turner of Buffalo, Thomas Walsh of Trenton, Michael Hoban of Scranton, James Hartley of Columbus, Denis O'Connell of Richmond, and Cardinal Dennis Dougherty of Philadelphia. Together with Hayes, Mundelein, and the six New England suffragans, they brought the total to fifteen, the number desired by Benedict. All agreed that if an election were held for the presidency at the upcoming meeting of the hierarchy, the vote would go almost unanimously against O'Connell. Some had told Walsh that they would be "astonished" to see the cardinal attend the gathering. "In my opinion," confided Walsh, "one can expect anything on his part, and it is necessary to prepare for every possible step."[23]

Several of the bishops, especially Dougherty, wondered if an election could be held without special Vatican intervention. First, there was the concession of 1858 that gave precedence to the archbishop of Baltimore; second, there was the canonical prescription that gave that honor to the senior cardinal, in this case O'Connell. It was the common opinion of the bishops that the first was superseded by the second, which only Rome could set aside. They counseled Walsh to make an urgent request to have the pope either appoint a presiding officer, give special permission for an election by secret ballot, or send other instructions.[24]

On 21 August, Walsh informed the pontiff that he had met with fourteen bishops and had written to four more. "I have expressed to all the mind of your Holiness," he said, "especially in connection with our next Episcopal assembly." All agreed that if an election were held,

Dougherty would almost certainly win, which "would be a very great humiliation for his Eminence of Boston and perhaps would be a way to open his eyes." On the other hand, elections often had troublesome consequences and created parties, both personal and official. If the Vatican failed to sanction the balloting, O'Connell would refuse to recognize the result, invoke his canonical right to preside, and appeal to Rome. This would throw the assembly into confusion and cause a delay, which no one wanted. Walsh begged the pope to wire instructions to Bonzano before 21 September, the day of the annual meeting.[25]

Meanwhile, Walsh heard from two of the archbishops to whom he had written: John Glennon of St. Louis and Austin Dowling of St. Paul. Without commenting on O'Connell's worthiness, the former held that the bishops had the right to elect their chairman.[26] Hailing from the New England province, the latter was more partisan. Replied Dowling, "I'm with you in pulling down Dagon—the big idol of Boston [cf. Judges 16:23–30]." He thought it would be shameful for the hierarchy "voluntarily to submit to the presidency of one who has been so openly contemptuous of decency & morality."[27] At a meeting with his suffragans, Dowling proposed that they stage a walkout with the New Englanders if O'Connell tried to preside over the annual convention. All but one of his suffragans agreed.[28] This news put the number of bishops opposed to O'Connell's presidency at well over fifteen. In fact, the historical record indicates that at this time at least twenty-two would probably have repudiated O'Connell, twenty-three if Dougherty could be counted on.

Bishop Schrembs informed Walsh that Archbishop Henry Moeller of Cincinnati refused to respond because he could not "bring himself to believe the facts in the case. He says that if these things [the Boston scandals] are true then why does Rome not act." Moeller was not alone. Schrembs related that others found it equally hard to believe. Still others, mostly in the West and South, considered the affair "a petty quarrel among the New England Bishops" and felt Rome's inactivity proved their point. Yet Schrembs claimed to know a great many prelates who would object to O'Connell's presidency. Like Walsh, he hoped for a Vatican instruction to forestall a floor fight. "There is no likelihood," he regretted, "of the Cardinal's remaining away from the meeting as delicacy of feeling in this matter is evidently foreign to his nature."[29]

On 25 August 1921, Gasparri sent a cablegram in cipher to Bonzano in response to Walsh's request for written confirmation of his instructions from the pope regarding O'Connell's removal. It seems that Benedict had since changed the rules regarding the ouster. Gasparri tersely reported: "His holiness responds that he would not have any difficulty in being of help in getting in touch with the cardinal if at least one-quarter of the bishops spontaneously [*spontaneamente*] express this wish to the Holy See."[30] Bonzano immediately perceived a difference between "the instructions Walsh maintained he had received from the Holy See and what the latter had really assigned to him." The number of bishops was not fifteen, but closer to twenty-eight, and the word "spontaneously" went against everything that Walsh was doing. Bonzano cabled to Gasparri the equally terse reply: "I fear that the bishop of Portland has exaggerated the situation." To Walsh, he wired that he had a communication for him from the Vatican, which he would give him orally at the consecration of Thomas O'Leary as bishop of Springfield, Massachusetts, on 8 September. Unfortunately, illness prevented Bonzano from participating in O'Leary's elevation to the episcopate, and he was unable to see Walsh until just before the annual assembly of the hierarchy.[31]

It is possible, though unlikely, that Walsh had misunderstood the instructions of Benedict and Gasparri. Unlikely, because shortly before his departure from Rome, Walsh had a meeting with Gasparri and Cerretti wherein they "all agreed upon the details of the procedure [for removing O'Connell]."[32] Any plan requiring details was one that necessarily ruled out spontaneity. As Walsh would later argue, the Italian word "*spontaneamente*" should have been translated as "voluntarily." Moreover, Walsh's description of his commission was consistent throughout the historical record: his letter from Rome back to his fellow suffragans; Bonzano's letter to Gasparri about what Walsh had originally said were his orders; Walsh's own letters to both Benedict and Gasparri keeping them abreast of the steps he was taking to fulfill their instructions; and later, as will be seen, his letter in defense of the actions he had taken to carry out their plan, even after he learned the contents of Gasparri's cablegram. In Walsh's view, the latter had simply adjusted the original instructions, and only in the minor detail of numbers.

After months of careful planning, things unraveled on the eve of the annual convention of the hierarchy. The day before it opened, Walsh visited Bonzano, who communicated the contents of the cable sent by Gasparri. Although Walsh considered it "clear enough and a good answer to my letter," it was also "impossible to carry out now at this late hour." Without calling an informal meeting of the hierarchy, there was no way to approach so many prelates. Concerned that Walsh had over-reached his instructions, Bonzano strongly urged against holding an election, "*turning completely* around from his own expressed judgment of a few weeks ago."[33] To Walsh's contention that the bishops did not want O'Connell as head of the hierarchy or even as nominal president of the annual assembly, the delegate replied that it would be incorrect to say that the cardinal would be head of the hierarchy. Each bishop was a "*prince*" in his own diocese, responsible to the pope alone. As for the presidency of the annual convention, Bonzano considered it "not a matter of much gravity or importance" because the bishops themselves decided all matters by majority vote. Finally, he reminded Walsh "of the unofficial stance" the pope intended to take toward O'Connell pro-vided that "one-quarter of all the Bishops spontaneously requested it." This position precluded "the imprudent propaganda" that the Portland prelate was "circulating among the Bishops." Even if Walsh's plan were to succeed, it would cause another scandal "because both the Clergy and the Faithful would hear about the moral slap in the face to His Eminence O'Connell."[34]

Walsh and Bonzano went to Catholic University where they con-ferred with several bishops gathered for the convention. Those they spoke with were prepared to join the New Englanders the next day in repudiating O'Connell by ballot. That evening Walsh met with his fellow suffragans, who agreed to proceed as planned, but were ready to yield if conditions called for it. According to Walsh, the day's events presented "a queerly confusing situation."[35]

Meanwhile, O'Connell paid his customary pre-convention visit to

Bonzano. During the interview, he made vague reference to the matter of his nephew, "looking to insinuate," the delegate later wrote, "that he had never known anything about him." In Bonzano's view, the cardinal appeared to be alarmed at the possibility that the scandals might be taken up at the meeting of the hierarchy, thereby humiliating him.[36]

O'Connell was not the only one concerned about such a turn of events. Several archbishops and bishops approached Walsh to express their "anxiety and fear of a break" that might occur during the meeting between the cardinal and his suffragans over that issue. Walsh assured them that the New Englanders "would sacrifice any and all of their personal views" if Bonzano "deemed it the proper course."[37]

The next morning, more than sixty prelates assembled at Catholic University for the annual convention.[38] Walsh reported that although a large number of bishops clearly favored the election of a presiding officer, the delegate directly intervened. Fearing scandal and division, Bonzano begged Walsh and several archbishops to block any movement against O'Connell. Even though the New Englanders believed they could muster the requisite number of bishops (Benedict's one-quarter of the hierarchy), the delegate's "very positive opinion against any election" caused them to yield. Boston's cardinal "*assumed* the chair."[39]

Although the convention that day passed without incident (it was spent in department reports), O'Connell created a scene outside the meeting room. He confronted Walsh in a residence-hall corridor and, to the amazement of passersby and those in their rooms, used vulgar language in blaming him for interference in the archdiocese of Boston. O'Connell went on to declare that Walsh had played a "low, mean, dirty trick" on him at the meeting of the suffragans in April 1921. The cardinal accused the Portland prelate and two other New England bishops of "attacking him and spreading scandal against him" at that gathering. In Walsh's view, the confrontation was simply O'Connell's public "attempt to falsify the facts and minimize the importance of what happened at the meeting." Walsh considered the encounter "an amusing specimen" of the cardinal's "dramatic artifice."[40] In short, a good offense was the best defense, and O'Connell had struck first by openly asserting that some of his suffragans had libeled him. Apparently, the ploy failed.

When the convention resumed, the cardinal "was wise enough to be modest" because "many were ready to put him and keep him in chains."[41]

The next day brought a discussion of the NCWC, which got quite a drubbing. A number of bishops were confused about its nature, some holding that it was merely the administrative committee, while others that it was the hierarchy operating through an executive branch. Espousing the former interpretation, both O'Connell and Dougherty were concerned about the authority of the committee; they argued that it had demonstrated a repeated tendency to usurp power beyond its portfolio. No doubt this had to do with various pronouncements issued during the previous year on progressive legislation in favor of unionization, funding for the newborn of indigent mothers, and state oversight of private schools to forestall compulsory public education. The cardinals admonished the committee and were supported by other indignant prelates.[42]

The tide turned, however, when it dawned on the assembly that the pair was minimizing the NCWC (however it was defined) in hope of dealing it a future death blow. Although the Welfare Council might need adjustment, obliteration was another matter. Archbishop-elect Curley became its champion. In a strong and direct address, he defended the NCWC as "organized leadership"; the day of "*one man leadership* [the de facto primacy of Gibbons] was gone." When he finished, noted Walsh, "the two [cardinals] sat dumb."[43]

Clearly, the gauntlet was down. A clash of ecclesiologies was taking place: deference to the cardinalate versus collegial authority. Each side had warned the other. Dougherty and O'Connell indicated that they intended (in Walsh's words) to "rule or ruin" the NCWC; the bishops made clear that the era of Gibbons was over, so do not try to assume his mantle. The issue was complicated by the scandal in New England. It was symbolic that when Dougherty resigned from the administrative committee, the hierarchy elected Walsh in his place. With the announcement of the vote, commented the new officeholder, "there were a few *tense* moments, when a word from Boston would have opened the gates."[44] Walsh was not about to let the matter of the chairmanship of the NCWC drop.

CHAPTER 7

Dueling to a Draw

IN THE DAYS AND WEEKS after the convention of the hierarchy, the principal parties reiterated and reinforced their positions. Before leaving Washington, the administrative committee of the NCWC met with the apostolic delegate, Archbishop Giovanni Bonzano. Archbishop Edward Hanna, chairman of the committee, gave what Bishop Louis Walsh considered a rather rosy picture of the proceedings. In the latter's view, "the real facts and feelings of our meeting were being veiled all too much." Only courtesy prevented him from objecting to Hanna's remarks.[1] Once back in Portland, Walsh sent the delegate a letter to say that the hierarchy had yielded on the election of its president only out of respect for Rome. Lamenting the belated reception of Cardinal Pietro Gasparri's instruction, he added, "If Your Excellency could have heard what was said to me by Archbishops and Bishops before, during and after our meeting, there would remain little doubt about the great ease with which the '*quarta pars*' [one-quarter] could have been '*spontanee*' [by free will] secured." Walsh explained that when the administrative committee had visited the delegate, "it was not opportune, nor would it have been courteous or dignified to mention the feeling of suppressed indignation, that pervaded the assembly of Bishops." He added that he wanted to acknowledge receipt of the cablegram sent by Gasparri and asked the delegate if he would send a copy of it.[2]

Simultaneous with Walsh's letter, Bonzano received one from Bishop Patrick Heffron of Winona, Minnesota, who had been prevented from attending the convention, but wanted to inform the delegate of what had occurred at a meeting of the province of St. Paul before the annual assembly. Heffron reported that the bishops of New England had sent a letter to certain archbishops urging them to participate in a walkout at the gathering if O'Connell presided. A resolution to that effect had been introduced and passed over Heffron's protest. Heffron considered the idea "childish." More to the point, he told Bonzano, "If the plan were carried out, the Catholic Church in the United States would have one of the most sensational scandals of its history." That was why he voted no.[3]

Heffron also informed O'Connell of the action of the bishops of St. Paul. "My purpose is self-justification," he said: "I strenuously opposed the resolution and voted against it. I considered the proceeding an intolerant piece of underhand ecclesiastical political chicanery. . . . I know nothing of the motives of those who wrote the letters, I know nothing of the animus of those who entertained the resolution. I consider the whole thing dastardly and treacherous, and I expressed myself very plainly, and I wish you to know that there was one at the meeting who would truckle to no such stuff."[4] Thankful for the intelligence, O'Connell replied that "time will bring you proof that what you did has God's blessing, as it will surely bring to those guilty of such unspeakable baseness the punishment due their treachery."[5]

Bonzano made effective use of Heffron's information in his reply to Walsh. He told the latter that many bishops had visited him at the time of the convention. Mistakenly thinking that Heffron had attended the assembly, he wrote, "While those who came before the meeting were alarmed over the possibility of an unpleasant occurrence, those who came afterwards showed delight over the avoidance of what one said would have been a most sensational scandal of the Church in America." This last clause was lifted almost verbatim from Heffron's letter. Bonzano continued by noting that he had been informed that the bishops of a certain province (St. Paul), in consequence of a letter from the Boston suffragans, had determined beforehand the action they would take against O'Connell in Washington. "This," said the delegate, "certainly does not express spontaneity, and I do not think it is in accord with the intention of the Holy See." Bonzano declined to send Walsh a copy of the cablegram from Gasparri because the latter had authorized only the oral communication of its contents, something that was untrue.[6] Given that most of the information contained in this reply came from Heffron's letter, one may justly wonder how many bishops really visited

Bonzano after the meeting.

In a draft response, Walsh argued that the word "*spontanee*" had to be understood as meaning "voluntarily"—in fact a perfectly good translation of the Italian *spontaneamente*— "because the Holy Father told me positively in both my audiences that I could approach any Archb[ishop]. & Bishop that seemed to me fitting."[7] Rather than quibble words with the delegate, he replied with a detailed account of his every step, beginning with his papal audiences in May 1921 down through the annual assembly, including his correspondence with Gasparri and Benedict XV. "That the 'quarta pars' Episcoporum . . . was present and ready to act by vote or in any other legitimate way," repeated Walsh, "cannot be doubted from what more than that number told me personally before and after our meeting." He admitted that there were indeed some bishops who expressed gratitude to the New Englanders for acceding to Bonzano's request of allowing O'Connell to preside, "while openly assuring us that they were entirely with us and of one mind on the important issue, that Boston should not and could not be our leader before the public."[8]

Meanwhile, O'Connell dropped the delegate "a line about the meeting of the hierarchy" in which "everything went most harmoniously." He reported, however, that some bishops expressed strong feelings against the usurpation of authority by the administrative committee, which in his mind was the NCWC. "Unless kept within safe limits," O'Connell cautioned, "the W[elfare]. C[ouncil]. could easily do harm. They were warned at the meeting. It remains to be seen whether the warning is heeded."[9]

In reporting to Gasparri about the convention, Bonzano recounted his successful effort to forestall O'Connell's rejection as president. "However, I am far from exonerating the Cardinal of Boston from all responsibilities," he added, "and I also know that the Bishops, although they did not want to pronounce any judgments against him during the assembly and with dignity tolerated him as President, do not intend to absolve him from such responsibility. His friends as well admit that unfortunately the 'deeds of Boston' are universally known by the Episcopate and all the Clergy in the United States." While noting that the convention had been conducted with apparent harmony, Bonzano attributed that outcome in part "to the humiliating condition in which it [the assembly] found the Eminent O'Connell," which precluded him from assuming "the attitude of a ruler, to which, unfortunately, he seems to be prone by temperament."[10]

Although the plan of the Boston suffragans to repudiate O'Connell's leadership through the NCWC had been sidetracked by the delegate, they intended to let their metropolitan know where they stood. Moreover, Walsh wanted to counter the cardinal's recent misrepresentation of what had occurred at their meeting in April 1921. In November, five suffragans sent O'Connell a letter reaffirming all that was said at that meeting about his responsibility for countenancing the scandals in his curia. They concluded by declaring that they did not consider him "a worthy or fitting ecclesiastic to be even a nominal leader among or for the Bishops of the country and we have so stated to the proper authorities."[11] This last phrase was Walsh's idea because he wanted to be able to demonstrate that the suffragans had repudiated O'Connell's leadership and had done so to the pope. He and his four colleagues each signed and imprinted with his episcopal seal two copies of the letter, one for O'Connell and one to be shown to bishops around the country "when the time comes."[12]

Walsh apparently intended to circulate a petition for O'Connell's removal among the bishops and archbishops of the nation. Accordingly, he drafted a letter to Pope Benedict XV in the name of the American hierarchy. Bearing witness that the scandals of the Boston curia were widely known among the clergy and only less so among the laity, "we, the archbishops and bishops . . . voluntarily and of our own free will [*voluntarie et spontanee*] declare," read the draft, that if a ballot for the presidency had been taken at the last assembly of the hierarchy, "in no way would our vote have been for the cardinal of Boston." The bishops wanted him as neither the "real" nor the "nominal" leader of the hierarchy. Moreover, there was a daily increasing peril that the scandals might be published in the press with grave and long-lasting injury to the church and the Holy See. Therefore, the bishops entreated the pontiff to "remove this danger from us and from our people in an appropriate way and as soon as possible."[13] Walsh was determined to prove to the pope that a quarter of the hierarchy, and perhaps more, had been ready at the assembly and were now willing to repudiate O'Connell's leadership. As will be seen, events were to preclude him from circulating the petition.

Meanwhile, O'Connell had made his own contact with authorities in Rome. He sent his old friend Cardinal Raphael Merry del Val money for 300 mass intentions and another $1,000 ($11,000 in 2006 terms) for his personal use, an amount it took the average American industrial worker nine months to earn. An exponent of the ecclesiology that distinguished sharply between the sacred and secular, and confined the church solely to the former, O'Connell remarked, "There is all around about an intangible something which would seem to emanate from too much politics, diplomacy and intrigue—too much mingling with affairs which don't concern us. But thank God it does not exist around me." This may have been an oblique reference to the NCWC which was certainly involved in the political process, and lately in intrigue against the cardinal himself. "How different in the wonderful days of Pio X [Pius X]," he rhapsodized, "—when the chief concern was God, and when cheap politics and free-masons were kept in their place. The memory of those days is a rare possession—conditions then were as near ideal as they ever can be. Will they ever return? For one thing I shall live in the spirit of that holy time and rate intrigue at its true value—just zero."[14]

A kindred spirit, Merry del Val found Benedict's politically active regime disturbing, especially Gasparri's effort to negotiate a settlement of the "Roman Question," that is, the political-religious conflict between the Vatican and the Italian government in the wake of the loss of the Papal States. Thinking that O'Connell referred to this, the Vatican cardinal praised his American counterpart's ability to realize "from a distance the prevalence of too much politics, worldly diplomacy and intrigue, that are hardly in keeping with the lofty ideals of our mission nor profitable to the best interests of God and of his Church." Merry del Val feared for the latter. "We are drifting," he warned, "how far we may drift I dread to think: and how hard it will be later on to get back to our only safe tracks, if we are to regain what we have lost." The safe track was pure doctrine and aloofness from the world. "A thousand thanks for your generous gift [of $1,000]," concluded Merry del Val.[15]

Here was a pair of reactionaries, pining for the good old days when churchmen kept to the sanctuary and avoided the halls of government. Given an opportunity to eradicate the politically involved NCWC, O'Connell would find his friend a ready ally.

While Boston's cardinal smoothed his way in Rome, Walsh also took his case to the Vatican. He reported to Gasparri about the events of the summer, namely, that fifteen prelates (the number required by the pope) had lined up against O'Connell, a number that could easily have been doubled. He had sent their names to Benedict XV along with a request for instructions about how to proceed at the annual convention. "I had hope of a response by cablegram before the assembly," he said, "but I now see that Your Eminence had thought that the 'cablegram in cipher' [of 25 August] . . . would be sufficient." Although it arrived in time, Bonzano had been prevented from delivering it until the day before the meeting.[16]

"The '*quarta pars episcoporum*' against the presidency of Boston was absolutely certain," reported Walsh, but the delegate, "interpreting the cablegram to his own liking," intervened to forestall an election. "These facts," he declared, "change nothing, neither the judgment of the bishops of the country, nor the hope of the bishops of the Boston province; and for myself, I alter in no way the position I took in conscience when His Holiness gave me the right, the duty, and the freedom to make known to him the sad situation in which we find ourselves." Walsh hoped that "according to the law of church and state, the freedom of election will be recognized before the next annual convention." He refused to criticize Bonzano for reversing himself on the matter of the election of the president of the assembly. Walsh was simply reporting the fact that the delegate had done so.[17]

What Walsh meant by "the law of church and state" became clear in the months that followed, at least the state part did. He planned to clarify the nature of the NCWC and the process of electing its chairman. From a study of pertinent documents, including the council's charter of incorporation and the minutes of the annual conventions, he constructed a constitutional outline of the NCWC and presented it orally to the administrative committee on 27 January 1922. The latter commissioned him to submit it in writing to the members for discussion at the next meeting. Meanwhile, the NCWC's general secretary, John Burke, was to check with the organization's attorney about the legality of O'Connell's assumption of the chairmanship at the last convention.[18]

A week and a half later, Walsh circulated a document demonstrating that the NCWC was the *hierarchy* of the United States, that the administrative committee was the hierarchy's executive arm, that the NCWC was incorporated in the District of Columbia, and that according to Washington's laws of incorporation, the president of the NCWC and all other officers must be elected. Since the administrative committee had charge of affairs between annual meetings, the board, not O'Connell, was to call the next convention. When the hierarchy met, moreover, the first order of business would be the election of officers, including the president of the convention.[19] If approved by the administrative committee, this statement of the situation was to be sent to all bishops. Thus, civil law was to be used in determining church order.

Walsh received responses from Archbishop Michael Curley of Baltimore, Bishop Peter Muldoon of Rockford, and Bishop William Russell of Charleston. All three agreed that his document aptly represented the organizational structure. Muldoon advised against mailing it to others until the administrative committee reconvened in April.[20] Curley wondered how far the issue could be pushed at the Vatican. "Rome," he warned, "knows little about civil corporations and will scarcely take such into account when it is a matter of electing or not electing Cardinals to positions of honor."[21]

The lucid outline of the organization moved Russell to regret and indignation. "We blundered egregiously last year," he proclaimed, "in allowing Boston to walk rough-shod over us [at the convention]. I did not rebel, because I did not know all the facts. I am determined however next year to take a stand, even if I stand alone. This temporizing policy is contemptible. Unless the [Apostolic] Delegate can show us his authority to foist this creature upon us, I am in favor of letting him know that we expect him to mind his own business."[22] Unfortunately, there would never be a second chance. Rome would settle the matter of the chairmanship, but only after it almost wrecked the NCWC.

Besides approving Walsh's document, Curley offered information and advice on the New England situation. A friend of his had learned from Monsignor Charles O'Hern, rector of the North American College in Rome, that "those who were objecting to, or bringing charges against Boston might just as well be knocking their heads against a stone wall." Bonzano was of like mind. Curley summarized the delegate's recent assessment of the case: "No facts and no proofs had ever been brought against Boston itself [i.e., O'Connell himself]. Action has been taken against the Curia [David Toomey and James P. E. O'Connell]. Now it is a question of taking action against the Head itself. That action will not be taken on his supposed responsibility for the Curia, but must be taken on evidence brought directly against himself personally. This might be otherwise were it a question of one in less authority, but the Holy See will be mighty slow in removing or punishing one so highly placed as he."[23]

In other words, Rome needed a smoking gun to proceed against a cardinal, especially one with such influential friends in the Vatican. Curley told Walsh that if the case was to go forward, "the men in Boston who state they have facts must be prepared to come out with those facts and take the consequences whatever they may be."[24] The archbishop was right: O'Connell would prove a very difficult man to undo.

The chairmanship debacle so incensed Russell that he began contemplating a drastic course of action. He sent Bonzano a letter threatening a public disclosure of the Boston scandals in order to force the Vatican to remove O'Connell. The delegate in turn threatened to summarily sack Russell from his diocese if he followed through with his intention. Bonzano's very definite stance caused Russell to calm down and retreat.[25]

Meanwhile, John Mullen was attempting to do exactly what Curley had argued must be done, that is, have priests in Boston come forward with tangible proof of O'Connell's wrongdoing. He invited four clergymen, including Michael Doody and Richard Neagle, both former chancellors under Archbishop John Williams, to meet about mounting a protest against O'Connell to Rome. "If these will have the courage and zeal to agree," he told Walsh, ". . . then we can see about securing additional names; but I have no hope of more than a dozen in any case. If these four will not make a beginning nothing can be done."[26] His plan quickly came to grief. Neagle refused to attend, stating, "I should like to be with you at such a meeting, but I find it more comfortable to forget some things and some people,—to keep them out of my thoughts as much as possible." Mullen concluded bitterly that if a priest of Neagle's caliber "will write in that strain, it seems absolutely futile to attempt to influence Washington [the apostolic delegate] or Rome through any action of the clergy of the Boston diocese. 'Say your little Mass; preach your little sermon; pocket your (little or big) collection; etc. etc.'" As will be seen in chapter ten, Mullen would not be the only priest to reach such a conclusion. He told Walsh that if the church in New England was to be saved, "hope must rest with the Bishops."[27]

The drive to unseat O'Connell took a detour on 22 January 1922 with the untimely death of Pope Benedict XV. When the latter went to the grave, his plan for bringing the Boston cardinal to Rome went with him. Two days after the pontiff's demise, O'Connell sailed on the *President Wilson* for Rome and the conclave. Arriving on 6 February, the day Cardinal Achille Ratti of Milan was elected Pius XI, O'Connell missed a chance to cast a papal ballot.[28] Yet all was not lost. A new face at the top offered an opportunity to start somewhat fresh and to recoup losses. O'Connell spent more than two months at the Vatican giving his sagging fortunes a badly need lift.

Contretemps in the career of Joseph Pelletier, district attorney of Boston, proved a boon for the cardinal. Pelletier had long been the target of Godfrey Cabot, treasurer of the Boston Watch and Ward Society, a civilian group that kept an eye on crimes, mainly of a sexual nature. In January 1922, the district attorney was accused of, among other things, collaborating in badger games with Daniel Coakley, a colorful if unscrupulous Boston lawyer. Typically, such a scam consisted of luring a wealthy, respectable man into a compromising situation with woman in order to extort money to keep the matter from going public or into the courts. In a separate trial, Coakley was acquitted by a sympathetic jury. In a highly controversial and politically charged civil suit, Pelletier was impeached, removed from office, and disbarred. He claimed that he had been tried "without the presumption of innocence" and that the court chose to believe the testimony of "crooks, libertines, and their kind" who had taken the stand against him.[29]

Historian James O'Toole suggests that as early as 1919 Pelletier may have been running a badger game on O'Connell on the basis of his knowledge of the nephew's marriage. This scenario seems unlikely. Mullen stated that in 1917, Pelletier had told him that he had gone to the cardinal to inform him of "the scandalous reports about the immoral life of Toomey and Msgr. O'Connell."[30] In running a badger game, one keeps the incriminating information secret. Disclosure to a known opponent of the intended victim, one who could make his own use of the knowledge, may directly undercut the blackmailer's intention of extorting money. Moreover, shortly after informing the cardinal in 1919 of the nephew's marriage, Pelletier began collaborating in an investigation conducted by Bonzano, Mullen, Michael Doody, and John Dunn of New York, none of whom were seeking to make money off O'Connell. Finally, in defending his nephew to the Vatican, the cardinal accused Toomey and his wife of attempting to extort money from him in return for their silence, and he further alleged that Doody and Mullen suborned perjury from them. Yet, O'Connell made no mention of any attempt at blackmail by Pelletier. Following the latter's conviction, however, the cardinal made skillful use of the situation.

Since Pelletier was a principal deponent against O'Connell and his nephew, his misfortunes were turned to good advantage. The cardinal attacked him as the chief instigator of the things said and done against the former chancellor. How, after all, could a man like Pelletier be trusted? If he was guilty of such deeds in the secular realm, why not in the ecclesiastical too? In this way, the cardinal weakened, if not seriously discounted, the entire affair. At least so reported Archbishop James Keane of Dubuque, who visited Rome in early spring.[31] Bishop William Hickey of Providence, who was at Rome in May, discovered that the Vatican cardinals had kept the new pontiff completely in the dark about the Boston scandal. Hickey himself had to inform him.[32]

Besides disparaging the case against the nephew, O'Connell wielded his influence. The first instance was an end run around the board of trustees of Catholic University in the reappointment of Bishop Thomas Shahan as rector. In September 1921, the board established a subcommittee to prepare a tentative *terna* and report back in April 1922. By right, the trustees alone had the power to nominate candidates and present them to the pope. Chaired by O'Connell, the subcommittee recommended Shahan, Bishop William Turner, and Reverend Patrick McCormick, in that order. Bypassing the board, the cardinal took the tentative *terna* to Rome and on 20 February submitted it to Cardinal Gaetano Bisleti, prefect of the Congregation of Seminaries and Universities. Declaring that the board of trustees had nominated the candidates (which was untrue), O'Connell asked that Rome reappoint Shahan, for neither of the others was qualified. Pope Pius did so; Bisleti issued the decree on 25 March 1922.[33]

More significant than the maneuver regarding the rectorship was O'Connell's action toward the NCWC. Because visiting American bishops manifested little interest in it, Rome had the impression that the organization was functioning without the active cooperation of the hierarchy.[34] As Father Giovanni Genocchi, a consultor for the pontifical biblical commission, reported to his friend Archbishop Hanna, "Some Bishops complained of what seemed to them a diminutio capitis [loss of rights] in their dioceses, in which the direction of too many affairs depended on the elected board of Bishops [the administrative committee] and no more on the Ordinarius [local bishop]." There were, moreover, a few prelates who were loath to attend the yearly conventions of the hierarchy because they "prefer not to move from their sees."[35]

Writing to Burke from Rome, Thomas O'Neill, procurator general of the Paulists, also warned that O'Connell wanted a larger role in the NCWC. Unless this was granted, "he will break up the whole organization or do a great deal to cripple it."[36] The Benedictines at the Vatican had worse news. They reported to Muldoon that O'Connell had declared "he would never leave Rome until he had a copy of the decree of condemnation in his pocket."[37] They were right. Supported by Cardinal

Dennis Dougherty, O'Connell planned to smash the NCWC, the Philadelphia cardinal acting from theoretical reasons, the Boston cardinal, from ideological ones, personal pique, and ambition.[38]

Through the good offices of Cardinals Merry del Val and Gaetano De Lai, the Consistorial Congregation issued a decree on 25 February 1922. The document embodied the Boston-Philadelphia view of the NCWC. The American bishops, said the decree, had inaugurated a new custom of annual meetings to deal with postwar affairs; they had established "a committee, known as the National Catholic Welfare Council," to manage business between conventions. "But at present," continued the decree, "since the times and circumstances have changed, several bishops [*nonnulli episcopi*], in their own name and in that of others, have advised that this custom and institute were no longer necessary or useful: wherefore they besought the Holy See to take the appropriate steps."[39]

In response, the Consistorial Congregation ordered a complete restoration in America of the authority of ordinary church law. In practical terms, the decree declared that the hierarchy could meet only in a plenary council convened by the pope for a special reason (canon 281). The annual conventions, therefore, must stop. In addition, "the institution and work of the said committee, the National Catholic Welfare Council, must cease." Although the document indicated that the Consistorial Congregation had decided these matters in a plenary session and by command of the pontiff, neither was true.[40] O'Connell had won. With the NCWC's demise, he inherited the mantle of Cardinal James Gibbons as dean of the hierarchy and de facto primate of the church in America. His victory, however, was short-lived.

On 22 March 1922, Bonzano stunned the American hierarchy with the news of the NCWC's suppression; he sent each bishop a copy of the decree.[41] It shocked members of the administrative committee. Commenting in his diary, Muldoon was both puzzled and dismayed: "Who are the '*non nulli*'? Very few. Why dissolve what Pope Benedict XV blessed? It is astounding and beyond belief that without a general consultation of the American Hierarchy such a decree should be issued. I cannot believe that the holy Father knew the import of the decree."

This last sentence proved only too true. Because Cardinals O'Connell and Dougherty were at the Vatican when the decree was issued, Muldoon suspected foul play. "Peculiar to say," he observed, "the decree wrongfully describes the Admn. Comm. as the N.C.W.C."—a view held by both cardinals. Muldoon believed that if published, the decree would harm the new pontiff's prestige, deaden the laity's enthusiasm, and raise suspicion among the hierarchy. "Well," he concluded, "we must make a protest, and ask to be heard, especially the Administrative Committee of the N.C.W.C." He felt confident that Rome would reverse itself.[42]

The committee's newest member, Walsh, experienced a similar reaction. "Letter at 2 P.M.," he noted in his diary, ". . . enclosing Decree from Consistorial, absolutely suppressing the *N.C.W.C.* at Washington—first decree under new Holy Father and evidently inspired by the Cardinals of Boston & Philadelphia. Not surprising to me but no less painful from *method* and *modus agendi* [manner of doing it]."[43] Like Muldoon, Walsh objected to the edict's misconception of identifying the Welfare Council with the administrative committee, and he almost brought the matter to Bonzano's attention.[44] Thinking better of the idea, he decided that a protest to Rome was the only course of action.

In St. Paul, Archbishop Austin Dowling was beside himself. After reading the decree, he fired off telegrams to many bishops but received replies from few except Walsh. To Father James H. Ryan in Washington, he reported: "Everybody seems knocked on the head. The Bishop of Portland [Walsh] a practiced gladiator is for protesting. I agree with him because by this the Bishops are swept off the boards *in saecula saeculorum* [for ever and ever]." Like Muldoon and Walsh, Dowling blamed the suppression on the two cardinals.[45] His advice to Muldoon was the same as Walsh's: protest. "Something must be attempted to lift this inhibition from us," he wrote. "We are adjudged almost to be schismatic. We may never meet unless convoked by Rome."[46] The chairman of the committee, Hanna, agreed that action had to be taken. "Protest must be made to the Holy See," he advised Muldoon, "and if necessary one must go to Rome. Our honor is at stake and the lives of those who sacrificed themselves for the work."[47]

The NCWC mounted a protest against the suppression, which was eventually signed by eighty bishops or four-fifths of the hierarchy. Its envoys, led by Bishop Joseph Schrembs, a member of the administrative committee recently transferred from Toledo to Cleveland, represented the case personally in Rome. There, the issue of the NCWC became the bone of contention in a Vatican power struggle.

The conclave of February 1922 found the college of cardinals split into opposing factions. The "Politicals," or progressives, led by Cardinal Pietro Gasparri, Benedict XV's secretary of state, wanted a strong international policy and a settlement of the Roman Question. The "Zealots," or reactionaries, led by Cardinal Merry del Val, Pius X's secretary of state, emphasized the church's spiritual mission and resisted any lessening of its dignity by overtures to the Italian government. In the early balloting, each side had maintained strength, resulting in a series of dead heats. On day three, both blocs slowly dissolved to form a coalition behind a neutral candidate, Ratti, who was elected the next morning and took the name Pius XI. His first blessing "*urbi et orbi*" (on the city and the world) came from the outer balcony of St. Peter's, where no pontiff had ventured since the loss of the Papal States. This action implied his intention to extend the olive branch to Italy, the policy of Benedict XV.[48]

The election of a non-aligned figure failed to heal the breach between the two blocs. Both took advantage of the new pope's first months in office to engage in a Vatican battle between Gasparri, the progressive secretary of state, and De Lai, the reactionary secretary of the Consistorial Congregation. This was the context confronting the legates of the NCWC.

They discovered that the new pontiff was unaware of what he had signed when he endorsed the decree abolishing the NCWC. He believed that the decree had gone through normal channels, that is, that the Consistorial Congregation had met in formal session with all cardinal members present and passed it—none of which had occurred. The decree was the work of De Lai, aided by Merry del Val. This fact became terribly evident to the NCWC legates as they queried each cardinal who belonged to that congregation, none of whom—except

Merry del Val and De Lai—had any knowledge of the decree of suppression. When Bisleti learned that O'Connell had lied to him about the reappointment of Shahan, he commented, "If one cannot believe a Cardinal, whom can one believe?" Bisleti now doubted everything O'Connell had ever told him. When Cardinal Donato Sbarretti, prefect of the Congregation of the Council, learned of the decree of suppression, he considered it invalid because according to canon law his congregation, not De Lai's, had responsibility for oversight of bishops' meetings. It soon became clear that the NCWC was caught in a fight that pitted De Lai and Merry del Val against Gasparri and other cardinals.[49]

Pius XI asked Bonzano to seek advice from both Dougherty and O'Connell about suspending the decree of suppression.[50] Dougherty replied that the decree should stand. Rome should allow the continuation only of those works of the NCWC which could not cease without seriously harming the church's reputation. Annual meetings of the hierarchy ought to stop because, as the decree observed, they violated canon law. It would be a sign of weakness if the Vatican were to reverse its decision. Dougherty's harshest criticisms were for the Washington secretariat, which he considered to be the NCWC. It retained laymen at extravagant salaries for work that had little to do with religion. A notable offender was the NCWC Press Department, which served as a national Catholic news service furnishing articles to diocesan papers. Dougherty warned that the administrative branch was "a small group of bishops, priests and laymen," who "have been usurping the place of the hierarchy."[51]

Although O'Connell's response to Bonzano is unavailable, it makes little difference because he took his case directly to Rome. Writing to both De Lai and Merry del Val, he was unrestrained in his criticism of the NCWC, which he considered to be only the administrative committee. Insinuating that the latter was bent on Americanism, O'Connell claimed it had deceived the pope in its appeal and was gathering the signatures of bishops for its protest, essentially threatening schism. "The *group* [administrative committee] is making every effort to have revoked the wise and just decree abolishing the famous N.C.W.C. of great pretenses and gigantic expenses," he wrote to De Lai.

I hope . . . that Your Eminence and the other Roman authorities will not let yourselves be *intimidated* by this "bluff.". . .

Now they are having a "plebiscite" [a vote] among the bishops in order to revoke the force of the decree.

The usual maneuvers that demonstrate again more clearly the wisdom of the decree.

Today we are in full "*Democracy*, Presbyterianism and Congregationalism."

If this maneuver succeeds, farewell to the authority of the Roman Congregations. We will make laws and decrees over here by means of "plebiscite" or method that naturally gains the most popularity, the idol of the day. . . .

And now it seems more than ever that this N.C.W.C. shows more clearly that it not only tends slowly to weaken hierarchical authority and dignity but still more it seeks to put into operation the same tactics toward the Consistorial. . . .

The plebiscite will certainly have many names of *those who profit.* But Your Eminence is there and guards for God both the faith and Rome. I am nothing but I am here and faithful.[52]

O'Connell's letter to Merry del Val was briefer, but identical in view.[53]

Both dispatches pictured O'Connell as the discounted but faithful defender of proper Roman church order against collegial, "democratic" in his terms, episcopal action, which was judged to be at heart heretical, that is, Presbyterianism or Congregationalism. At issue was American-ism in its worst form. His words were aimed to incite. The correspon-dence was self-serving, for if the NCWC were swept off the board and if true "hierarchical authority and dignity" were enforced, O'Connell as senior cardinal would sit atop the church totem in the mantle of Gibbons, virtual primate and spokesman of American Catholics.

Back at the Vatican, both sides in the power struggle were searching for a compromise. The issue beneath the conflict from the point of view of the Zealots became clear when Schrembs met with De Lai's personal secretary, Monsignor Giuseppe Tondini. Rather than allow annual conventions of the hierarchy to continue, Tondini proposed that the bishops of each ecclesiastical province hold an annual meeting followed by a gathering of the American archbishops. Schrembs angrily demanded to know why the hierarchies of other countries could meet, but not the American hierarchy. "You have such a large country," replied Tondini, "so many bishops, the power of them." Schrembs vented his wrath on the man, who then recanted the compromise and apologized profusely. "There you have it in a nutshell," concluded James H. Ryan, Schrembs's fellow envoy. "Cardinal De Lai is afraid of the American bishops. . . . They are always talking about the autonomy of the single bishops. It's a smoke screen. What they mean is, as the dear Monsignor said, it is easier to deal with one bishop than with a hierarchy."[54]

In the end, the pope demanded that the Consistorial Congregation hold a true plenary session on the issue of the NCWC. Convinced by Gasparri of the justice of the Welfare Council's cause, the pontiff was determined to override a negative vote and reinstate the NCWC. He armed Gasparri with a papal veto in the event that the cardinals of the congregation upheld the original decree. As it turned out, the veto was unnecessary. The Consistorial cardinals voted five to two in favor of restoring the NCWC; the eighth cardinal voted to defer the decision to a later date. Zealots cast all three unfavorable ballots: De Lai and Merry del Val voting nay and Basilio Pompili voting to defer. The NCWC was to operate in the future, however, in accord with a set of Vatican-imposed guidelines.[55]

In fact, there were two versions of the guidelines, representing the views of each side of the Vatican power struggle. Immediately after the plenary session of the Consistorial Congregation, Gasparri recounted his version to Bishop Schrembs. The published version was issued several weeks later by De Lai. Both stipulated that the chairmanship of the annual convention was to be determined according to the canonical rule of precedence, meaning there would be no election; the senior cardinal present was to preside. Both left it up to the hierarchy to decide how often it wished to meet. The two differed markedly, however, over the nature of the NCWC. Gasparri warned that the administrative committee was not a "super-hierarchy," but the executor of the resolutions passed by the annual assembly. His advice accorded with the NCWC's self-understanding, that is, the Welfare Council was a voluntary association of the hierarchy meeting in annual convention, and the administrative committee was its executive arm. Adopting the O'Connell-Dougherty view that the NCWC was simply the administrative committee, De Lai declared that since the name Welfare Council was not accepted by everyone and gave rise to misunderstandings, the bishops ought to change it to something like the National Catholic Welfare Committee. "In the mean time, however," he cautioned, "all should know that this institution is not the Catholic hierarchy of the United States." De Lai's version also included a stipulation that any NCWC agent who interfered in a diocese was to be dismissed.[56] Given the two versions, misunderstanding and conflict between O'Connell and the administrative committee were sure to continue.

CHAPTER 8

Nominalism Twentieth-Century Style

IN AUGUST 1922, Archbishop Giovanni Bonzano sent the written guidelines on the reinstatement of the NCWC, issued by Cardinal Gaetano De Lai, to Cardinal William O'Connell.[1] "I am delighted to see from this decree," responded the latter, "that we are to return to the traditional method of meeting, which will now be safeguarded as it should have been from the beginning." What he meant is unclear. He probably understood a combination of things: the right to the chairmanship was to be determined by canon law; the meetings were for "friendly conference"; the NCWC was not to be identified with the hierarchy; its name was to be changed, perhaps to the National Catholic Welfare Committee; and agents of the NCWC were to be dismissed for interference in diocesan rule. With regard to the frequency of assemblies, continued O'Connell, "I trust that the Bishops will decide to meet not oftener than once in three years." Clearly, as historian Gerald Fogarty observes, he hoped to minimize the council.[2]

O'Connell soon heard from both contenders in the Vatican quarrel. No doubt to let him know where the power lay, Cardinal Pietro Gasparri, whose appointment as secretary of state did "not please some," sent him a copy of a recent letter of support from the pope, which was published in *Civiltà Cattolica*. "Wishing to cut short behind the scenes maneuvering," wrote Gasparri, Pius XI had given it to him on the feast day of St. Peter, the cardinal's namesake. The secretary of state was certain the letter would please O'Connell.[3]

Within days the Boston cardinal heard from De Lai regarding the instructions putting the NCWC in its place. "I hope you will have found the manner satisfactory," he remarked.[4] The outcome was excellent, replied O'Connell. Thanking De Lai for his care and firmness, the American assured him that he had "saved a very dangerous situation."[5] A pleased De Lai responded that this was the solution he had been working for "after the mistaken direction given the matter by some of those in the Secretariat of State." "It is really a scabrous business that you have given me to do," he concluded. "And I thank God that he has given us a way of resolving it discreetly. The credit belongs in the beginning to Your Eminence and to Cardinal Dougherty."[6] Here was admission from De Lai himself that the two American cardinals had engineered the suppression of the NCWC.

Bishop Louis Walsh's reflections on the Vatican guidelines are noteworthy because his line of thinking foreshadowed the course of action to be taken by the administrative committee, of which he was a member. He drew the battle line in a memorandum that insisted that the NCWC was indeed the hierarchy, not as a canonical body, but as a voluntary association. Because it was incorporated under the title National Catholic Welfare Council, the name could not be changed. Moreover, the council must meet annually to maintain episcopal interest.[7]

On 11 August, the administrative committee met and scheduled the September meeting of the hierarchy for the twenty-seventh of that month at Catholic University. It was decided that the committee chairman, Archbishop Edward Hanna, should convoke the convention. Following Walsh's thinking, the board passed a series of motions regarding the new guidelines. First, meetings of the hierarchy should be held annually. Unwilling to change the NCWC's name, the committee made provision in case the hierarchy demanded it. In that event, Hanna was to report that after considering the words "congress," "committee," and "conference," the board recommended the last because De Lai's instructions used it in describing the purpose of the annual convention, namely, "friendly conference."[8]

This recommendation bespoke the committee's understanding that the NCWC was the hierarchy as a voluntary, not a canonical, body in yearly session, a position counter to De Lai's instructions which embodied the view of O'Connell and Cardinal Dennis Dougherty that the NCWC was simply the administrative board. This was the heart of the matter. Thus, the committee was preparing to go head to head with O'Connell.

Since the Vatican guidelines vindicated O'Connell's position, he tried to bring the administrative committee in tow. On 1 September, he sent Hanna a lengthy letter urging harmony at the upcoming annual convention. Some bishops avoided past meetings, said O'Connell, because of "too much rhetoric and declamation and too little sentiment of harmony." Many prelates expected great good from the 1922 meeting "if only we can succeed in keeping out discord and dissension. . . . At all costs, therefore, harmony and not oratory must prevail." He wanted Hanna to communicate this to his colleagues who were to give department reports. "The wise thing to do now," concluded O'Connell, "is to ignore absolutely past differences of opinion."[9]

While the cardinal spoke of peace and harmony, his thoughts ran in quite another direction: an assault on the administrative committee. In a memorandum written for use at the annual convention, he rehearsed a series of questions and demands. Why was there no detailed financial report of the NCWC's expenses? How much were officials of the press bureau being paid and what editorial work were they supposed to be doing? What did the hierarchy have to say about all this press activity? What good had it done? Was the NCWC incorporated? "By whom, when, and by what right?" Who appointed the American Board of Catholic Missions (ABCM), and why had it antagonized Propaganda Fide? Why did it still refuse to implement the latter's directions? Did not the Legal Department run the risk of becoming an ecclesiastical lobby in Washington? Would it not be safer to let individual bishops work through their congressmen and senators at home? Within this avalanche of questions was one suggestion, itself antagonistic. O'Connell thought there ought to be a committee of bishops other than the administrative committee to audit the entire operation and counsel the hierarchy about the prudence of continuing various programs.[10]

Some of these questions were calculated to irritate, for O'Connell himself must have known the answers. For example, he had attended the meetings at which the hierarchy had established the ABCM (1919), allowed it to organize contrary to Propaganda's plan (1921), and gave the administrative committee permission to incorporate the organization (1920). The memorandum revealed O'Connell's belligerent attitude and his determination to rein in the NCWC, if not kill it. The night before the convention, he began his attack by privately confronting Hanna with the prepared questions and objections.[11]

On 27 September, O'Connell, as senior cardinal, chaired the fourth annual assembly of the hierarchy. Fifty-nine bishops were in attendance but the number eventually climbed to sixty-one. A notable absentee was Cardinal Dougherty. At the outset, O'Connell declared that an essential matter of business was "to give full adhesion and execution to the instructions of the Holy See and to safeguard the rights of dioceses, especially in national meetings." Taking the bit, Archbishop Michael Curley averred that he found Rome quite interested in the annual conventions and moved that O'Connell send the pope a formal letter thanking him for the consideration shown the American hierarchy and pledging its loyalty. The motion carried unanimously.[12]

Although the *Minutes* indicate that the department reports were accepted with hearty approval and without criticism, Walsh noted that there were sharp exchanges in which O'Connell let "no occasion go by to butt in with his notions," all of which were rebuffed. The bishops maintained and supported all that was done by the administrative committee, while they opposed many of the "positions and innuendos of the presiding officer" and thoroughly routed his attempt to dismantle the Press Department, over which Walsh presided.[13] The session also included some fun at O'Connell's expense. Unseen by those on the podium (the cardinal included) were Hanna's antics—"head, lips, hands, feet and smiles . . . saluting His Eminence 'fifty' or more times" during the course of his report as chairman of the administrative committee. "Truly," noted Walsh, "it was comical in the extreme, but he [Hanna] was not to be suppressed."[14]

When the bishops took up the Vatican guidelines, Hanna immediately moved that there be a convention of the hierarchy in the following year and that a decision on the principle of holding annual assemblies be deferred to a later date. The action carried. The matter of yearly meetings was tabled and never reopened; the conventions simply continued annually as if by tradition. Next on the agenda was the nature of the Welfare Council. O'Connell explained that in the mind of the

Consistorial cardinals, the hierarchy was not identical with the NCWC. The latter was simply the administrative committee. To judge by the *Minutes*, his opinion went unchallenged.[15]

Walsh, however, recorded that there "was a plain and open discussion on what was and is the N.C.W.C." Although some of the nonnulli bloc gave O'Connell support, the vast majority of bishops, according to Walsh, held that the NCWC "was and is the Body of Bishops as a voluntary association, incorporated in order to take and hold property exempt from taxation, and *of which body*, the 7 Bishops, forming the Administrative Committee, are the Trustees of the Corporation and the Executive administrators for various works." Sharp words were exchanged, but no harm done.[16]

Following the discussion, Walsh moved that because "the name 'Council' and the Act of Incorporation of The National Catholic Welfare Council involve[d] some delicate and difficult points of Civil and Canon Law," the matter be referred for study to the administrative committee which was to report at the next convention. The motion was amended by Archbishop Patrick Hayes of New York to include that the hierarchy preferred the name National Catholic Welfare Conference. The action carried as amended.[17]

Almost as if planned to irritate O'Connell, who wanted no rhetoric or fancy speeches, Bishops Joseph Schrembs and Michael Gallagher closed the convention with "feats and shrieks of oratory, never before witnessed in Washington or perhaps in the United States, while the audience stared in amazement and were so intent that they forgot to applaud." Most bishops considered the speech-making "real recreation,"[18] and by almost all accounts, the convention was a success. Many prelates departed Washington with a good feeling about the meeting, the NCWC's accomplishments, and the future of the work.[19]

The implacable Walsh was still intent on ousting O'Connell from the chairmanship. In a letter to Curley, Walsh admired the patience of the hierarchy in tolerating the cardinal's "dictatorial methods, 'innuendoes,' 'sotto voce,' and attempt to force his arbitrary notions and interpretation" on the recent assembly. It was obvious to one and all that O'Connell came to the meeting with "hopes and plans to undermine or starve out the N.C.W.C." Although Walsh was not averse to changing the name of the Welfare Council, he insisted that it must be clearly understood that the NCWC was not simply the administrative committee; it was the body of bishops considered as a voluntary association. He thought the entire matter could be settled amicably "if the Boston dictator is silenced." Because the latter would soon destroy the morale of the hierarchy, something had to be done. Convinced that O'Connell had to be removed from the chair, Walsh suggested a round-table conference including Curley, Dougherty, Hayes, Archbishop Austin Dowling, and a few of the New England suffragans to devise an effective plan.[20]

Curley shared some of Walsh's views. He was certain that O'Connell opposed any assembly of bishops, held the entire work in contempt, had "little respect for any member of the administrative board, or for that matter any member present," and had attended the recent convention only to deal the NCWC "a fatal blow." Although he failed, the council might still disappear because too many bishops stayed away from the meetings and declined to contribute money for the organization's support. Despite a strong belief in collegial action, Curley felt doubtful about the NCWC's future.[21]

He was also pessimistic about a roundtable conference. In the first place, Dougherty would never cooperate. Even if he did, the matter could not be resolved on this side of the Atlantic. The situation called for drastic action which would create in Rome "something of the shock that Charleston's [Russell's] letter produced," that is, his threat to make public the scandals. There was only one way to settle the Boston mess, concluded Curley, and that was "by a figurative bomb shell thrown into the heart of the Eternal City." Turning to the name change, he was convinced that the Vatican considered the administrative committee alone to be the NCWC, no matter what the American bishops might think. In Rome's view, the annual convention, whether attended by a few or by all of the bishops, was the hierarchy, and the committee was the Welfare Council. For Curley, it made little difference how the NCWC was defined or named, so long as the work continued.[22]

In mid-November, Walsh met in New York with Bonzano, who was departing for Rome for his elevation to the cardinalate. Recently, the apostolic delegate had grown more bitter toward O'Connell. Although planning to inform the pope of the true situation in New England, Bonzano doubted that the Vatican would remove the cardinal, even though everyone considered that action desirable.[23] Some of the Boston clergy also visited the departing delegate to importune him to rid them of O'Connell. Bonzano commissioned Father Thomas McCarthy of St. Clement's parish in West Somerville to gather evidence. Once in Rome, the new cardinal proceeded slowly.[24] The case would not get off the ground until summer when the Vatican initiated an investigation.[25]

While Walsh sought O'Connell's ouster, the cardinal worked to minimize the NCWC by insisting on a name change that would identify it with only the administrative committee. He informed De Lai that the hierarchy had referred the renaming of the council to members of that board with a recommendation that the title be changed to "Conference" rather than "Committee" as the instructions suggested. De Lai replied that after consulting with the pontiff, the two preferred the name "Committee." O'Connell was directed to confer with Dougherty and report back.[26]

Because Dougherty had missed the annual convention, O'Connell recounted to him how he had hammered home the point that "Committee" was the proper term. Most prelates either agreed or were indifferent, claimed the cardinal. "The few who seem to be running the machine—especially at present—Muldoon and Walsh especially resent even a suggestion about any change—even of the name." They thought "Committee" diminished the authority of the administrative board. Yet such diminishment was precisely what had to be done. The committee *was* the NCWC and needed to be put in its place.[27]

Dougherty could hardly agree more. "The proponents and defenders of the title 'Council,' that is, the body of seven prelates [the administrative committee]," he replied, "consider themselves the hierarchy." They even incorporated themselves as that and issued statements in that name without consultation. "As if a few members of the hierarchy could be the whole hierarchy," concluded Dougherty. "It would be running against the divine constitution of the Church for such a thing to be true. . . . They are nothing but a committee; and that it [*sic*] what they should be called."[28] Contrary to Dougherty's contention, the corporation was the hierarchy of the United States. The act of incorporation named every bishop in the country and applied the instrument to their successors.[29]

At the risk of belaboring the point, it should be noted that the problem of naming the council arose from conflicting views about its nature. Dougherty, O'Connell, and others of the nonnulli bloc considered it to be only the administrative committee posing as the hierarchy and dictating to it. Those on the committee, supported by the majority, saw it as the hierarchy considered, not as a canonical body, but as a voluntary association carrying out its decisions through the administrative committee and its departments. Although both sides agreed fundamentally about how the hierarchy and the committee were to relate, they differed radically about which was to be called the NCWC.

O'Connell sent Hanna a mighty epistle reminding him that De Lai's instructions recommended changing the name to "Committee." Unfortunately, the hierarchy had compromised and suggested "Conference." "You must remember," he told Hanna, "my last words to you were, 'please see to it that this name is changed to Committee,' which is the name properly indicating the condition and function of the seven Bishops." O'Connell informed Hanna of De Lai's letter stating that the pope himself wanted the word "Committee" used. Practically ordering Hanna to alter the title as soon as possible, the cardinal concluded, "I take it for granted that the expressed wish of the Holy See will now be all-sufficient and that the name will be immediately changed from 'Council' or 'Conference' to 'Committee.'"[30] He then reported to De Lai about the action he had taken.[31]

Hanna gave assurance of the committee's willingness to accept the pope's wish, provided O'Connell would produce the letter that expressed it. Before the cardinal could respond, the committee met in Chicago and reconsidered the Vatican directive that recommended the name National Catholic Welfare Committee. Schrembs remarked that the pope had never mentioned this in any audience dealing with the NCWC. As a matter of fact, Gasparri's version of the instructions contained no such stipulation. Schrembs suspected that De Lai added it. When Hanna read O'Connell's letter to the committee, the bishops unanimously declined to accept his dictum.[32]

They believed, in Walsh's words, that the cardinal was simply trying "to wreck the whole association, in hopes of being the sole intermediary between Rome and the Bishops." They decided to remind him that the hierarchy had not empowered them to alter the name, but only to report if "Conference" was a suitable substitute for "Council." The committee deemed it quite apt because it was the word used in canon 250, article 4, which gave the Vatican Congregation of the Council jurisdiction over "bishops' meetings or conferences [*episcoporum coetus seu conferentias*]." The committee would so report at the next convention and let the hierarchy decide.[33]

On Hanna's return to San Francisco, two letters from O'Connell awaited him. In the first, dated 6 January 1923, the cardinal included the appropriate quotation from De Lai's dispatch. Because it left no room for debate, O'Connell trusted that the change of name to "Committee" would be "made prudently and without commotion."[34] The second was a follow-up requesting the committee's decision, for he had promised the information to De Lai.[35] Hanna reminded the cardinal that the hierarchy had not authorized the board to modify the name, but only to make a recommendation. "Of course the name must be changed," admitted Hanna. "We shall submit our report and the Bishops will give final solution."[36]

In April, he reported this exchange to the administrative committee, which passed two resolutions. First, at the next convention of the hierarchy, it would present a motion that "the voluntary meeting of the Bishops be called the National Catholic Welfare Conference and that the name of the committee which shall administer its affairs be called the Administrative Committee of the National Catholic Welfare Conference." Second, the committee was to recommend that the hierarchy maintain the five existing departments of the executive branch.[37] There the matter rested until September.

The ideological differences separating the administrative committee and its supporters on the one hand from O'Connell, Dougherty, and their supporters on the other, were wide indeed. The former were committed to collegial, episcopal action. In their view, the NCWC was the hierarchy, implementing its decisions through the administrative committee and its secretariat. O'Connell and his supporters were committed to preserving the autonomy of individual bishops and deference to cardinals by lesser prelates. In their view, the NCWC was the administrative committee and its secretariat, who represented nothing more than themselves. Hence the importance of what the NCWC was called: nomenclature bespoke the essence.

O'Connell's attempt, with the backing of De Lai and allegedly the pope, to order the committee to alter the name of the organization indicated his understanding that, as senior cardinal, he was in charge. Authority ran from the pope through the Roman congregations to the senior cardinal and on down. Hanna's response that the committee could not change the name because it had been commissioned by the hierarchy to make recommendations back to that body about appropriate nomenclature, attested to the committee's understanding that the hierarchy collectively was the NCWC, whose agents the committee and secretariat were. The hierarchy collegially, if informally, was in charge.

The stage seemed set for a mighty confrontation at the next meeting of the bishops. Yet, the anticipated eruption never occurred. As Father James A. Walsh of Maryknoll had observed to the apostolic delegate in 1919: "One weakness noted [in O'Connell] is a positive fear, on . . . [his] part, of any one who opposes him. He is known not to be brave, and his boldness is so easily repulsed that even curates do not hesitate to speak their minds plainly when confronted by him." Biographer James O'Toole has pointed out that, despite the cardinal's authoritarianism, if one had the courage to stand up to him, resistance often won out, the more so in the wake of the scandals in his curia.[38] In fact, O'Connell was a bully, who, like other bullies, was a coward at heart. That the administrative committee defied him on the matter of the name change caused him to view the issue as Americanism alive again, with his nemesis the Sulpician community acting as the driving force.

CHAPTER 9

A Sulpician Plot

THE EVE OF THE 1923 CONVENTION of the hierarchy found Cardinal William O'Connell in a black, anti-Sulpician mood. The embattled prelate was still the object of a drive to oust him from both Boston and a leadership role in the American hierarchy. Leading the charge were some of his clergy, most of his suffragans, and two members of the NCWC administrative committee, Bishop Louis Walsh and Archbishop Austin Dowling. The last two mentioned had been trained by the Sulpicians and taught with them on the faculty of St. John's Seminary in Brighton. Thus, O'Connell came to believe that the drive against him was inspired by the Sulpicians, whom he had summarily dismissed from the seminary in 1911 and had publicly belittled a year later in the Boston College speech. In 1920, at the height of his campaign to defend his nephew against the charge of concubinage, the cardinal tried to mend fences with the Sulpicians, an overture that suggested a connection in his mind between the scandal over the clerical marriages in his curia and his expulsion of the Sulpicians from Boston.

His attempt at reconciliation with them revolved around their new seminary in the nation's capital. In 1919, the Sulpicians had completed construction of present-day Theological College at Catholic University in Washington, D.C. In the following year, O'Connell offered to help the new seminary in whatever way he could (no doubt monetarily). While admitting his mishandling of their dismissal from Boston, he defended the action as substantially correct. Their friends—no doubt Walsh and Dowling among them—however, considered it a mistake, wished it had never happened, and blamed the cardinal for it. O'Connell regretted the ill will and wanted to make amends.[1]

The Sulpician provincial, Edward Dyer, was not to be placated. Holding the cardinal responsible for the Sulpicians' exile from New England, he reminded O'Connell of his address at Boston College in 1912. The cardinal objected that he had spoken off the cuff and had no recollection of his words. Dyer reminded him that his speech had been printed in the Boston *Pilot* at the time and reprinted more recently in the cardinal's own published *Sermons and Addresses* (1915). The Sulpician promised to look it up for him.[2] There was no forgiveness and no love lost between them.

The first episode of O'Connell's dark mood occurred in winter 1923. Monsignor Joseph Tracy, who had served on the faculty of St. John's Seminary with the Sulpicians and remained a friend and supporter, was then pastor of St. Columbkille's parish in Brighton. During a turbulent face-to-face encounter, O'Connell accused Tracy of participating in "Sulpician intrigue" against him. The charge, allegedly supported by facts and indisputable proof, was denied by Tracy, who defended his own and the Sulpicians' honor.[3]

Four days before the annual meeting of the hierarchy in fall of 1923, a bizarre confrontation occurred, revealing the frame of mind in which the cardinal would view the convention. The annual meetings took place at Catholic University. As was his custom, O'Connell was lodging in the Oblate College across the street from the Sulpician Seminary in Washington. He summoned Father Joseph Nevins, a priest of the archdiocese of Boston whom, in 1909, he had released for service in the Society of St. Sulpice. Sulpician priests belonged to their diocese of origin and were essentially on loan to the Sulpician community for life, unless recalled by their bishop.[4]

When Nevins arrived, he found O'Connell "in a state of more or less suppressed fury." The cardinal pretended not to know him. Having ascertained that the priest taught at the seminary across the road, O'Connell accused him of disrespect and badgered him unmercifully in an obvious attempt to provoke some fault that would justify recalling him to Boston. Realizing this, the Sulpician maintained his composure. "Do you know that you [are] in a nest of intriguers over there?" asked the cardinal. Nevins said nothing, which riled O'Connell to abusive language about the Sulpicians. He concluded by telling Nevins to expect a letter recalling him to Boston at the end of the year. Still, the visitor remained quiet. "Don't you know I can recall you to the diocese?" asked the cardinal. Yes, admitted Nevins, but he would appeal to Rome, and the Vatican would surely support him. This brought more verbal abuse on the Sulpicians.[5]

Finally, "as though speaking to a mongrel cur that had committed a nuisance in the princely apartments," O'Connell told Nevins, "Get out!" The priest genuflected to kiss the cardinal's ring, but O'Connell turned away yelling, "Get out! get out of this house!" Pursuing Nevins to the door, he roared, "Get out!" When Nevins turned at the threshold to say good-bye, O'Connell stepped close and "laughing with a demoniac sneer said, 'Will you please convey a message for me to your superiors and associates—tell if you will, please, that they are a bunch of intriguers—a gang . . . will you tell them that?'" Nevins bowed and replied, "I think Your Eminence would do better to convey that message in person, I couldn't!" As he walked across the lawn, the cardinal, with "a cruel, contemptuous voice and a demoniac laugh, shouted, 'You poor little intriguer, ho, ho, ho, ho!'" Nevins described the audience as "the experience of my life."[6] The cardinal's deep feelings against the Sulpicians were to resurface after the convention of the hierarchy.

Just before the annual assembly, the administrative committee reaffirmed its intention to recommend that the NCWC's name be changed to the National Catholic Welfare Conference, thereby maintaining that the organization was, in fact, the hierarchy. The board further agreed to urge a continuation of the present departments.[7] Two days later, sixty-six bishops assembled at Catholic University for the fifth annual convention of the hierarchy. Archbishop Edward Hanna introduced the administrative committee's two motions: one regarding the name change and the other regarding the five departments of the executive branch. Both received unanimous approval, and the bishops budgeted another $200,000 ($2,318,000 in 2006 dollars) for the work.[8]

The Ruthenian question, which arose during the meeting, merits special note for the difficulty it would create between Hanna and O'Connell after the convention. In 1913, Pius X erected a Ruthenian Catholic diocese covering the entire United States. Its bishop had died in 1916 and the see lay vacant thereafter. The American Ruthenians were demanding that Rome appoint another ordinary. Bishop Joseph Schrembs recommended that they be placed under some form of episcopal rule, be it Roman or eastern. The hierarchy directed the "chair" to present the matter to the new apostolic delegate, Archbishop Pietro Fumasoni-Biondi.[9] Both Hanna and O'Connell heard this instruction as directed at himself, the former as chairman of the administrative committee and latter as chairman of the annual convention. Confusion and recrimination would follow.

O'Connell offered closing remarks. Expressing delight at the privilege of presiding over a meeting that was so frank, encouraging, and unanimous in its decisions, he felt that all difficulties with regard to the convention were firmly settled and the principles of action clearly defined. There was no reason, he declared, why every bishop should not give the NCWC financial backing and moral support.[10]

His words greatly surprised Bishop Walsh, who commented in his diary: "I came really prepared for a serious opposition and perhaps a final break, but it did not show its face at all, the Boston Cardinal really capitulating on every side after his three years of attack. Is it really calm before another and different form of attack? In any case he promised to pay up."[11] Walsh's questioning spirit was well-advised. O'Connell was as opposed as ever to the NCWC and made no financial contribution to support its work.

While all passed smoothly within the convention, an event outside came to O'Connell's attention. Father John Fenlon, a "Sulpician . . . in some vague way connected with the N.C.W.C.," as the cardinal expressed it (Fenlon was secretary of the administrative committee), conversed in the corridor with Monsignor George Waring of New York and Monsignor Richard Haberlin, O'Connell's chancellor. They chatted about Rome. Allegedly speaking of the duplicity of the Vatican curia, Fenlon illustrated his point with several recent instances. "You can make Rome do anything if you *get the crowd behind you*," he concluded. If true, these were reckless words for someone who must have known they would be repeated to O'Connell. Haberlin was shocked that Fenlon, the spiritual director of Catholic University, would make such a remark.[12]

After his glowing public remarks at the close of the convention, O'Connell undermined the administrative committee in his post-convention report to the apostolic delegate. He claimed there was a general feeling that vast sums were "being expended and large contributions rather liberally levied upon many dioceses." "As any reference to this has always immediately aroused disagreeable incidents," said the cardinal, "the Bishops prefer to make no further comments at the meeting, though very many of them speak plainly enough among themselves. . . . So the few leaders in this matter do as they wish."[13] These sentiments, of course, ran counter to O'Connell's public declaration at the meeting's conclusion that the NCWC was worthy of the hierarchy's full monetary and moral support.

His report also pointed out that the bishops of the administrative committee were reelected at the final session with only thirty prelates present. "This fact must be well noted," stressed the cardinal. "30 is less than a third of the hierarchy . . . those thus elected were *not elected by the hierarchy*, as of course will be claimed always. And therefore only in an extremely limited sense can they be said with truth to *represent* the American hierarchy."[14]

As for the committee's way of operating, O'Connell recounted Fenlon's conversation about getting favorable Roman action by mobilizing a crowd. Alluding to the circular that protested the suppression of the NCWC and had been signed by eighty bishops, the cardinal remarked: "We are familiar enough with the methods of these people, but it is well to know that Fr. Fenelon [*sic*] had the rashness to formulate them. We have had plenty of evidence lately that that particular group [the administrative committee] have learned their lessons from such experienced teachers, and know how to put them into practice."[15] Clearly, O'Connell was warning the delegate that the committee was imbued with democratic principles imbibed from the Sulpicians.

He made the point more clearly to Cardinal Dennis Dougherty, who had missed the final session of the convention. Recounting how the administrative committee, "this N.C.W.C.," was reelected by only a fraction of the hierarchy, he emphasized that Dowling, Walsh, and Bishop Peter Muldoon "were made by the Sulpicians"; the first two had even taught with them at St. John's Seminary in Brighton. This "little clique" was "distinctly the central force of all the planning and scheming." Others on the committee counted for nothing. "It is unquestionably the continuation of Sulpicianism contra mundum [against the world] but especially contra nos [against us]," O'Connell told Dougherty. In view of Fenlon's remarks, he concluded: "The centre of all these things, say what they will, is S[t]. Sulpice and the purpose is obvious—to keep the power in their hands by demolishing us and our prestige. We are obviously the intruders and must be kept in our place—by the crowd."[16]

In O'Connell's mind, the issue was Sulpician intrigue against deference to the cardinalate. The way to smash the latter was with democracy, the crowd. That being the case, O'Connell wanted to exchange views with Dougherty before future meetings so that they could present a united front. "For with S[t]. Sulpice," he warned, "we can see only an enemy not merely personal but in principle. And any sign of lack of unity between us would of course only strengthen them and their clique."[17] Dougherty assured him of "cooperation and harmonious action."[18]

O'Connell's attitude toward the Sulpicians and the administrative committee was incredible. Certainly, he differed with the board on many issues, but it was unfair to limit opposition to Dowling, Muldoon, and Walsh. Hanna, Schrembs, and Bishop Edmund Gibbons, who also sat on the committee, shared the views of the other three. If O'Connell was concerned about a scheme to undo him, he was correct. Walsh was leading it, but not as part of a Sulpician conspiracy. His support on the administrative committee was limited to Dowling. Walsh's major backing came from the Boston suffragans and some of the cardinal's own clergy who wanted his removal for scandal and malfeasance in office. To be sure, the Sulpicians rejoiced at O'Connell's woes, but nothing indicates that they played an active role against him. At most, they kept Walsh's "secret archives"— his papers relating to the cardinal and other matters—and probably came into possession of those only after the bishop's death.[19]

Within weeks, O'Connell had fresh reason to suspect the administrative committee. As mentioned, he and Hanna each believed they were to take up the Ruthenian issue with the delegate. Both did. Before leaving Washington, O'Connell wrote to Fumasoni-Biondi and laid the matter before him. On the day after the convention, the administrative committee paid its customary visit to the delegate and did the same. Fumasoni-Biondi instructed Hanna to write a letter to every bishop whose diocese contained a sizeable number of Ruthenians to request that the prelates advise the delegate if these Catholics should be placed under a bishop of their own rite or under the local Roman ordinary. Hanna sent the letter on 6 October 1923.[20]

When Dougherty received a copy, he replied to Hanna rather than Fumasoni-Biondi. As a member of the Vatican Congregation for Oriental Affairs, which had charge of Eastern Rite Catholics, the cardinal disqualified himself from expressing an opinion. He advised, however, "that the Holy See would prefer to be entirely at liberty in the matter and not be in any way pressed from without to take a course of action which it has hitherto not deemed advisable." No doubt, this was a warning against pushing to have Ruthenians subjected to Roman bishops. Too, it may have been a warning against trying to impress the Vatican by the number of bishops who might support this action. Informing O'Connell of the letter, Dougherty thought the mailing of such a circular "would devolve upon the ranking Cardinal," that is, O'Connell.[21]

The latter fired back: "*I* was the one requested by the Bishops to lay the matter before the Delegation. . . . It is simply a trick, and a contemptible one at that, to attempt to force the recognition of the N.C.W.C. by the Delegation, which has never been given before." Agreeing that Rome should be left free in this matter, he hoped Dougherty would take the opportunity "to let the Delegate know of this trap into which he has evidently unwittingly fallen."[22] It is unknown if Dougherty did so. When Hanna learned of O'Connell's objection, he confided to John Burke, "He seemingly forgot that I was ordered by the body of Bishops to present the matter to the Apostolic Delegate."[23] In any event, this misunderstanding gave further proof of O'Connell's hostility toward the NCWC and of his belief that it was a rival to his authority as senior cardinal.

In December 1923, the Boston prelate fired another salvo at the Sulpicians. In that month, he formed the Academy of St. Thomas, a theological society at St. John's Seminary. Opening the first meeting with words about the importance of upholding correct doctrine, O'Connell recalled that on arriving as coadjutor archbishop, he had attended classes at the seminary to learn what was being taught. He was shocked by the false teachings being given to the students. On a visit to Rome, he exposed the matter to Pius X, who bound him under pain of mortal sin to drive the professors from the seminary. This O'Connell did—he expelled the Sulpicians.[24]

Vindication of this newest aspersion came later that month when Rome condemned the revision of the *Manuel biblique ou Cours d'Écriture Sainte a l'usage des Séminaires* (*A Biblical Manual or Course of Sacred Scripture for Seminary Use*) done by the Sulpician Augustin Brassac. In December 1923, Cardinal Raphael Merry del Val, head of the Holy Office which oversaw doctrinal matters, placed the *Manuel biblique* on the index of forbidden books because it was "so riddled with errors that it is hopeless to correct it." "Neglecting to a high degree the positive explanation of integral Catholic doctrine [that is, the interlocking philosophical-theological system of Thomas Aquinas]," said the decree, Brassac espoused the new method of "higher criticism," that is, the application of historical and literary criticism to the Bible. His views on scriptural inerrancy and inspiration were obviously erroneous. Moreover, he seemed "to care nothing for decisions of the pontifical biblical institute." Almost totally devoid of piety, the work had no redeeming qualities and was, therefore, unfit for use in seminaries.[25] Referring to this condemnation, Cardinal Gaetano De Lai congratulated O'Connell for being "on target when he removed the Sulpicians from his seminary!"[26]

Marginally pleasing to O'Connell was word from Vatican Secretary of State Pietro Gasparri that the pope was sending each cardinal a book entitled *De Dignitate et Officio Cardinalis* (*On the Dignity and Office of the Cardinal*). The Boston cardinal commented to his friend, Merry del Val, that their counterparts around the world would probably rejoice to learn that the Holy Father publicly acknowledged that there was such a thing "as Dignity now attached to the Cardinals [*sic*] office." American cardinals had a tradition, said O'Connell, that their dignity consisted in "wearing the red and bearing insults." Referring to the previous delegate, Giovanni Bonzano, who had literally backed O'Connell against the wall at their last meeting, he added that princes of the church needed no convincing about their dignity, but the same could not be said for apostolic delegates, at least those in America, "who made it their chief duty to affront us whenever it was possible." The book, concluded O'Connell, ought to be sent to them.[27]

From the foregoing, it is clear that O'Connell came to view the drive for his removal as a Suplician plot. Despite the absence of truth in the matter, his association of the Sulpicians with his troubles was understandable and enabled him to redefine the issue away from the scandals he had countenanced. There was a long history of bad blood between him and the Sulpicians, beginning with his days at St. Charles' College, his removal of them from St. John's Seminary, his Boston College speech, his failed attempt at reconciliation in 1920, and finally his near-repudiation by the NCWC and its successful reversal of the decree of suppression.

The restoration of the NCWC had been spearheaded by the administrative committee, which at the time boasted four members who were Sulpician-trained, two of whom had taught with the Sulpician faculty at St. John's. The traditional Gallicanism of the Sulpicians, that is, their respect for the national characteristics of the church, made it possible for O'Connell to see the matter as Sulpician intrigue to democratize the American church through the NCWC and their allies on the administrative committee. In his view, this attempt undermined the hierarchical nature of the church, especially deference to the cardinalate and particularly deference to himself as dean of the American hierarchy. In essence, he continued to interpret events through his traditional perspective of Romanism versus Americanism.

CHAPTER 10

Walsh's Last Stand

IN LATE 1922, Cardinal Giovanni Bonzano, the former apostolic delegate, carried to the Vatican the fight for O'Connell's removal from office. He had enlisted Father Thomas McCarthy to gather evidence. Having labored at the task for a year, the priest confided to Bishop Louis Walsh that he found his investigation "depressing at times, and I have grown heart sick." He was terribly disappointed in his fellow clerics. "Priests whom I respected, and for whom I had affection," he told Walsh, "trembled with fear at the very thought of giving evidence, while others, looking for promotion, avoided the issue. . . . God expects decent clean-living priests to assist in bringing to justice the scandal-giver." This lack of cooperation caused McCarthy to state that he knew of no clergyman in the archdiocese "worthy to be archbishop" as successor to O'Connell.[1]

In the summer of 1923, David I. Walsh, U.S. senator from Massachusetts unrelated to Bishop Walsh, and Joseph Pelletier, former district attorney of Boston, went to Rome where they had personal interviews with Pius XI about the Toomey-O'Connell scandals, but they could reveal nothing of their conversation because the pontiff had sworn them to secrecy. McCarthy had been informed by Rome that the pope was reviewing all the evidence, which both "shocked and grieved" him. As yet, however, he gave no indication of his intended course of action.[2] In mid-December, Louis Walsh met with Bishop Joseph Rice of Burlington to discuss Cardinal O'Connell. They agreed to go to Italy in the winter of 1924 to "make another attempt to straighten out our affairs."[3]

In preparation, Bishop Walsh gathered information from Father John Mullen, one of the cardinal's principal accusers. Mullen was not sanguine about the chances for success in unseating O'Connell. "As far as I can learn, Rome does not wish to take any drastic action," he told Walsh. ". . . I feel their intention at most is [Pontius] Pilate's Emendatum ergo illum dimittam [He has been corrected therefore I will let him go (cf. Luke 23:17)]. They will go no further than they are obliged to go;

because they fear a world scandal; and they do not know what to do with him; and because he has friends at Rome working for him." In Mullen's view, Cardinals Raphael Merry del Val and Gaetano De Lai would do all in their power to save O'Connell, and they would work to weaken Cardinal Pietro Gasparri's influence on the pope with regard to the Boston prelate. Although other cardinals had no use for O'Connell, "they are not anxious to burn their fingers, especially when they have no immediate interest in the case." Finally, O'Connell had religious orders in Rome that supported him, particularly the Augustinians. Father Charles Driscoll, who was assistant general of that order, served for years in the cardinal's chancery in Boston and was loyal to him. "All this means much in Rome," concluded Mullen.[4]

Despite his misgivings about success, he advised that the case against O'Connell already had a strong foundation in the proven marriages of David Toomey and James P. E. O'Connell, especially since the latter had been degraded and excommunicated by Benedict XV. The uncle knew about the nephew's marriage, lied about it, and had two witnesses (Charles Sullivan and Richard Haberlin) perjure themselves in the nephew's defense. With regard to the cardinal himself, Mullen suggested three lines of attack: mal-administration in both temporal and spiritual matters, personal immorality, and *mala fama* (ill repute).[5]

The charge of mal-administration of temporalities included the Portland finances, the archdiocesan insurance scam, obligatory subscriptions to the *Pilot* (O'Connell's personal paper), and the expectation of gifts and "Christmas wishes" (checks, sometimes blank) from priests who wanted ecclesiastical honors or better parishes. Mal-administration of spiritualities included O'Connell's avoidance of celebrating mass on major church festivals (or shortening them when he did), his refusal to take part in the blessing of new churches and schools, and his assignment of the married chancellor to give spiritual conferences at the seminary.[6]

On a more personal level was the matter of O'Connell's own faith and morals. According to Mullen, it was widely known that the cardinal rarely said daily mass, was never seen going to confession, made truncated annual retreats, and kept company with immoral men, especially Dr. William Dunn, a known homosexual. For all this, O'Connell suffered ill repute: the bishops of his own province rejected him, as did many others around the country; most professional people in New England opposed him, and the common folk, despite "the old Irish loyalty to anything priestly," were "cold, murmuring and sullen" about him.[7]

McCarthy also urged Walsh to argue some of these same points. He sent the bishop a list of charges that could be backed up with proof. Among them were O'Connell's "reputation for immorality and avarice among priests and laymen," his truncated annual spiritual retreats, his missing of daily mass, and his protection of bad priests.[8]

Meanwhile, O'Connell was taking countermeasures to secure his position. At the urging of Driscoll, he had increased his Peter's Pence collection from $30,000 to $60,000 annually beginning in 1921 ($332,000 to $664,000 in 2006 dollars), a sum he maintained throughout the decade. On the advice of Cardinal Merry del Val, he sent to several Vatican cardinals a seven-volume set of his collected addresses and sermons as evidence of his labor in the vineyard of the Lord. To further burnish his image, O'Connell made a survey of his accomplishments as archbishop of Boston, showing that he had erected eighty-one new parishes, twenty-five mission stations, two colleges, and two retreat houses, all debt-free. The account of these achievements was printed and spread abroad. "H[is] E[minence] is playing a desperate game and will stop at nothing," wrote Mullen to Walsh. "All this advertising in the Pilot . . . about his wonderful administration gives the authorities in Rome a colored title at least to put off radical action. . . . How true was my prediction that H[is] E[minence] would concoct a glorification of his administration in an attempt to bluff Rome."[9] As will be seen, the bluff and money would pay off handsomely.

In mid-December 1923, O'Connell notified the apostolic delegate, Archbishop Pietro Fumasoni-Biondi, of a forthcoming trip to Rome. His route would be circuitous, via the Holy Land, where he intended to make a pilgrimage. His translation of De Lai's book, *Passion of Our Lord,* had rekindled in him a lifelong wish to visit there. In January 1924, O'Connell bade farewell to his flock gathered in the cathedral. "Visualizing the accomplishments of the past fifteen years, stupendous as they are," reported the *Pilot,* "His Eminence stated that he would lay them all at the foot of the Cross of Calvary as a mighty tribute of the love and fidelity of his priests and people who had worked in a bond of close union with him during those fruitful years." The pilgrimage was not simply to offer to God the past fruits of his ministry. O'Connell would use the journey to Palestine as a time for reflection to mature new plans for making the archdiocese even greater. "I shall then, laying these plans on Calvary, ask God to approve of and bless them," said the cardinal; "later, proceeding to Rome, I shall lay them before the Holy Father. No, I look forward to the pilgrimage to Jerusalem as not a waste of time—far from it." This last remark was odd and seemingly out of place in an address from a man who viewed the upcoming trip as the fulfillment of a lifetime dream. Was it really so, or was it something else? Was he trying to convince his people or himself that the visit to the Holy Land was not a waste of time? Speculation abounded, as will become clear. Still, the cardinal urged the laity to join him in spirit by meditating on the scenes depicted in De Lai's *Passion of Our Lord.*[10]

The volume had been rendered into English the year before by O'Connell—at least that was the official story. It was said that the translation had been done by Father Joseph Murphy, a professor at St. John's Seminary. Published by the *Pilot* and recommended as Lenten reading, the book sold for $1.00 ($11.50 for hardbound in 2006 dollars) so that most Catholics could afford it. Promising De Lai all the proceeds, O'Connell sent "the first advance of one thousand dollars" in March 1923. Within a year, the book had gone through nine editions, grossing $23,018—the equivalent of $266,000 in 2006. After deducting the cost of printing, O'Connell sent De Lai, over the course of a year, a total of $9,560—seven-times the annual salary of an average American industrial worker in that day, with a purchasing power of $110,800 in 2006. Such benefaction was certainly not misplaced, for if there were to be formal proceedings against Boston's cardinal, De Lai's Consistorial Congregation was the Vatican department that would handle them.[11]

Mullen took a cynical view of O'Connell's pilgrimage. "It is common gossip here," he wrote to Edward Dyer, "that he has been called to Rome; and the Holy Land idea is only a camouflage." Yet, according to a story later handed down from a priest in whom the cardinal had allegedly confided, the pilgrimage was a penance imposed on him by Benedict XV for his cover-up of James O'Connell's marriage. The cardinal was to make it on foot in full episcopal regalia, a humiliation he deeply resented. A remark of Archbishop Austin Dowling at the time also suggests the penitential nature of the trip.[12]

The truth is difficult to gauge. O'Connell was then under investigation, and it is unlikely that he lacked knowledge of it. If he had not been summoned to Rome, he was certainly going there to protect his interests. If the pilgrimage was not a penance, it may have been the camouflage that Mullen thought, though perhaps not to cover up a summons to the Vatican. It may have been a bluff to demonstrate to the Vatican the sincerity of O'Connell's faith because the *Pilot* had been careful to state that De Lai's *Passion* had been instrumental in rekindling the Boston cardinal's early desire to make a pilgrimage to the Holy Land. The knowledge of this would certainly ingratiate him with De Lai, along with the ample financial rewards that accrued to the latter from the translation of his book. If in fact it was a penance, O'Connell covered its significance by declaring that the pilgrimage had been a lifelong dream, one now undertaken for the good of the archdiocese. In any case, as will be seen, the brevity of his stay in Palestine would suggest that he, in fact, considered the visit perfunctory.

Shortly after O'Connell sailed, McCarthy wrote to Bonzano: "The majority of priests, nuns, and seminarians are praying that he may never return. His return to Boston will mean only one thing, and that is, that Rome approves of his mal-administration, scandalous life and hypocrisy."[13] Mullen warned Walsh that O'Connell was using money to smooth his path. The cardinal was bringing a $50,000 mission collection—in fact, more than $88,000 ($1,020,000 in 2006 terms)—to present to Cardinal Willem Van Rossum, prefect of Propaganda. There was also De Lai's *Passion*. If the aged cardinal knew that the American public believed that O'Connell "was simply playing him (DL) in all this, and were laughing at the colossal bluff," said Mullen, "he (DL) would not be too well pleased. . . . DL needs waking up. He is no fool. If shown the bluff, he will recognize it."[14]

Mullen was too sanguine about De Lai, who informed his Boston friend of a recently received anonymous letter that read in part: "Word is spreading especially in America, that you are the paid agent of Cardinal O'Connell—that . . . he provides you continuously with money and that the translation into English of the book is only another pretext for him to continue to send you money, which he claims has come from the sale of books." De Lai considered the idea "wickedness." O'Connell's translation was, he wrote, a good deed carried out with much fatigue, and "I certainly enjoy the ample benefits from it." Stating that the news of such a letter must certainly cause the Boston prelate sorrow, De Lai advised that "it is good to be warned about these shady maneuvers, and so to be on guard against dangers."[15] By the time De Lai's letter arrived, O'Connell had left Boston. To date, however, he had already sent his Roman friend $8,560 ($99,200 in 2006 terms) in clear profit, with more to come.[16]

The cardinal was attended on the pilgrimage by two close associates: Monsignor Richard Haberlin, chancellor of the archdiocese, and Monsignor Michael Splaine. The term "pilgrimage" usually connotes a reflective and reverential visit to a holy site. Though O'Connell wrote feelingly to his brother about the experience, and reporters described the cardinal's piety, the Holy Land tour appeared to be less a pilgrimage than a lightning jaunt through Palestine in the company of two Boston newspaper men brought specially for the occasion: Joseph Toye of the *Traveler* and David Shea of the *Post*.[17] No doubt, the presence of newsmen accorded with the cardinal's public style of office-holding, but to bishops like Walsh it smacked of a publicity stunt.

O'Connell arrived in Palestine on 12 February 1924 and motored to Nazareth in his personal car, transported from Boston on the ship. The next morning he said mass in that town and then drove to Cana, the Sea of Galilee, and thence to Jerusalem where he arrived later in the day.[18] "A Prince of the Church clothed with Roman purple [cardinal's robes] . . . was about to enter the Holy City," reported the London *Tablet*. "He was Cardinal O'Connell . . . majestic in stature, noble in bearing, yet so humble in heart that his personal wish, as expressed in his own words, was 'to crawl in' unobtrusively, as a lowly pilgrim." O'Connell entered the city on foot through the Jaffa gate, where he was met by an escort that walked him to the church of the Latin patriarch, with whom he stayed. Later, at a dinner celebrated in his honor, the patriarch decorated the cardinal with the Grand Cross of the Holy Sepulcher.[19]

The following morning put O'Connell on the road to Bethlehem. At the boundary of the parish, he was met by the pastor. When the occupants alighted from the car, he escorted them on foot to the basilica and then to the grotto of the stable of Bethlehem where the cardinal said a low mass and spent time in silent prayer. "As he himself said afterwards," reported the *Tablet*, "those moments passed kneeling in the stable were more precious to him than hours seated on his archepiscopal throne had been." The cardinal then returned to Jerusalem for a visit to the seminary; lunch with the patriarch and Sir Herbert Samuel, British high commissioner for Palestine; and then high tea with the latter at Government House. O'Connell had reserved that evening, Thursday, for his visit to the Garden of Gethsemane. He entered there as evening fell, and a lantern was necessary to light the path.[20]

On Friday morning, O'Connell walked from the patriarchate to Mount Calvary where he said another low mass at the Church of the Holy Sepulcher. After mass, he visited the sepulcher itself and made the way of the cross. He spent the rest of the day visiting the Pool of Bethesda, the birthplace of the Virgin Mary, the Dome of the Rock, and the upper room (site of the Last Supper). On Saturday morning, he left for Rome, via Constantinople and Athens.[21]

O'Connell spent three days in the Holy Land, prompting Mullen to marvel: "Our pilgrim . . . arrived in Palestine Tuesday—and leaves today!!! . . . Can you beat it! 'The longings of years to see the Holy Places' and he stays three days!! Wouldn't you think H[is] E[minence] would know that everyone would see through his bluff?" Bluff or no, Mullen had reason to believe that it would work. Monsignor Patrick Supple, who had formerly been close to the cardinal but had since fallen from grace, told him that Sante Tampieri had written from the Vatican to say that O'Connell "is sure to leave Rome with flying colors."[22]

When the *Pilot* carried several articles rhapsodizing the pilgrimage, Walsh, who chaired the NCWC Press Department, ordered the general secretary, John Burke, "to cease staging the *Boston Cardinal*" on the picture page of the nationally syndicated NCWC news service. "He has paid nothing [in dues to the NCWC]," said the angry prelate, "he deserves no favors. I realize fully the commercial side of featuring him, but the latest *nauseating series* of *self-advertising* has become a boomerang. I will be responsible for ignoring him in our service."[23]

Late in January 1924, Bishops Rice and Daniel Feehan departed for the Vatican where Walsh was later to join them. The three intended to make a last stand to have O'Connell removed. Dowling, already in Rome to report on his archdiocese and to conduct NCWC business, planned to remain there and support their effort. In early February, he confided to Burke that the cardinal was due "at the end of the month with all his penitential merits [from the pilgrimage] thick upon him. I sense nothing here of the high things that were whispered in America in his regard."[24] Foul weather and poor accommodations, however, forced Dowling's early departure. He left Walsh a letter stating that he had tried to broach the topic of O'Connell with the pope, who either misunderstood or failed to notice because he took the conversation in a completely different direction.[25]

Walsh came to view his trip to Rome as an attempt to uphold the rights of the national episcopate against "Italianization and centralization." When he reached France, he met up with Cardinal Francis Bourne of Westminster, England, who was also on his way to the Vatican. Walsh found Bourne equally emphatic about the need for the church to decentralize. The two of them called on Bishop Henri Chapon of Nice. Both Chapon and Bourne favored the calling of a council in Rome "to come back to 'normal right and law'—our right and duty to demand not only Episcopal dignity but [the] right of [the] 'Episcopate' in each country—to inform [the] Holy See and govern the Church, subordinate to [the] Holy See, but not merely subservient." All three believed that the hierarchy of a country ought to rule as a collegial body. They agreed that the time had come to settle the matter of the "Divine Episcopate," that is, that the office or position of bishop had been instituted by God. They reached the conviction that the pendulum had "swung too far from political Gallicanism which *lowered Divine Authority* and [the] Infallibility of [the] Pope to another equally dangerous theory and practice of *lowering* & degrading the Episcopate, individuals & as a body—done by such men as De Lai & Del Val [*sic*]." In Walsh's view, "the dignity and vitality of the Holy See in any country now depends on creating a sound Episcopate in each country and letting such Episcopate govern." Otherwise, the church in each country risked being dubbed "an Italian Mission," as Archbishop E. W. Benson of Canterbury referred to the Catholic church in England.[26] As James O'Toole observes, Walsh thus joined the two issues that consumed him: "Deposing O'Connell was the first step toward 'creating a sound Episcopate' in America; relying on the fledgling cooperative structure of the NCWC was the means for giving that episcopate its full authority to govern."[27]

On the evening of 21 February 1924, Walsh arrived at Rome and was met at the train station by Feehan and Rice, who had already seen Pius XI and found him both interested in, and sympathetic about, the Boston situation and hopeful of being able to find an appropriate solution. Feehan and Rice told Walsh that they had not been able to glean much information from any of the Vatican cardinals and avoided broaching the Boston question with De Lai. They hoped that their silence with him would not be misinterpreted.[28]

Two days later, Walsh visited Monsignor Giuseppe Pizzardo, under-secretary of state, who informed him that the pope was current on most aspects of the Boston situation, but that supporting documentation the pontiff wished to review could not be located in the Vatican archives. Pizzardo urged Walsh to speak freely with the pontiff about O'Connell and address all the major points. He promised to arrange a papal audience for the bishop as soon as possible. The following morning, Walsh visited Cardinal Bonzano to discuss the "Boston imbroglio." Like Pizzardo, Bonzano encouraged him "to speak plainly on all important points, as the Holy Father was really anxious to know and ready to do his duty."[29]

The next day, Walsh spent nearly an hour and a half recounting for Pius XI O'Connell's intrigue to become metropolitan, his shady financial dealings in both Portland and Boston, the scandal of the nephew, the universal lack of confidence in the cardinal, and the fear of a "volcanic eruption" if the scandals became public. He gave the pope a copy of the petition, signed by seven of the eight New England suffragans back in 1920, requesting O'Connell's removal. The pontiff was very interested and attentive. Like Pizzardo, he told Walsh that he "could not find nor get 'the documents.'" Still, Pius proposed the same solution to the problem as Benedict XV: give the Boston cardinal a sinecure in the Vatican, provided the American bishops would urge it. When Walsh expressed the fear that American bishops had about a man of O'Connell's caliber representing the church of the United States at the Vatican, the pontiff responded that Roman authorities could control his influence. He told Walsh to broach the matter prudently with the hierarchy. Pius wished to see him again but wanted him to confer first with De Lai and urge upon him the necessity of bringing O'Connell to Rome.[30]

Two days later Walsh met with De Lai. The bishop found the cardinal cordial and "unexpectedly open." They had a frank discussion about Boston and the danger a public disclosure of the scandals posed for the American church and the Holy See, but De Lai opposed giving O'Connell a position in the Vatican. Still, he promised to think it over and asked Walsh to return. Walsh found De Lai "very serious and cautious about Boston, [an issue] *difficult* to solve."[31]

He got a more receptive hearing from Gasparri the next morning. When Walsh told the cardinal that some bishops feared having O'Connell as American representative in the Vatican, Gasparri replied: "In my opinion, he will have no special influence in Rome and will live an ordinary life—and the only *remedy* will be applied; try then to *make* them *accept* this remedy." Walsh then returned to Pizzardo with a request that he search the archives again for two important documents: the letter sent by the New England suffragans in July 1920 requesting O'Connell's removal; and the sworn deposition of Joseph Pelletier.[32] The latter document was particularly important because it showed that O'Connell had been informed of the marriage of his nephew and had done nothing until forced to by the Vatican. There is no indication that the either document was located.

On the afternoon of 28 February, O'Connell arrived in Rome where he had prearranged for an audience with the pope two days hence. With regard to the audience, the *Pilot* reported that the pontiff "expressed much interest in the pilgrimage of the Cardinal," but the paper remained curiously silent about a discussion of O'Connell's future plans for the archdiocese, one of the alleged purposes of the Holy Land tour. During his stay, the Boston prelate saw his friends Merry del Val and De Lai and presented Van Rossum with a check for more than $88,000 ($1,020,000 in 2006 dollars) to be used for the worldwide missions. Other Vatican officials received donations in the form of stipends for mass intentions. O'Connell then had a second audience with the pope on 8 March.[33]

Shortly after O'Connell's arrival, the political winds shifted. Although De Lai had come around to the pope's position about giving the Boston cardinal a Vatican sinecure, the first step would have to be a request from an overwhelming number of the American bishops asking for a cardinal in the Vatican curia, "then the door is open—yes but—the way is long." No doubt De Lai's acknowledgment of the pope's desire was an act of real politick that in fact signified no change of heart. Walsh himself admitted that O'Connell's touting of his accomplishments as archbishop was paying off: "The *bluff record* of the Pilot has done its work and filled up the heads of De Lai etc. . . . [T]he reason for the Pilot hot air is now clear, the 'Loyal Coalition' machine was put into action and the *tomfoolery* was believed."[34] The loyal coalition was, no doubt, De Lai, Merry del Val, Van Rossum, Tampieri, and company.

In preparation for his next meeting with the pope, Walsh placed his argument for O'Connell's removal in the form of a long syllogism. The major premise stated that if a public official was convicted of *mala fama*, he ought to be removed from office if at all possible. Accepting this as axiomatic, Walsh simply had to establish that ill repute attached to O'Connell. After naming thirteen bishops who had served in New England after 1901, he declared that all were "*of one mind* in regard to O'C[onnell]. that he was not *straight*, but *crooked*, that he was not *honest*, but *dishonest*, that he would or has disgraced the Church and the Holy See and the Episcopal office and Cardinal's dignity, and the *living* among these Bishops believe that he is an *incubus* and *curse* to

149

Boston, New England, and to the Church in the United States." Walsh had heard all but one of his fellow suffragans (George Guertin) express their "sad mind and heart" at O'Connell's appointment to Boston and his deeds there. Finally, the cardinal's history from 1901 to 1924 was "one continuous *suggestion*, or *insinuation*, or *suspicion*, or proven fact that he was and is *a malhonnete* [dishonest] man, *a crooked ecclesiastic*." Walsh considered the documents in his possession sufficient proof. His conclusion? "*Remove O'Connell quickly*, without promotion if possible, with *artificial* and *superficial exaltation* if more expeditious."[35]

The bishop had his second audience with the pope on 12 March. It seems both De Lai and O'Connell had weakened papal resolve. Pius confronted Walsh with evidence of all the construction O'Connell had done in Boston, something that indicated he had good administrative ability and enjoyed confidence. Walsh countered that the cardinal's ability as a builder had nothing to do with the point at issue. Pope and bishop argued and explained until Pius put Walsh under pontifical secrecy about the matter. The situation was under investigation, said the pontiff, so for the present "*prudence* and *silence* were necessary."[36]

Rather than ask for a third interview, Walsh submitted his final thoughts to the pope in a letter. First, he declared that he was the only bishop to witness the Boston affair from its beginning in 1901. During that time, he knew thirteen bishops of the province, eight now dead and five living. Each had expressed his view of O'Connell's character and methods, and all were of one accord. If the pontiff desired, Walsh was prepared to put on paper under oath "the sad and scandalous history and to prove with absolutely incontestible evidence the more important facts," though this might be difficult because "some documents given to His Holiness Benedict XV seemed to have disappeared." He admitted that a few matters eluded him, like the enormous debt that O'Connell claimed to have inherited from his predecessor, Archbishop John Williams. Without pretending to know the details, Walsh claimed it was a calumny, for the list of debts submitted by O'Connell was absolutely denied by both of Williams's chancellors.[37]

Furthermore, because he, Feehan, and Rice had argued that a great number of American prelates had no confidence in the cardinal, Walsh begged to be allowed to compile a register of bishops who repudiated O'Connell in order to establish their position with incontestible evidence. If Pius doubted the suffragans, he should consult Bonzano or the two new American cardinals, Patrick Hayes of New York and George Mundelein of Chicago, soon to arrive in Rome. The Americans, in particular, could testify to the sentiment of the hierarchy in the United States. Most especially, however, the pope should speak with Archbishop Bonaventura Cerretti, who served at the American delegation between 1906 and 1914, who knew thirteen New England bishops past and present, and who was the only man "who knew everything that Pope Benedict XV had said and had intended to do [about O'Connell] just before his death." If these witnesses could not convince the pontiff of the attitude of the American hierarchy, declared Walsh, it was useless to try to prove it.[38] A disappointed Walsh sailed for home in April. Within a month he was dead at sixty-six. His passing removed O'Connell's most ardent critic and impassioned foe. No one stepped forward to fill his shoes.

After Walsh's death, O'Connell claimed the discovery of documents, which remain unlocated, proving that his late suffragan was plotting with the Sulpicians against him. The cardinal informed De Lai of his suffragan's demise and the incriminating papers. His friend found the news "most welcome." "For Your Eminence it has been a liberation," wrote De Lai. "It is also a just judgment of God. But makes one tremble for him [Walsh] before the tribunal of divine justice! Let us hope that good faith has saved him somewhat to an act of repentance. But with a spirit thus formed it is frightening. . . . I believe that God has begun to reward you somewhat by freeing you from your untrustworthy suffragan of Portland, and by putting into your hands the sad plot of infidelity."[39]

Clearly, De Lai backed his American patron 100 percent. Both were among the last of an older guard. Perhaps a common viewpoint, friendship, and money blinded the Roman to the faults of his American ally. Although Walsh might fairly be accused of relentlessness in his pursuit of O'Connell, it seems equally fair to say that the cardinal should have been removed from office.

With regard to Walsh's successor, De Lai promised to be more than usually vigilant "because of the very special circumstances of the case. Y[our]. E[minence]. ought to have a faithful suffragan at Portland."[40] The two certainly made the succession difficult; the see lay vacant for an entire year. After consulting the bishops of the province, Fumasoni-Biondi recommended a *terna* nominating James Cassidy, vicar general of Fall River; Edward Carr, a pastor in the same diocese; and William Doran, a pastor in Providence, in that order. Cassidy was especially hostile to O'Connell. Meanwhile, O'Connell was promoting his own set of candidates in hope, as Fumasoni-Biondi expressed it, that the election of one of his men would be "a new affirmation of his authority." The cardinal's slate included John Peterson, rector of the seminary; Joseph McGlinchey, diocesan director of Propagation of the Faith; and Richard Haberlin, the chancellor. Under O'Connell's pressure, De Lai's Consistorial Congregation unanimously rejected Fumasoni-Biondi's *terna*.[41]

Fumasoni-Biondi vented his frustration to his superior Gasparri. He thought that the Consistorial cardinals "put too much faith in the words of a man like O'Connell" because they were unaware of the true situation in Boston. Given the secrecy of the investigation, the delegate did not feel at liberty to inform them about the character of the New England cardinal. So he turned to his superior, Gasparri, for help. In the first place, advised Fumasoni-Biondi, if opposition to O'Connell meant the automatic rejection of a candidate, "it will be very difficult to make provision now for the diocese of Portland, or for any other in the province that may eventually fall vacant."[42]

With regard to the cardinal's nominees, the delegate considered none of them suitable. Allegedly, Peterson was somehow involved in the scandalous life of the nephew-chancellor. Moreover, his elevation would leave vacant the rectorship of the seminary, which, according to rumor, would go to Michael Splaine, "a person very close to the cardinal and quite deplored." The second candidate, McGlinchey, was unsuitable for the episcopate. The final one, Haberlin, had perjured himself in the nephew's case.[43]

In Fumasoni-Biondi's opinion, the best man for Portland was John Murray, auxiliary bishop of Hartford, omitted from the original *terna* because it was unfair to rob Connecticut when Maine could be provided for otherwise. Now there was no choice, but the Consistorial had to cease giving credence to O'Connell. "I understand the desire to leave Cardinal O'Connell at the head of the very important diocese of Boston," admitted the delegate, "but it would seem to me that he should not be given favored treatment, which is considered by some as Rome's approval of a regime that is regarded as harmful to the interests of the Church." He asked Gasparri to intervene with the pope.[44] Two months later, Murray was transferred from Hartford to Portland. Unable to bestow that diocese on a favorite who might support him, O'Connell would spend the next two years attempting to bring the NCWC to heel and assert himself as spokesman of the hierarchy.

CHAPTER 11

The Ecclesiastical Politics of Child Labor

CARDINAL WILLIAM O'CONNELL successfully managed damage control at the Vatican by publicizing his administrative accomplishments and by making generous monetary contributions to the causes of, if not directly to, his cardinal friends. Though the investigation of his regime in Boston might continue, it would come to nothing. Having salvaged his career, he sought to assert a measure of dominance over the affairs of the American church by subjugating the NCWC, or at least by making it acknowledge deference to Boston. Two interrelated matters, the Child Labor Amendment and the federal education question, afforded him the opportunity to do so.

An issue close to the heart of Father John A. Ryan, co-director of the NCWC's Social Action Department, was the abolition of child labor. Because many states refused to prohibit this evil, Congress had passed the Owen-Keating Act (1916) forbidding the employment of children under fourteen in the production of goods intended for interstate commerce. When the Supreme Court struck down the law two years later, Congress passed new legislation levying a 10 percent tax on articles made by children and shipped interstate. This law too was invalidated. Given the Court's track record, Ryan felt the only recourse was to amend the Constitution. Many congressmen agreed. Throughout 1923 Congress entertained as many as eighteen Child Labor Amendments but without taking action.[1] In January of that year, John Burke, general secretary of the NCWC, asked the administrative committee if it wished to advocate the passage of any of them. Although deploring the evil of child labor, the bishops preferred to leave the matter with the states.[2] If the committee refused to put the NCWC behind the movement, Ryan would seek support from one of its branches: the National Council of Catholic Women (NCCW).

Established by the hierarchy in 1920, the NCCW sought to bring together all societies of Catholic women under one umbrella. Because

154

its foundation coincided with the drive by the New England bishops for the removal of O'Connell, ecclesiastical politics had plagued the institution from the start. Sharing many New Englanders' distaste for the cardinal, Father John Cooper, the founding director of the NCCW, had given Lillian Slattery, O'Connell's personal representative, an unfriendly welcome to the organizing convention. Fearing that she would simply be the cardinal's puppet within the NCCW, representatives from New England threatened to boycott the fledgling council if she was elected to its executive committee. In an effort to smooth matters over, Bishop Joseph Schrembs, who headed the NCWC Department of Lay Activities, praised Slattery and the Boston Archdiocesan League of Women. When delegates elected her to the executive committee, Cooper resigned in protest, and the NCCW found it difficult to gain support in New England. For her part, Slattery gave O'Connell a negative report on the convention, which caused him to give the NCCW a vote of no confidence.[3]

In autumn 1923, Ryan submitted to the annual convention of the NCCW a resolution calling for the passage of a Child Labor Amendment. Although adopted, the endorsement lacked binding force. Local branches remained free to accept or reject it, a characteristic of all resolutions issued by the women.[4] Despite its advisory nature, the resolution would carry weight with a Congress ignorant of the fine points of NCCW policy.

A few weeks later, Ryan joined Senator Thomas J. Walsh, a Catholic Democrat from Montana, Grace Abbott of the U.S. Children's Bureau, and others in drafting a Child Labor Amendment, submitted to the new Congress in December 1923. One among many similar measures, it empowered the federal legislature to limit and to prohibit the toil of persons under the age of eighteen.[5] When Congress held a hearing on the several versions of the amendment, Agnes Regan, executive secretary of the NCCW, appeared in support of such a measure. By June, both the House and Senate agreed on wording that gave Congress "the power to limit, regulate, and prohibit the labor of persons under eighteen years of age."[6] The amendment then went to the states for ratification.

Because the NCCW had called for such legislation, the National

Child Labor Committee enrolled it on the list of supporters of the measure, but without asking permission to do so. This upset some members of the NCCW. The council's president, Gertrude Hill Gavin, hastened to assure them that the resolution adopted by the women in 1923 was of a general nature, calling for the passage of *a* Child Labor Amendment, but not *this particular* one. She also reminded them that the NCCW's resolution lacked binding force.[7] Although accurate, her advice would bedevil the organization at its next convention.

In September 1924, the NCWC Social Action Department released two newsletters on the amendment. Without endorsing the amendment, both letters defended it against misrepresentations and explained why advocates cited the Bishops' Program of Social Reconstruction (1919) in its favor.[8] These articles set the NCWC on a collision course with Cardinal O'Connell, who was working hard to have Massachusetts voters repudiate the amendment in the November referendum. Chief spokesman of a position described by historian Thomas Greene as "the conservative radicalism of Catholic social thought," O'Connell considered the measure Bolshevik, an attempt to assert a federal control over children that would ultimately lead to the usurpation of parental rights in education.[9]

Indeed, at the time there was a two-pronged educational movement afoot in the land: one for compulsory public education and the other for the establishment of a federal department of education with a sizable subsidy at its disposal for various purposes. In the mind of most Catholics, the success of either of these drives would mean the eradication of parochial schools, directly by the first and indirectly by the second.[10]

Two renegades in O'Connell's flock opposed him on child labor: Senator David I. Walsh of Massachusetts and Mayor James M. Curley of Boston, who was also the Democratic nominee for governor. Both had successfully pressured their party's state convention to endorse the amendment and then began championing the measure. On Sunday, 5 October, O'Connell had every pastor denounce it from the pulpit; he also demanded that each parish send two women to a mass rally against it later in the day. With that, Walsh lapsed into silence. On Monday, Curley affirmed that "he could not do otherwise than take the side of his party, no matter what action was taken by the Catholic Church." Within twenty-four hours, however, he changed his mind. Over the radio and in the press, he completely reversed his position of the previous day. He had since discovered that the amendment was a Bolshevik plot.[11]

Curley's sudden about face is puzzling. That it resulted from direct intervention on O'Connell's part is unlikely because their relationship was antagonistic and turbulent.[12] Perhaps the mayor feared that an organized opposition by the church would have a negative impact on his gubernatorial campaign.

In any case, Curley's mercurial switch caused wonder among editors and reflected badly on O'Connell and the church. The *Boston Herald* snidely remarked that if such an ardent advocate of the amendment had changed his mind, perhaps the Democratic party should rewrite its state platform.[13] The *Christian Science Monitor* considered the *Herald's* solution "too incomplete a remedy for so grave a fault." Reminding readers that the recent Democratic national convention had nearly split asunder over the issue of condemning the Ku Klux Klan by name, an organization which held that Rome dictated politics to American Catholics, the editor commented sarcastically: "Why not recall all state conventions that the opinion of the Democrats may accord with inspired infallibility? Even that would leave the national organization somewhat inharmonious, so that a reassembling of the national convention seems imperative. Why not summon it to meet in Rome?"[14]

The *New Republic* lamented O'Connell's playing field marshal regarding the Catholic position on the amendment because it threatened to ignite the "fires of religious prejudice and passion" in "what ought to be a non-partisan, non-political question of human welfare." Although the editor admitted that the cardinal may be sincerely motivated "by the absurd fear he professes that the child labor amendment will abolish the church's schools, he has certainly done their cause far more harm than good."[15]

While bringing the Boston church into line on the amendment, O'Connell attempted the same with the NCWC. In mid-October 1924, he wrote to Bishops Edmund Gibbons and Joseph Schrembs, chairmen of the Departments of Laws and Legislation and Lay Activities, respectively. In the letter to Gibbons, the cardinal accused Burke, Ryan, and Regan of being "tied up with some of the dangerous influences at the Capital" in favor of "that nefarious and bolshevik" Child Labor Amendment and of crediting their views to the hierarchy. Unless corrected very soon, warned O'Connell, they were "driving fast toward a public condemnation."[16]

He told Schrembs that the three were "lacking in certain fundamentals and had better be watched." "Bureaucracy knows how to get a hold of some of our agents—who want a job," continued the cardinal, "and unless their loyalty is beyond question, before we know it we shall be compromised and involved." He wanted Schrembs to investigate "whether our agents are on the right side."[17] Assuring the cardinal that he would, the bishop tried to distance the Welfare Conference from Ryan with the unbelievable statement that the priest did not "in any manner represent the N.C.W.C. though at times he has worked with the Social Action Department." In fact, he was the co-director of that department. Immediately, Schrembs sent copies of O'Connell's letter to Burke and Bishop Peter Muldoon with an urgent request for information.[18]

Schrembs summarized his views on the situation for Gibbons. "I believe Boston must be suffering from a brain storm at the present time," he wrote. Not only had the administrative committee "sidetracked any official pronouncement on the subject of child labor," but it had also ensured that "nobody, speaking for the Conference, has ever made any declaration on the subject." In Schrembs's opinion, O'Connell had forgotten that he was only one member of the hierarchy and had no more right to speak for it than anyone else. "Dr. John Ryan, as an individual, has a perfect right to his own opinion and I don't know that any of us has any authority to silence him," concluded Schrembs. "To my mind, Boston is simply seeking an opportunity to impose his views on the National Catholic Welfare Conference or to discredit us in Rome. I believe the whole thing is much ado about nothing."[19] As Schrembs understood it, the cardinal was trying to dictate policy to the hierarchy.

Without awaiting reply from NCWC officials, O'Connell sent his friend, Monsignor Michael Splaine, to Washington to secure recantations from the offenders. He stopped in New York to ask Gavin to have the upcoming national convention review the NCCW's endorsement of the amendment. Refusing to do so herself, Gavin responded that O'Connell's representative to the assembly, Slattery, was free to introduce the question. In Washington, Splaine urged Regan to call an emergency session of the NCCW executive board to have it rescind the endorsement of the amendment. When she refused, he became indignant, using "language that a gentleman does not ordinarily employ in addressing a lady." Splaine then saw Ryan, who countered with the charge that O'Connell's propaganda about the Socialist origins of the amendment was a flat lie. Backing off, Splaine went to William Kerby, professor of sociology at Catholic University, who also favored the legislation. He too refused to alter his view.[20]

Two days later, the *Pilot*, O'Connell's personal paper, ran an editorial quoting the Roman instructions of July 1922 that the NCWC was not to be identified with the American hierarchy. "Therefore," declared the editor, "the expressions of this Conference, particularly in the press and social action departments, cannot be viewed as the authoritative expression of the Hierarchy of the United States." Even though those departments functioned under bishops, agents carried out the routine business, and "reports, mistaken and unfortunate, [were] sometimes sent forth for publication which have no other sanction than the personal and individual honest purpose of the writer or reporter." For example, the Press and Social Action Departments had recently released articles commending the so-called Child Labor Amendment. "Immediately," said the *Pilot*, "the true position was strongly and fearlessly taken by many distinguished Prelates through the nation, condemning roundly this proposed amendment and by conclusive proofs demonstrating its disastrous effects upon the state and family." In this case, the NCWC agents aired views that were "wholly unrepresentative of the true position of the Hierarchy."[21]

This was an artful piece of deception and insinuation—a complete misrepresentation of the situation. It identified O'Connell's view with the hierarchy's when, in fact, the bishops had never taken a stand on the Child Labor Amendment. At the same time, it suggested that the NCWC had endorsed the legislation, which was also untrue.

Acting as general secretary of the NCWC for the ill and convalescing Burke, James H. Ryan complained to Bishop Gibbons, "Boston is acting like a wild man, & with utter disregard of the facts."[22] To Schrembs, he reported that neither the Press nor the Social Action Departments had issued official statements on the amendment. Since the congressional hearing, Regan had been silent on the legislation, and both Burke and himself opposed it. In light of the *Pilot* editorial, "a very unfair statement," Ryan suggested that someone ought to inform Rome of the true situation "as Boston will unquestionably make a great deal of this matter." As a precautionary measure, he had already explained the facts to Father George Leech, the secretary of the apostolic delegate.[23]

Abreast of the affair, Burke too responded, especially protesting the *Pilot* editorial whose "hidden and chief falsity" was the supposition "that the Hierarchy has taken a positive position on the Child Labor Amendment and that that position is against." Furthermore, the editorial accused the agents of the NCWC of misrepresenting the bishops and, therefore, of disloyalty. Like James Ryan, he feared that Rome might be misinformed.[24]

John Ryan informed Muldoon that while he and Raymond McGowan, assistant director of the Social Action Department, had issued two letters aimed at correcting "some extraordinarily mistaken interpretations" of the amendment, neither statement endorsed it. "Of course, the general tone of my letter," he admitted, "would be construed as favorable to the amendment." Still, it did not sanction it. Ryan told Muldoon of a recent conversation with Edward McGrady, legislative representative of the American Federation of Labor (AFL). He and other labor leaders feared a split in unionism if other bishops adopted O'Connell's view. The cardinal had imposed on Boston's Catholic unionists the choice between following either the church or the AFL, which supported the amendment. Although Ryan told McGrady that other prelates probably would not oppose the legislation, this was uncertain. "I am afraid," he confided to Muldoon, "we are going to confront a nasty situation."[25]

As NCWC agents defended themselves, O'Connell widened his attack. In late October, he addressed Archbishop Michael Curley, chancellor of Catholic University, because Kerby and both Ryans, John and James, were faculty members. The cardinal asserted that John Ryan was compromising the university's status "by his queer stand and his queer utterances and letters." He wanted the three restrained and their public activities stopped. They were "hurting the University and the Catholic position—which is certainly not theirs." Curley promised to look into the matter.[26] Archbishop Austin Dowling, who by now was fully aware of the situation, commented to Archbishop Edward Hanna, "Boston is doing his *damndest* [*sic*] to bust the N.C.W.C. once more."[27]

On 1 November 1924, three days before the people of Massachusetts voted on the amendment, the affair worsened when Edward Keating, the Catholic co-sponsor of the Owen-Keating Act and at this time editor of *Labor*, the journal of the railway brotherhood, flooded Boston with 100,000 copies containing the reprint of an earlier article by John Ryan in support of the amendment.[28] Furious, O'Connell fired off letters to Curley and Muldoon.

To the former, he told how the "queer and crooked views" of Ryan had inundated the city of Boston. Convinced this was intentional, O'Connell charged that Ryan knew his opinion would be used "to offset the position taken by me and all my priests here during these trying days before the voting." The alternatives were few, declared the cardinal, "either abandon weakly our duty and turn it all over into the hands of the Ryans the Kerbys and the Regans . . . or demand that these servants of the University and paid agents of the N.C.W.C. either cease their crooked and false activities or leave the University and the offices of the N.C.W.C." He demanded that Curley remind the offenders of their obligation.[29]

O'Connell held Muldoon responsible for allowing subordinates to take the reins. Professing affection for him personally, the cardinal scolded: "Really Bishop, if everybody lets these people . . . run things entirely their own way we shall all get ourselves in trouble. . . . Everybody outside the N.C.W.C. knows that these people have radical views on the social questions—we are and ought to be conservative."[30]

161

Rather than reprimand the three professors, Curley explained their positions. He failed to see how James Ryan figured into the situation at all: his academic field was education and he had never expressed a view on the amendment. While Kerby grudgingly supported the amendment as the "worst possible way to do a good thing ... [that] ought to be done," his writings were confined to the field of charitable institutions. Curley acknowledged that John Ryan did back the amendment, but noted that he charted this course long before O'Connell organized the fight in Massachusetts. Ryan never "had a single thought of taking a stand merely to be in opposition to any one, particularly, to the Senior Cardinal Archbishop of the Country," said the chancellor. In his opinion, Kerby and James Ryan should be troubled no further. That left only John Ryan, and Curley believed that O'Connell would give him a hearing before condemnation.[31]

Desirous of being "as indulgent as possible," O'Connell advised that the professors be more careful and warned that John Ryan was "steering a slippery road." "His whole trend," said the cardinal, "is *toward* a socialistic tendency, and I think he takes himself too seriously." If the three had learned their lesson from this experience, O'Connell was willing to let the matter drop.[32] As noted earlier in this study, if one had the courage to stand up to the cardinal, he would back down, especially in the wake of the scandals. Although he let Curley off the hook, the NCWC was another matter.

While O'Connell corresponded with Curley, the infirm Burke rose from his sickbed to consult personally with several members of the administrative committee about the best course of action. Both Dowling and Schrembs wanted to present the case to Rome, if only informally. Muldoon disagreed. In his view, the issue was a tempest in a teapot. At present, only the apostolic delegate need know the truth, preferably by word of mouth. Given the mixed opinion, Burke, James Ryan, and Schrembs decided to draft a letter of explanation to the Holy See and submit it to the entire committee for approval. The proposed document summarized the NCWC's non-involvement with the Child Labor Amendment.[33] Preferring Muldoon's course, the committee scotched the letter.

On 9 November, eight days after the people of Massachusetts went to the polls on the amendment, the NCCW opened its annual convention. When the executive committee met the following evening, O'Connell's representative, Slattery, insisted that Regan had overstepped her authority by appearing at the congressional hearing on Child Labor and by allowing the National Child Labor Committee to use the NCCW's name. In proof, she presented Gavin's letter stating that the organization's resolution of 1923 was not an endorsement of the present amendment. This was unfair because the correspondence had been written *after* Congress passed the measure. Slattery demanded that the board have the convention withdraw the use of its name from the Child Labor Committee. When her request was tabled, she appealed directly to Schrembs, who disallowed the motion until the NCWC's administrative committee could vote on it.[34] He was not to dodge O'Connell's bullet so easily; he would face another salvo the next day from the convention floor.

Sentiment in the assembly was divided over the Child Labor Amendment and came to the surface during Slattery's report on Boston's League of Catholic Women. Her entire account focused on the amendment. Cardinal O'Connell, she said, had organized a statewide committee to educate the public on the dangers of it, and the League had registered voters. In five days it enrolled 100,000 Catholic women to cast dissenting ballots. Voters killed the amendment, said Slattery, by a four to one margin—in fact, three to one. The Catholics of her state, she concluded, were proud to follow not only "Mother Church but ... Massachusetts in all its public activities, when it is against bureaucracy in Washington." Her words won applause.[35]

A voice from the floor asked how the NCCW could endorse an amendment opposed by O'Connell and his entire archdiocese. Schrembs recounted the story of the resolution and Regan's appearance before the congressional committee in support of *an* amendment. Rightly or wrongly, said the bishop, the National Child Labor Committee had registered the NCCW's name on the roll of supporters for *this particular* amendment. If the convention disapproved, its only recourse was to pass a motion for the removal of its name from the literature, "and thereby clearly indicate that you are not in favor of the Child Labor Amendment."[36]

Despite applause, Schrembs refused to allow such a motion because it would constitute an official statement that the NCCW opposed the legislation. "Such a pronouncement," he declared, "is unauthorized by the Bishops of the country, as they have not expressed themselves on this subject." If it was wrong to have endorsed an amendment in the first place, it would be equally wrong to withdraw the endorsement now. Those favoring the amendment now clapped. "Do not applaud," Schrembs told the convention. "This is too serious for partisan feeling." He refused to take sole responsibility for any further action on this matter. The convention was not to withdraw its support until and unless the entire administrative committee of the NCWC approved.[37]

Apropos of Boston, Schrembs said that O'Connell had exercised his right to speak for his own archdiocese. "His Eminence . . ." he concluded, "is the first one to recognize that other Bishops . . . may possibly disagree with him. . . . He is the first one to allow them the liberty of expressing themselves in their own Diocese [*sic*] and in their own States. . . . And unless the Hierarchy, unless the Bishops as a whole would commit themselves to a pronouncement, he would certainly be the last one to ask that his pronouncement be taken for the entire country."[38]

This was turning the tables on O'Connell. Clearly, the cardinal wanted the NCCW endorsement rescinded, which would have amounted to a declaration against the amendment. It is also obvious that he considered his view to be that of the hierarchy. Schrembs invoked the principle of autonomy of a bishop, much vaunted by O'Connell, against him. The cardinal's opinion was not that of other prelates; each was free to decide for himself, until and unless, all decided otherwise. Because Schrembs refused to support Slattery and because the executive committee declined to make her president of the NCCW, she resigned from the board.[39] Gavin was glad to see her go: "As long as she represented that province, we never could have gone ahead in any part of New England."[40]

Without bringing to the administrative committee the question of the National Child Labor Committee's use of the NCCW's name,

Schrembs quietly let the issue drop. Nor did the NCCW agitate the matter further. On 21 November, James Ryan presented to the apostolic delegate a memorandum explaining the amendment, the NCWC's position on it, and O'Connell's accusations. Early the next month, he reported to the absent Burke that "Boston is still making noise but I think that everybody is on to him."[41]

The apostolic delegate, Archbishop Pietro Fumasoni-Biondi was certainly "on to" O'Connell. The child labor debacle, the Portland succession, and a few other incidents had given him a good reading of the Boston prelate. Writing to his superior, Cardinal Pietro Gasparri, Fumasoni-Biondi summarized it thus: "Cardinal O'Connell, from the time of the election of the present Supreme Pontiff, has sought and seeks with all his power, combined with an intimate knowledge of the Roman Curia, to reestablish his authority in the diocese and province of Boston, and his ascendancy in relation to the American hierarchy. . . . The letter, written in rather strong terms by Your Eminence to Cardinal O'Connell, dated 22 April 1921 . . . toward the end of the pontificate of Benedict XV, in which was condemned his tacit connivance with the scandals that occurred in his household, has unfortunately not had the desired effect. His Eminence regards all that as a simple incident of the past [pontifical] administration."[42]

To be sure, the Vatican continued to investigate O'Connell. In Spring of 1925, Pope Pius XI ordered Fumasoni-Biondi to make a visitation of Boston. While the delegate intended to obey, he felt the effort would be useless. To Gasparri he confided: "The priests, who, believing that no one, not even the Holy See, can act against the Eminent Ordinary, not only do not wish to give the least appearance of going against him, but also find many pretexts to refuse to come to see me so as not to fall into the Cardinal's displeasure." Though the visit issued in no decisive result, O'Connell's influence over the church was greatly diminished. Fumasoni-Biondi reported that the "dislike of the episcopate for him remains unchanged and total. . . ."[43]

CHAPTER 12

Americanism Redivivus

WITHIN MONTHS OF THE IMBROGLIO over child labor, Cardinal William O'Connell crossed swords with the NCWC for the last time over the closely related issue of the establish of a federal department of education. For almost a decade, the church had opposed the creation of one out of fear that such an agency would assert federal control over children and eradicate Catholic schools. In 1925, the NCWC had just completed a successful fight in the Supreme Court against compulsory public education. In that same year, the National Education Association (NEA) introduced into Congress its new Curtis-Reed bill, the latest measure proposing the creation of a department of education. The NEA dropped from this present legislation the huge subsidy contained in its predecessors, which was considered the lever for asserting federal dominance over education, in keeping with the axiom that federal control always followed federal funds.[1]

The elimination of aid from the measure caused the Catholic hierarchy to reexamine its position toward the creation of a department. At its annual convention in 1925, progressives like Bishop John P. Carroll of Helena, Montana, Archbishop Austin Dowling of St. Paul, and Cardinal Patrick Hayes of New York, advocated that the hierarchy take a positive stand toward some degree of federal participation in schooling, perhaps even the NEA bill itself. On the other hand, conservatives like Bishop William Turner of Buffalo, Bishop Hugh Boyle of Pittsburgh, and Bishop Francis Howard of Covington, Kentucky, warned that the NEA was the church's principal enemy on educational matters. Once it secured the establishment of a department of education, it would attempt to enlarge the agency's scope with a view to asserting control over all schooling. Conservatives argued that since the public at large opposed further federalization, the hierarchy should not take a contrary position.[2]

Sensing the drift in opinion, Dowling, who chaired the NCWC's

Department of Education, inquired if the bishops wanted to oppose the Curtis-Reed bill openly or informally. The former course, he cautioned, was likely to ensure its passage because the church had gained a reputation for obstructionism on the issue of public schools. In the end, the hierarchy decided to take no formal stand against the legislation, though it wanted the NCWC informally—quietly—to oppose any move toward the federalization of education. O'Connell, who chaired the assembly, emphasized that Dowling's department was "not to be hampered in any way in its activity, but may use its discretion informally to direct its course of action."[3]

Clearly, the majority of the hierarchy considered the NEA bill dangerous because it threatened to federalize education. The bishops' failure, however, to take a decisive position with regard to the measure was destined to compromise the position of the NCWC's administrative committee. The latter was left in the untenable spot of trying to forestall enactment of the NEA bill without violating the hierarchy's instruction to avoid public opposition. In keeping with the bishops' wishes, the committee directed the NCWC's general secretary, John Burke, to make no propaganda against the legislation, but to quietly resist the measure. If open action became necessary, he was to consult with the board.[4]

In accordance with the committee's instructions, Burke met with Father Wilfrid Parsons, editor of the Jesuit-published *America* magazine, one of the most ardent opponents of federalization. He urged Parsons to abate the journal's antagonism until the situation might warrant it, thereby maximizing its impact at the appropriate time. When Archbishop Michael Curley, who had not attended the convention of the bishops, informed Burke of his intention to make a pronouncement against the Curtis-Reed bill, the priest advised him that the hierarchy wanted no open opposition. Disagreeing with Burke about the hierarchy's intention, Curley relented only because the general secretary told him that President Calvin Coolidge gave the bill no chance of success during the current session of Congress.[5]

Meanwhile, an anonymous source had given Parsons the erroneous information that "some sort of a deal is on foot at Washington by which the N.C.W.C. is favoring, or to favor, the Federal Department of Education, either publicly or privately." Parsons took Burke's request for an abatement of criticism as corroboration of the truth of this misinformation. The Jesuit warned both Curley and O'Connell of the situation.[6]

Not long afterward, Burke received a letter from Monsignor Richard Haberlin, O'Connell's chancellor, with word that the cardinal had heard that "the N.C.W.C. is about to come out in favor of the Federal Department of Education or, at least, has given assurances in legislative circles that the [NCWC's] Department of Education favors the Curtis-Reed Bill." O'Connell wanted to know the truth. Burke quickly replied that neither the NCWC nor any of its departments had endorsed the measure or intended to do so. The Washington secretariat was abiding strictly by the instructions of the administrative committee.[7]

Although Burke had no idea how the rumor started, he began to suspect its origin when *America*'s lead editorial in the New Year's edition raised "An Alarm and a Warning" about an alleged deal to put the Curtis-Reed bill across and questioned, "Are the guardians of our interests betraying them?"[8] In *America*'s view, the NCWC was more than soft-peddling opposition to the measure; it was conniving at securing its passage.

Although there was no truth to the rumor, the church's silence on the legislation left its attitude toward the measure open to misconstruction. Curley himself was growing increasingly frustrated with the inaction of the NCWC and held Dowling responsible for failing to give direction. In fact, interpreting the NCWC's public silence on the bill as consent, Congress prepared to pass the legislation. With that, Dowling's Department of Education sprang into action. It recommended that the NCWC openly oppose the Curtis-Reed bill and, if need be, propose alternative legislation for the expansion of the U.S. Bureau of Education as a way of demonstrating Catholic support for public education while stopping short of endorsement of a federal department.[9]

Accepting this advice, the administrative committee mobilized open opposition. The situation seemed so desperate that in Burke's estimation, the only course left was to fight fire with fire. Following the advice of Dowling's department, he had the NCWC draft an alternative bill to upgrade the Bureau of Education and secured Senator Lawrence

Phipps of Colorado, chairman of the Committee on Education and Labor, to introduce the measure as his own, thus masking the NCWC's involvement. Dowling issued a press release praising the Phipps bill as "a forward looking, constructive . . . statesmanlike measure," which would make the Bureau of Education "the most important educational research agency in the United States."[10] Thus, the church supported a competing measure, one that stopped well short of the establishment of a federal department of education while at the same time advancing the cause of schooling. These actions displeased the prelate of Boston.

Three days before the 1926 convention of the hierarchy, Cardinal O'Connell summoned Burke to Oblate College in Washington. On arrival, the priest was unaware that he was in for a rambling three-hour interview. O'Connell was concerned about the Phipps bill and wanted to know what the NCWC secretariat had done about it. He had heard that Burke had "sold out" on the education question by yielding to the federalizers. Moreover, he asserted that Phipps was anti-Catholic.[11] Not a Klansman himself, the senator was friendly to the Invisible Empire and received its backing in the 1924 election.[12]

Without mentioning that the NCWC had drafted the proposed legislation, Burke explained the events leading to the endorsement of it as an alternative to the Curtis-Reed bill. He noted that the NCWC's Department of Education approved the Phipps bill, and the administrative committee concurred. Again, O'Connell asked what the Washington office had done about it. Burke carefully sidestepped any admission that the secretariat had authored the bill. "If your Em[inence].," he said, "means what have we done . . . in pushing the Phipps Bill, beyond what I have told you, I would answer 'nothing.'" He added that the administrative committee would press for it only if the Curtis-Reed seemed likely to pass.[13]

O'Connell reminded Burke that the hierarchy had instructed the secretariat to make no public antagonism against the Curtis-Reed bill, but to stand squarely against further federalization. In his view, the secretariat had violated this directive in every respect. It had actively opposed the Curtis-Reed bill and supported the Phipps bill, which he clearly considered yielding to federal control. Burke explained that the hierarchy's orders had put the Washington office in an untenable position. When it failed to oppose the Curtis-Reed measure, Congress interpreted the NCWC's silence to mean the legislation was acceptable to the church. The administrative committee had no choice but to oppose it. The endorsement of the Phipps bill was a tactical maneuver to ensure defeat of the Curtis-Reed bill because most Catholic educators favored a larger budget for the U.S. Bureau of Education and an increase in its investigative abilities.[14]

This set O'Connell off on a long dissertation about the two schools of American Catholics—actually, a disquisition against Americanism in which the cardinal indiscriminately blended Archbishop Dowling and others with the Americanists of the 1890s. To know the church and to have the traditions that enabled one to keep the faith intact, said O'Connell, came from Roman and international experience. Nobody educated solely in America could have this. Dowling was a good man. O'Connell admired him in many ways. Why, the cardinal was not even speaking about Dowling personally. "All were good men," he said. "But their very zeal, lacking as they did the solid traditions of Catholic practice and positions, led them to surrender unknowingly on matters of principle. That is to some extent they were brought up in America. They realized how generous America was to the C[atholic] Church; how the Church flourished under its institutions—therefore they must remain at peace with America—they must not forfeit good will of Americans—they had a minority complex, unknown to themselves."[15]

When *Testem Benevolentiae* had been issued condemning Americanism, continued O'Connell, he had been shocked because it dealt with men he admired. "But let one read the books of those men today—Hecker, Ireland, Gibbons—and he would have to confess that they did not know the finer distinctions of Catholic teaching, the difference between natural and supernatural virtues." America was a Protestant country, built on the principles of that religion. A Catholic must always distrust the government, said the cardinal. "Anyone who is looked upon with favor by Gov[ernment]. authorities and officials is ipso facto suspect." The state would always oppose the church on education. There were men in the 1890s who would "though they were

Catholics have compromised our position. There were those who would do it today."[16]

Turning to the NCWC, O'Connell declared that it was just a committee of bishops. Nor would it last. "Nothing like that ever lasted," he said. "Things came and went. The C[atholic]. Church is organized. Why get up another organization? The Pope looked after the Bishops. This N.C.W.C. is a work of supererogation." It was dangerous, too, warned O'Connell, unless properly directed. For instance, John Ryan had supported the Child Labor Amendment, while the cardinal had opposed it. Moreover, Mrs. Francis Slattery, his personal representative to the NCCW, had been prevented "by a cabal engineered by Miss Regan" from bringing the amendment before the board of directors of the NCCW. Said O'Connell, Agnes Regan had fallen under the spell of Grace Abbott, director of the Children's Bureau in the Department of Labor. Having vented his spleen, he concluded the interview: "Father Burke no government has ever used a priest without squeezing him dry as a lemon and then throwing him out."[17]

This interview revealed the mind of the man. At issue was Americanism redivivus. Dowling, his colleagues on the administrative committee, Burke, and the other agents at the NCWC headquarters were the new Americanists, lacking Roman experience, wanting in Catholic tradition, suffering from too close contact with the government, and therefore unwittingly forfeiting church principle. O'Connell, on the other hand, was the new Michael Corrigan, Roman-trained, loyal son of the church, and an upholder of the true faith. He was re-fighting the school controversy of the 1890s in a new dress. The Curtis-Reed bill, the Phipps bill, the Child Labor Amendment were all attempts to gain federal control over children. Like the first Americanists, the agents of the NCWC were attempting to reconcile church and society, attempting to repay the nation for its generosity to the church, but they were giving up cherished Catholic principles. O'Connell knew better. Although church and country might stand side by side, the two could never be mixed because their foundations were diametrically opposed, one Catholic, the other Protestant.

There was something settled about the interview, something peaceful, even paternal, in the cardinal's attitude. Perhaps it sprang from his belief that the NCWC would never last. In any case, his antagonism toward its endorsement of the Phipps bill was to be his swan song of opposition. To be sure, he continued to refuse to give monetary support for the NCWC, but at least he ceased his harassment of it. When Burke informed his confidant, Bishop Peter Muldoon, of the audience, the latter replied: "Your Boston experience was unique—yes almost incredible. How do people get that way? What a farce it must all seem to him & he the chairman [of the Welfare Conference]. I think the Lord will take care of the N.C.W.C."[18]

And so it came to pass. O'Connell's day in the sun had really been eclipsed with the accessions of Benedict XV and Pius XI. The last vestiges of his Roman patronage were stripped from him with the deaths of Cardinals Gaetano De Lai in 1928 and Raphael Merry del Val in 1930. His influence within the hierarchy was nil, at least among those who had long dealt with him. "Many of us older bishops who know him do not believe him," wrote Archbishop John T. McNicholas of Cincinnati to the apostolic delegate; "we do not trust him; we consider him a most dangerous Prelate."[19]

As for the NCWC, it outlived O'Connell and served as a prototype for the future organization of the church. By the 1930s, the Catholic hierarchies in various countries began to organize conferences of bishops like the NCWC. In 1965, Vatican II mandated their establishment in nations where they did not already exist.[20] The council even gave such conferences canonical status, thus making them part of the organic structure of the church. O'Connell's view of the NCWC as a work of supererogation, something that would never last, proved to be absolutely wrong. In fact, it became a model. The NCWC continues to this day under a new name: the United States Conference of Catholic Bishops.

In the years and decades that followed O'Connell's swan song, there occurred a series of symbolic events. In 1928, the cardinal settled with the Sulpicians in a final outrage. Without informing them, he exhumed the bodies of their men buried at St. John's Seminary in Brighton and transferred them to one of the archdiocesan cemeteries.[21] Having expelled their living confreres from the seminary in 1911, he ridded the premises of every vestige of the order by removing their physical remains. Still, O'Connell continued to inveigh against them. On the eve of his seventieth birthday, he publicly repeated his earlier slur that Pius X had given him the "disagreeable task" of ordering the Sulpicians out of the seminary.[22]

In 1932, the Vatican did to O'Connell what it had done to his predecessor, Archbishop John Williams. As will be recalled, O'Connell engineered his appointment as coadjutor archbishop through powerful Roman connections, even though his name appeared on neither of the *ternae*. Similarly, the Vatican gave him, unasked and without consultation, Francis J. Spellman as auxiliary bishop, a man himself with strong Roman patrons. Prior to departing Italy for America, Spellman had been assured that he would become the next archbishop of Boston. Thus came full circle the treatment meted out to Williams. True to form, O'Connell believed that Spellman's appointment had been accomplished by Sulpician machination.[23]

Sixty years after O'Connell's death, there occurred a final emblematic event. The Italianate mansion, built as the archbishop's residence by O'Connell with money from the Keith bequest, had become an enduring symbol of arrogance. In late 2003, facing $85 million in costs to settle sexual abuse claims against pedophile priests, the archdiocese of Boston decided to sell it to neighboring Boston College. In the end, the sale consisted of the mansion and forty-three surrounding acres, which include O'Connell's burial site. O'Connell's body is to be exhumed and removed from the property once arrangements are made with his surviving relatives.[24]

Salvation Comes to the Archbishop

LATE IN LIFE, Cardinal William O'Connell may have come to recognize, if only at a subliminal level, the emptiness of his climb to power. In fall 1929, on the eve of his seventieth birthday, he penned his *Recollections* while residing at his vacation house in Centerville on Cape Cod. They were published in 1934 for the public and triumphal celebration of the fiftieth anniversary of his ordination to the priesthood.[1] In them, he recounted the story of the visit paid to him thirty years earlier by Cardinal Francesco Satolli. For reasons explained below, the description of Satolli suggests that O'Connell was unconsciously characterizing himself in the person of his Roman friend. "Once, after his elevation to the Sacred College [of Cardinals]," began the account,

> he [Satolli] visited me while I was Bishop of Portland in 1903.[2] He had already exhibited the symptoms of a fatal disease. To one so full of vitality the discovery was an awful shock, and in a desperate effort to shake off the melancholy and apprehension which possessed him at the thought of death, while still so young relatively, he fled to America, with the hope that some celebrated physician would be able to ward off the dread disease, and that at the same time the sight of old friends would give him cheer and courage. When he arrived in Portland, I at once saw that he was a completely changed individual. He stayed with me a week and seemed to find under my roof something of the peace of mind and tranquillity of soul he had been seeking so eagerly. In the long evenings, as we sat together in my study, he went over as in retrospect the whole review of his active life. In the shadow of death all the illusions of promotions and titles and honors seemed to vanish, and he found,

I think, immense relief in going over the story of his eventful career. With his head drooped upon his breast he no longer employed the vivid imagery and language with which as a student I had always associated him. He dropped all that as a sort of superficial mantle and revealed to me in the simplest and clearest words the inner soul of a luminous mind and a naturally generous character. It was a pathetic story of utter disillusionment in an hour when all the world believed that he had touched happiness in reaching his glorious goal. I listened, astounded at the revelation, a revelation which did him far more credit and which brought me nearer to him in respect and reverence than anything I had ever seen of him in the days when he appeared to be a phenomenal success. He looked pale and worn and tired, and I could see that his very soul had become weary of a long, hard battle up the heights where at last he stood triumphant. Now, all that was like a dream to him, a dream that would suddenly pass. With almost frightened eyes he saw the littleness of earthly glory in the sudden realization that now it was all over and that the grim figure of death had touched him on the shoulder. As a pupil I had drunk in many draughts of his intellectual knowledge, and here in this little room he appeared to me still in the rostrum teaching, in infinitely clearer language, a lesson of far deeper importance than any I had ever heard before from his lips.

. . . The next day, at my request, he was examined thoroughly by a physician of very high reputation. The result of this examination proved only too truly that restoration to health was hopeless. He might live some months, but as the disease was progressive the end was certain. I bade him good-bye at the station. He tried to be cheery, but I saw with what effort. He went back to Rome, only to await for a few months the final summons.[3]

175

In April 1904, Satolli informed O'Connell that he would be coming in June to the United States in "a private manner" (for reasons unspecified) and hoped to end his visit in Portland. He made no mention of illness. Nor did Francis MacNutt, who considered Satolli's forthcoming American journey "rather annoying," given that at that moment he was O'Connell's most ardent promoter for the coadjutorship of Boston. The layman feared that Propaganda might take action on the Boston succession in the absence of Satolli. One suspects that if Satolli were actually visiting the United States for medical reasons, MacNutt would have been solicitous, rather than annoyed about the trip. Similarly, Antonio Savelli-Spinola wrote to O'Connell about Satolli's upcoming visit to America without mentioning issues of health. Rather, he viewed it as an opportunity for Satolli and O'Connell to fully inform each other about the Boston succession.[4]

When Satolli came to the United States, it was not in a private capacity but as Pius X's special envoy to the St. Louis World Fair. He traveled far and wide, first visiting Cardinal James Gibbons in Baltimore, then proceeding to St. Louis for the fair, afterward heading north to St. Paul for a sojourn with Archbishop John Ireland, then to Newport, Rhode Island; Portland, Maine; Albany, New York; New York City; Newport again; and back to New York—hardly the schedule of a dying man.[5]

If he were really looking for quality medical advice, any of the major cities he visited would probably have afforded better physicians than Portland, Maine. Again, when Satolli returned to Rome, he wrote to thank O'Connell and bring him up to date on events surrounding the Boston succession—with not a word of gratitude for medical assistance. To be sure, Satolli suffered a lingering illness during his final years, but death came, not in 1904, but in 1910.[6] These facts make one hesitate to give full credence to O'Connell's account, especially in light of his penchant for embroidering the truth.

O'Connell's account reads like an unconscious self-portrait, a way of catching a glimpse of the true inner man by projecting his feelings on Satolli. "In the long evenings, as we sat in my study, he went over as in retrospect the whole review of his active life." O'Connell was known to while away long evenings in his study, in this case writing his memoirs:

going over as in retrospect the whole review of his active life. "In the shadow of death all the illusions of promotions and titles and honors seemed to vanish, and he found, I think, immense relief in going over the story of his eventful career." Aged seventy-five when his *Recollections* were published, O'Connell must have felt the breath of death on the back of his neck.

Moreover, the first 318 pages (83 percent of the book) were devoted to his rise from poor Irish-American boy to priest to rector of the American College to bishop of Portland to papal envoy to Japan to archbishop of Boston to cardinal of the Roman church: his eventful career of promotions, titles, and honors. It was a career that even by his own reckoning ended with his elevation to the cardinalate; the final pages of the volume tell little of his accomplishments after 1912, the year he received the red hat. The rise to power was all.

In these few lines from an otherwise fabulous tale of a meteoric career, O'Connell "dropped all that as a sort of superficial mantle" and saw the "inner soul of a luminous mind and naturally generous spirit" that had succumbed to ambition. "It was a pathetic story of utter disillusionment in an hour when all the world believed that he had touched happiness in reaching his glorious goal." At this moment in some unconscious way, salvation may have come to the archbishop. "With almost frightened eyes he saw the littleness of earthly glory in the sudden realization that now it was all over and that the grim figure of death had touched him on the shoulder."

Death, however, delayed coming for O'Connell for another fourteen and a half years. Although marginalized in the hierarchy after the scandals of his nephew and David Toomey, the cardinal remained a powerful presence in Boston. His longevity served him well. By the time of his demise, a quarter of a century after the discovery of the marriages, many of his pursuers had already gone to the grave. With the emergence of no new scandals, the dust from the original ones had long settled. In April 1944, O'Connell suffered a stroke and soon thereafter developed pneumonia. He died quietly in his residence in Brighton on the twenty-second at age eighty-four.[7]

Conclusion

BORN INTO A lace-curtain Irish, Catholic family in New England, William Henry O'Connell was a man who craved respectability in a society that had long denied it to those of his ethnic background. His experience in Rome, first as a seminarian and later as rector of the North American College, exposed him to a vastly different world from the one in which he was reared. Catholicism, not Protestantism, was the norm. His position as rector placed him in intimate contact with the Vatican curia and those of his wealthy countrymen who chose to live in or visit the Eternal City. Befriending the powerful and assisting the well-to-do had to be intoxicating. It must have given O'Connell a taste of what might be if he were to attain something of equal rank. Had he remained in Boston as a simple parish priest or perhaps even as a pastor, the likelihood of his becoming a bishop would have been remote, and the church may have been spared what later occurred.

O'Connell owed his appointment as bishop of Portland, Maine, to his friend Cardinal Franceso Satolli. Nothing indicates that the American rector had promoted his own cause. His appointment to Boston was a different matter. The condemnation of Americanism gave him the fulcrum with which to lift himself onto the archiepiscopal throne of that city. O'Connell deliberately tarred with the brush of that heresy those who were nominated to the see of Boston in his stead. In his view, the church in New England and elsewhere in America suffered from a local or national spirit that jeopardized catholicity. He portrayed himself as the Vatican's faithful son in what he pictured as a sea awash in disloyalty to Rome. And the ploy worked. His Vatican allies secured the archbishopric for him. Once in power, he sought to bring Roman discipline to the province of New England.

O'Connell's excessive Romanism and his rise to power through Vatican, rather than American, channels marked him as an outsider in the American hierarchy. The vast majority of American bishops balanced loyalty to the Vatican with a desire for appropriate accommodation of the church to local circumstances. This difference between O'Connell and his colleagues became unbridgeable when it was embodied in the postwar NCWC, a collegial, national organization of the episcopate, one that violated O'Connell's Roman-focused, top-down understanding of the church in almost every respect. The NCWC was too democratic; it was rule by the "crowd." In O'Connell's view, the senior prelate—the ranking cardinal—ought to speak for the national church, which in large measure had been the case in the days of Cardinal James Gibbons. In the years following World War I, however, relatively few bishops shared this position.

While ideology separated O'Connell from his episcopal colleagues, it was administration that offered them the opportunity to unseat him. The irregularities that surfaced in the Portland finances pointed to a lax conscience with regard to money. O'Connell's payment of the deficit he left in that diocese was tacit admission of guilt in what amounted to embezzlement. The many lucrative schemes he then employed in the archdiocese of Boston made him a wealthy man, though neither his accusers nor historians have been able to prove exactly how much money came to him. It is certain, however, that he garnered a fortune by his mandates and through his manipulation of church policies.

 Equally as serious as O'Connell's blend of personal and official finances were his errors in judgment in his choice of personnel and his turning a blind eye to the secret marriages of his nephew James P. E. O'Connell and David Toomey. Coupled with those scandals was his own worldliness. These matters provided his suffragans with a way to vent the frustration pent up over their church-related differences with O'Connell.

Unfortunately, the drive for his removal was tied intimately to the NCWC, which was to be the instrument of his rejection. Thus, what had begun as a problem in the Boston province became an issue with repercussions for the church nationally. At least for the three principals in the fight, O'Connell, Bishop Louis Walsh, and Archbishop Austin Dowling, philosophical differences over the nature of the American church were inextricably linked with the campaign for the cardinal's removal. The two issues became indistinguishable.

O'Connell later personalized the conflict by identifying it with an old enemy, the Sulpicians, who had tendered Americanism quiet but strong support. In his mind, they were "intriguing" to unseat him in Boston and to replace proper deference to the cardinalate with collegial rule by the NCWC. His 1926 interview with John Burke made it evident that he considered that organization a new and dangerous Americanist experiment.

The question, however, that begs an answer, is why did the Vatican fail to remove O'Connell from office? The truth may never be fully known because it went to the grave with Benedict XV and Pius XI. That said, there are a number of plausible explanations. For his part, O'Connell maintained a steady flow of money to the Vatican on two levels. At the official level, his Peter's Pence collections were always high and, during crisis times, especially so. The $88,000 collection for the worldwide missions in 1924 was an apt specimen of monetary largess to the Holy See through legitimate means. On a personal level, O'Connell kept his Roman friends stocked with stipends for masses and financial benefactions sufficient to ensure a favorable hearing. Most of his beneficiaries were ideological colleagues, like Cardinals Gaetano De Lai and Raphael Merry del Val, and, in the case of the former, occupied a position of power capable of saving the errant prelate of Boston.

Moreover, O'Connell was a past master at maintaining appearances. His public manner of office-holding served him well. The highly advertised accomplishments of his tenure as archbishop and the well-timed Holy Land pilgrimage made Pius XI think twice about sacking so able an administrator and so apparently repentant a subject.

Despite the Boston cardinal's distaste for ecclesiastical democracy, both Benedict XV and Pius XI were willing to consider informal intervention for O'Connell's removal if the numbers were right. The former initially set the figure at fifteen members of the hierarchy who were willing to reject his leadership, a number later raised to twenty-eight. Pius XI, too, briefly considered removing O'Connell to Rome at the request of the American hierarchy. In 1921, there had been enough bishops, including Cardinal Dennis Dougherty, prepared to reject O'Connell's leadership to satisfy Benedict XV, save for a misunderstanding about the meaning of a cablegram from the Vatican. Yet by 1924, only the stalwarts remained dedicated to the ouster of the Boston cardinal. Though Rome continued to investigate O'Connell, nothing came of it, and the matter lapsed into oblivion.

This last result was probably the greatest tragedy of this sad episode. By permitting the problem to quietly disappear, no lessons were learned. The ecclesiastical agencies that should have held O'Connell accountable for his administration, failed to do so. This failure caused laypeople and priests to believe that the Vatican had to be sharing in the cardinal's harvesting of funds or it would have addressed the matter. And to a degree, they were right. The failure to move against O'Connell also worked in the other direction by discounting the believability of the scandals. For example, Archbishop Henry Moeller refused to accept the facts of the case because, as he said, "If these things are true then why does Rome not act?"

There was a canonical process for holding offenders accountable, but it was not invoked, no doubt because it involved an ecclesiastical trial that would have been difficult to hide. Given O'Connell's high station, the Vatican probably feared that this process would be as sensational as if the scandals themselves broke. Hence, Rome opted for informal action. The problem with informal action is that it is open to misunderstanding and political log-rolling, and therefore ineffective. Witness the debacle regarding the Roman cablegram of August 1921 and later Pius XI's asking Bishop Walsh to co-opt Cardinal De Lai into agreeing to bring O'Connell to Rome. Even if the process had been used, De Lai, a man tied to O'Connell by ideology, friendship, and money, would have been responsible for handling it. Given De Lai's pliability in the matter of the suppression of the NCWC, one can imagine the result of his pliability in a trial.

There are two lessons that might have been learned from the foregoing. First is the need for rules that forbid the acceptance of monetary or other gifts and favors by Vatican officials from anyone within or outside the church. Such officials must be absolutely impartial and above reproach in their dealings so that they can faithfully carry out their duties. Second is the need for a rule that requires that serious allegations always be handled through a formal process, regardless of the publicity that might result. Better to deal with an issue in an effective, fair manner that shows willingness to hold people accountable than to risk repeat because of ineffective, informal procedures. Such a rule should be uniformly applied to all church personnel, including cardinals and all Vatican officials without exception. Had lessons been learned from O'Connell's "Boston tragedy and comedy" and had measures like these been put in place as a result, the church might have been spared subsequent scandals.

Archival Abbreviations in Endnotes

AAB	Archives of the Archdiocese of Boston
AAP	Archives of the Archdiocese of Philadelphia
AANY	Archives of the Archdiocese of New York
AASF	Archives of the Archdiocese of San Francisco
AASL	Archives of the Archdiocese of Saint Louis
ACUA	Archives of Catholic University of America
ADA	Archives of the Diocese of Albany
ADCh	Archives of the Diocese of Charleston
ADCl	Archives of the Diocese of Cleveland
ADP	Archives of the Diocese of Portland, Maine
APF	Archives of the Congregation for the Propagation of the Faith
ASV	Archivio Segreto Vaticano (Vatican Secret Archives)
AUND	Archives of the University of Notre Dame
DAUS	Delegazione Apostolica Degli Stati Uniti (Apostolic Delegation of the United States)
AASMSU	Associated Archives at St. Mary's Seminary and University (Baltimore)

Endnotes

PROLOGUE

1. Robert Aidan O'Leary, "William Henry O'Connell: A Social and Intellectual Biography" (Tufts University: unpublished doctoral dissertation, 1980), 42–44; James M. O'Toole, *Militant and Triumphant: William Henry O'Connell and the Catholic Church in Boston, 1859–1944* (Notre Dame: University of Notre Dame Press, 1992), 9–12; Dorothy Wayman, *Cardinal O'Connell of Boston: A Biography of William Henry O'Connell, 1859–1944* (New York: Farrar, Straus and Young, 1955), 3–15; William Henry O'Connell, *Recollections of Seventy Years* (Boston: Houghton Mifflin, 1934), 1–10, 47.

2. O'Leary, "O'Connell," 44–45; O'Toole, *Militant and Triumphant*, 9–13; Wayman, *Cardinal O'Connell*, 3–15; O'Connell, *Recollections of Seventy Years*, 1–10, 47.

3. O'Connell, *Recollections*, 46–70 (the quotations are on 50 and 54).

4. Ibid., 70–71.

5. Notes on a conversation with Arsenius Vuibert by an unnamed Sulpician, 5 January 1919, AASMSU, RG 9, box 6; O'Toole, *Militant and Triumphant*, 13–14; Christopher J. Kauffman, *Tradition and Transformation in Catholic Culture: The Priests of Saint Sulpice in the United States from 1791 to the Present* (New York: Macmillan Publishing Company, 1988), 229–30.

6. O'Connell, *Recollections*, 71–80; O'Toole, *Militant and Triumphant*, 14–15; Wayman, *Cardinal O'Connell*, 18–19.

7. O'Connell, *Recollections*, 81, 110–39; O'Toole, *Militant and Triumphant*, 15–18; O'Leary, "O'Connell," 45–47; Wayman, *Cardinal O'Connell*, 22–31.

8. O'Connell, *Recollections*, 141.

9. Wayman, *Cardinal O'Connell*, 53–54; O'Toole, *Militant and Triumphant*, 18–23.

CHAPTER 1

1. James Gaffey, "The Changing of the Guard: The Rise of Cardinal O'Connell of Boston," *Catholic Historical Review* 59 (July 1973): 228.

2. Roger Aubert, *The Church in a Secularized Society*, trans. by Janet Sondheimer, vol. V of *The Christian Centuries*, ed. by Louis Rogier et al. (New York: Paulist Press, 1978), 56–57; Roger Aubert et al., *The Church between Revolution and Restoration*, trans. by Peter Becker, vol. VII of *The History of the Church*, ed. by Hubert Jedin (New York: Crossroad, 1981), 104–13; Roger Aubert et al., *The Church in the Age of Liberalism*, trans. by Peter Becker, vol. VIII of *The History of Church History*, ed. by Hubert Jedin (New York: Crossroad, 1981), 3–9.

3. Aubert, *Church in Secularized Society*, 76–69 (the quotation is on 59); Aubert et al., *Church between Revolution and Restoration*, 273–79; Aubert et al., *Church in Age of Liberalism*, 304–30; Kauffman, *Tradition and Transformation*, 154–59.

4. William O'Connell, *Sermons and Addresses of His Eminence William Cardinal O'Connell, Archbishop of Boston*, 11 vols. (Boston: The Pilot Publishing Company, 1915 and 1938), 2:238; John F. Broderick, S.J., ed. and trans., *Documents of Vatican Council I, 1869–1870* (Collegeville, Minn.: The Liturgical Press, 1971), 53–63.

5. O'Connell, *Sermons and Addresses*, 4:30–31.

6. Ibid., 10:68. As Jay Dolan points out, in the late nineteenth and early twentieth centuries the church considered authority and obedience cardinal elements of Catholic life (*American*

Catholic Experience: A History from Colonial Times to the Present [Garden City, N.Y.: Double-day & Company, 1985], 221–25). Yet conservatives like Archbishop Michael Corrigan of New York and Bishop Bernard McQuaid of Rochester, while upholding papal authority, could be critical of and cynical about it (R. Emmett Curran, *Michael Corrigan and the Shaping of Conservative Catholicism in America, 1878–1902* [New York: Arno Press, 1978], 505–06). It was O'Connell's excessive ultramontanism that marked him as the first of a new breed of prelate.

7. O'Connell, *Sermons and Addresses*, 4:64.

8. Ibid.

9. Ibid., 3:173–74. This is decree nineteen of the archdiocesan synod (1909). See also O'Leary, "O'Connell," 124–26.

10. O'Connell, *Recollections*, 124–25, 132–33, 323–24 (the quotations are from 132–33, 324); O'Toole, *Militant and Triumphant*, 16–17.

11. Gabriel Daly, O.S.A., *Transcendence and Immanence: A Study in Catholic Modernism and Integralism* (Oxford: Clarendon Press, 1980), 7–25; Roger Aubert et al., *The Church in the Industrial Age*, trans. by Margit Resch, vol. IX of *The History of the Church*, ed. Hubert Jedin and John Dolan (New York: Crossroad, 1981): 18–19, 307–11. For a rhapsody on the "Roman mind," see O'Connell, *Recollections*, 133–34.

12. Thomas Wangler, "Emergence of John J. Keane as a Liberal Catholic and Americanist (1878–1887)," *American Ecclesiastical Review* 166 (September 1972): 457–478; same, "John Ireland and the Origins of Liberal Catholicism in the United States," *Catholic Historical Review* 56 (January 1971): 617–29; same, "John Ireland's Emergence as a Liberal Catholic and Ameri-canist: 1875–1887," *Records of the American Catholic Historical Society of Philadelphia* 81 (June 1970): 67–82; same, "The Birth of Americanism: 'Westward the Apocalyptic Candlestick,'" *Harvard Theological Review* 65 (July 1972): 415–36.

13. John Ireland, *The Church and Modern Society: Lectures and Addresses*, 2 vols. (St. Paul: Pioneer Press, 1905), 1:71–101 (the quotations are on 73, 88, 90, and 99). See also Dolan, *American Catholic Experience*, 309.

14. Ireland, *Church and Modern Society*, 1:75; Josiah Strong, *Our Country: Its Possible Future and Its Present Crisis* (New York: Baker and Taylor Company, 1885 and 1891), chapter 14 (the quotation is on 213–4 and 222); Sidney Mead, "American Protestantism Since the Civil War," *Journal of Religion* 26 (January 1956): 1–16; Emily S. Rosenberg, *Spreading the American Dream: American Economic and Cultural Expansion, 1890–1945* (New York: Hill and Wang, 1982), 3–13, 38–48; Sydney E. Ahlstrom, *A Religious History of the American People* (New Haven, Conn.: Yale University Press, 1972), 877–78.

15. Ireland, *Church and Modern Society*, 1:71–101 (the quotations are on 75 and 93).

16. Ibid., 82–83; James H. Moynihan, *The Life of Archbishop John Ireland* (New York: Harper and Brothers, 1953), 49; John T. Farrell, "Archbishop Ireland and Manifest Destiny," *Catholic Historical Review* 33 (October 1947):295–301. For Keane and Denis O'Connell's com-mitment to democracy and the separation of church and state, see Patrick H. Ahern, *The Life of John J. Keane, 1839–1918* (Milwaukee: Bruce Publishing Company, 1955), 94; Gerald Fogarty, S.J., *The Vatican and the Americanist Crisis: Denis J. O'Connell, American Agent in Rome, 1885–1903* (Rome: Universita Gregoriana, 1974), 266–67.

17. Gregory XVI, *Mirari Vos* (1832) and Pius IX, *Syllabus of Errors* (1864), in Colman J. Barry, O.S.B., *Readings in Church History*, 3 vols. (New York: Newman Press, 1965), 3:37–44, 70–74; Aubert, *Church between Revolution and Restoration*, 279–88; Vatican II, *Dignitatis Humanae* (1965) in Austin Flannery, O.P., *Vatican Council II: The Conciliar and Post Conciliar Documents* (Northport, N.Y.: Costello Publishing Company, 1975), 799–812.

18. Ireland, *Church and Modern Society*, 1:91; Margaret Reher, "The Church and the Kingdom of God in America," (Fordham University: unpublished doctoral dissertation, 1972), 125–26.

19. Thomas McAvoy, C.S.C., *The Great Crisis in American Catholic History, 1895–1900* (Chicago: H. Regnery Co., 1957), 79–83; Christopher Kauffman, "The Sulpician Experience in the United States: From Gallicanism to Americanism," a paper delivered at the Cushwa Conference on American Catholicism, Notre Dame University, 4 October 1985; Kauffman, *Tradition and Transformation*, 154–71, 179–88; Isaac T. Hecker, *The Church and the Age: An Exposition of the Catholic Church in View of the Needs and Aspirations of the Present Age* (New York: Catholic Book Exchange, 1896), 7–87; John Farina, *An American Experience of God: The Spirituality of Isaac Hecker* (New York: Paulist Press, 1981); Edward J. Langlois, C.S.P., "Isaac Hecker's Political Thought," in John Farina, ed., *Hecker Studies: Essays on the Thought of Isaac Hecker* (New York: Paulist Press, 1983), 49–62; Joseph F. Gower, "Democracy as a Theological Problem in Isaac Hecker's Apologetics," in Thomas M. McFadden, ed., *America in Theological Perspective* (New York: Seabury Press, 1976), 39–42; David J. O'Brien, "An Evangelical Imperative: Isaac Hecker, Catholicism, and Modern Society," in Farina, *Hecker Studies*, 102–15; Joseph P. Chinnici, O.F.M., *Living Stones: The History and Structure of Catholic Spiritual Life in the United States* (New York: Macmillan Publishing Company, 1989), 91–92, 100–09; Martin J. Kirk, C.F.M., *The Spirituality of Isaac Thomas Hecker: Reconciling the American Character and the Catholic Faith* (New York: Garland Publishing, Inc., 1988), 143–74, 199–214; Margaret Mary Reher, *Catholic Intellectual Life in America: A Historical Study of Persons and Movements* (New York: Macmillan Publishing Company, 1989), 45–49, 57–59.

20. Quoted in Curran, *Corrigan*, 50.

21. Ibid., 333–34; Dolan, *American Catholic Experience*, 311.

22. Quoted in Chinnici, *Living Stones*, 121; Joseph Chinnici, O.F.M., ed., *Devotion to the Holy Spirit in American Catholicism* (New York: Paulist Press, 1985), 11.

23. Curran, *Corrigan*, 505–06.

24. Ibid., 316.

25. John Tracy Ellis, ed., *Documents of American Catholic History* (Milwaukee: Bruce Publishing Company, 1962), 457–59; John T. Ellis, *The Life of James Cardinal Gibbons, Archbishop of Baltimore, 1834–1921*, 2 vols. (Milwaukee: Bruce Publishing Company, 1952), 1:307–09. Prior to the mid-twentieth century, there were three ranks of cardinals: cardinal deacons, cardinal priests, and cardinal bishops. The rank of cardinal deacon consisted of laymen and priests elevated to the cardinalate. The ranks of cardinal priests and bishops consisted of actual bishops elevated to the cardinalate. Cardinal priests were named titular pastors of churches in Rome. Cardinal bishops were named titular bishops of one of the dioceses of Rome.

26. Gerald Fogarty, S.J., *The Vatican and the American Hierarchy from 1870 to 1965* (Wilmington, Del.: Michael Glazier Press, 1985), 45–49; Colman Barry, *The Catholic Church and German Americans* (Milwaukee: Bruce Publishing Company, 1953), 62–73, 289–96; Marvin R. O'Connell, *John Ireland and the American Catholic Church* (St. Paul: Minnesota Historical Society Press, 1988), 217–26.

27. Henry J. Browne, *The Catholic Church and the Knights of Labor* (Washington, D.C.: The Catholic University of America Press, 1949); Wangler, "John Keane," 466–68; same, "John Ireland," 76–78; Fogarty, *American Hierarchy*, 87–92.

28. R. Emmett Curran, "Prelude to 'Americanism': The New York Accademia and Clerical Radicalism in the Late Nineteenth Century," *Church History* 47 (March 1978): 48–65.

29. Ireland, *Church and Modern Society*, 1:217–32; Bernard J. Meiring, *Educational Aspects*

of the Legislation of the Councils of Baltimore, 1829–1884 (New York: Arno Press, 1978), 219–49; Harold A. Buetow, *Of Singular Benefit: The Story of Catholic Education in the United States* (London: Macmillan Company, 1970), 152–61.

30. La Vern J. Rippley, "Archbishop Ireland and the School Language Controversy," *U.S. Catholic Historian* 1 (Fall 1980): 1–16; Barry, *German Americans*, 184–85; O'Connell, *Ireland*, 289–90; Lloyd P. Jorgenson, *The State and the Non-Public School, 1825–1925* (Columbia: University of Missouri Press, 1987), 187–201.

31. For the complexities, nuances, and politics needed to flesh out this highly distilled account of the school controversy, see Curran, *Corrigan*, 339–83; Ellis, *Gibbons*, 1:667–707; Fogarty, *Americanist Crisis*, 198–218; same, *American Hierarchy*, 69–85; Joseph H. Lackner, S.M., "Bishop Ignatius Horstmann and the School Controversy of the 1890s," *Catholic Historical Review* 75 (January 1989): 73–90; O'Connell, *Ireland*, 322–74; C. Joseph Nuesse, "Thomas Joseph Bouquillon (1840–1902), Moral Theologian and Precursor of the Social Sciences in The Catholic University of America," *Catholic Historical Review* 72 (October 1986): 603–06; Daniel F. Reilly, O.P., *The School Controversy* (1891–1893) (Washington, D.C.: Catholic University Press, 1943), 74–232; Frederick J. Zwierlein, *The Life and Letters of Bishop McQuaid*, 3 vols. (Rochester, 1925–1927), 3:160–98. The quotation is taken from Satolli's fourteen points printed in Reilly, *School Controversy*, 272.

32. Ellis, *Documents*, 495–507 (the quotations are on 498, 501, and 504).

33. Austin Flannery, O.P., ed., *Vatican Council II: The Conciliar and Post Conciliar Documents* (Northport, N.Y.: Costello Publishing Company, 1977), 766–812.

34. O'Connell, *Recollections*, 160–61.

35. Ibid., 161.

36. Ibid., 128, 161–62.

CHAPTER 2

1. Fogarty, *Americanist Crisis*, 252–54.

2. O'Toole, *Militant and Triumphant*, 23–28; O'Leary, "O'Connell," 49–54; Robert F. McNamara, *The American College in Rome, 1855–1955* (Rochester, N.Y.: The Christopher Press, 1956), 337–38; Robert H. Lord, John E. Sexton, and Edward T. Harrington, *History of the Archdiocese of Boston: In the Various Stages of Its Development, 1604-1943*, 3 vols. (New York: Sheed and Ward, 1944), vol. 3:461–62. Regarding Satolli's intervention, see Notes on a conversation with Arsenius Vuibert by an unnamed Sulpician, 5 January 1919, AASMSU, RG 9, box 6; remarks by Father Alexis Orban, S.S., in Diary of Louis Walsh, 22 November 1909, ADP; Wayman, *Cardinal O'Connell*, 70–71; Brendan A. Finn, *Twenty-four American Cardinals: Biographical Sketches of Those Princes of the Catholic Church Who Either Were Born in America or Served at Some Time* [Boston: Bruce Humphries, 1947], 278); Francesco Satolli to Cardinal Miecislaus Ledochowski, Prefect of Propaganda, 4 October 1895, copy, APF, Acta della Congregazione, 265 (1895): 524r.

3. McAvoy, *Great Crisis*, 154–203; Fogarty, *American Hierarchy*, 141–61.

4. McAvoy, *Great Crisis*, 204–10; Fogarty, *American Hierarchy*, 161–64; O'Connell, *Ireland*, 442–52; Frank T. Reuter, *Catholic Influence on American Colonial Policies, 1898–1904* (Austin: University of Texas Press, 1967), 1–19; Walter LaFeber, *The American Search for Opportunity, 1865–1913*, Vol. II of *The Cambridge History of American Foreign Relations*, ed. by Walter I. Cohen (New York: Cambridge University Press, 1995), 129–64; William Appleman Williams, *The Contours of American History* (New York: W. W. Norton and Company, 1988), 360–70; Thomas G.

Paterson, et. al., *American Foreign Relations*, 2 vols (Lexington, Mass.: D. C. Heath, 1995), 2:11–33; Rosenberg, *Spreading the American Dream*, 38–62.

5. Fogarty, *American Hierarchy*, 73, 143–84; McAvoy, *Great Crisis*, 155–291.

6. O'Connell, *Recollections*, 181–93, 205–06, 209–11; McNamara, *American College*, 349–52; Francis MacNutt, *A Papal Chamberlain: The Personal Chronicle of Francis Augustus MacNutt*, ed. by John J. Donovan (New York: Longmans, Green, and Company, 1936), 1–223; O'Leary, "O'Connell," 57–59; O'Toole, *Militant and Triumphant*, 27–32.

7. O'Leary, "O'Connell," 51; O'Toole, *Militant and Triumphant*, 28–29.

8. Satolli to O'Connell, 14 September 1898, ADP, O'Connell Papers.

9. Satolli, Relazione con Sommario Sulla Elezione del Nuovo Vescovo di Portland, APF, Acta della Congregazione, 272 (1901): 41–48, 352–53; Fogarty, *American Hierarchy*, 195–96; O'Toole, *Militant and Triumphant*, 34–37.

10. Satolli, Relazione con Sommario Sulla Elezione del Nuovo Vescovo di Portland, APF, Acta della Congregazione, 272 (1901): 41–48, 352–53; Fogarty, *American Hierarchy*, 195–96; O'Toole, *Militant and Triumphant*, 37–38.

11. Quoted in Gaffey, "Changing of the Guard," 228.

12. O'Leary, "O'Connell," 57–59 (the quotation is on 58).

13. Alfred J. Ede, *The Lay Crusade for a Christian America: A Study of the American Federation of Catholic Societies, 1900–1919* (New York: Garland Press, 1988), 64–75; O'Leary, "O'Connell," 61–64; O'Toole, *Militant and Triumphant*, 40–41.

14. Francis MacNutt to O'Connell, 20 February 1902, ADP, O'Connell Papers; McNutt to O'Connell, 5 April 1902, ibid.; Curran, *Corrigan*, 510–12.

15. Sante Tampieri to O'Connell, 23 December 1901, ADP, O'Connell Papers; Tampieri to O'Connell, 16 November 1902, ibid. Tampieri openly expressed his hope of becoming vicar of O'Connell's titular church if his patron received the red hat.

16. Giuseppe Marucchi to O'Connell, 15 July 1901, ADP, O'Connell Papers.

17. Mariano Rampolla to Diomede Falconio, 17 April 1903, ASV, DAUS, IV, Liste Episcopali 61; Falconio to O'Connell, 17 April 1903, ibid.; Falconio to Rampolla, 20 April 1903, ibid.; Ellis, *Gibbons*, 2:119; O'Toole, *Militant and Triumphant*, 62–64; Wayman, *Cardinal O'Connell*, 104–07.

18. O'Connell to Leo XIII, 21 April 1903, copy, ASV, DAUS, IV, Liste Episcopali 61.

19. Ibid.

20. MacNutt to O'Connell, undated [June 1903], ADP, O'Connell Papers; LaFeber, *American Search for Opportunity*, 156–68; Paterson, *American Foreign Relations*, 2:24–29.

21. MacNutt to O'Connell, 18 December 1903, ADP, O'Connell papers; MacNutt, *Papal Chamberlain*, 136–52. In this letter, MacNutt suggested that Satolli's star was waning: "The Pope said apropos of him, that he liked no man who did not look him in the eyes when he talked. You are familiar with the jackal-like glance of our friend from Perugia and may imagine the degree of confidence it awakens in Pius Xth!" Nothing indicates that Satolli fell from grace.

22. Diary of Matthew Harkins, 23 November 1903, copy, AUND; O'Toole, *Militant and Triumphant*, 64.

23. Tampieri to O'Connell, 15 March 1904, ADP, O'Connell Papers; Satolli to O'Connell, 22 November 1903, ibid.

24. O'Leary, "O'Connell," 64–66; O'Toole, *Militant and Triumphant*, 67–69.

25. Statement of Archbishop John Ireland of St. Paul and Bishop Denis O'Connell of Richmond, undated [but after 1910], AASMSU, RG 9, box 6. With war imminent, William O'Connell must have condoled with his Spanish friend, Monsignor Merry del Val. "I have been

affected by the thought and delicate feeling which were expressed in the token you sent me this morning," the latter replied. "Many, many thanks. I wish I could express in words how much I value this act on your part. My personal acquaintance with the Queen and my knowledge of her admirable character . . . make me feel deeply for her at this crisis" (Merry del Val to O'Connell, 22 April 1898, ADP, O'Connell Papers). Throughout the text, the current dollar amounts are computed using the Consumer Price Index.

26. Minutes of the Meeting of Suffragan Bishops of the Province of Boston, 7 April 1904, copy, AASMSU, RG 9, box 6; Lord, Sexton, and Harrington, *Archdiocese of Boston*, 3:421; O'Toole, *Militant and Triumphant*, 65.

27. Michael Glazier and Thomas Shelley, eds., *The Encyclopedia of American Catholic History* (Collegeville, Minn.: The Liturgical Press, 1997), 614.

28. John Williams to Diomede Falconio, 20 April 1904; Patrick Riordan to Falconio, 21 April 1904; Patrick Ryan to Falconio, 21 April 1904; Alexander Christie to Falconio, 22 April 1904; James Gibbons to Falconio, 22 April 1904; John Keane to Falconio, 23 April 1904; Sebastian Messmer to Falconio, 24 April 1904; William Elder to Falconio, 25 April 1904; John Farley to Falconio, 29 April 1904; Ireland to Falconio, 29 April 1904—all in ASV, DAUS IV, Liste Episcopali 73. At the time, there were fourteen archbishops in the United States. The remaining four chose not to express an opinion.

29. Quoted in Gaffey, "Changing of the Guard," 229–30.

30. Antonio Savelli-Spinola to O'Connell, 26 May 1904, ADP, O'Connell Papers (emphasis in original).

31. Tampieri to O'Connell, 21 May 1904, ADP, O'Connell Papers.

32. Falconio to O'Connell, 18 May 1904, copy, ASV, DAUS, IV, Liste Episcopali 73.

33. O'Connell to Falconio, 23 May 1904, copy, ASV, DAUS, IV, Liste Episcopali 73.

34. [O'Connell], *Terna* of Consultors and Rectors, and Bishops *Terna*, unsigned, undated [April or May 1904], copy, ASV, DAUS, IV, Liste Episcopali 73.

35. Ibid. O'Toole, *Militant and Triumphant*, 64–65; Fogarty, *American Hierarchy*, 201–02.

36. William H. O'Connell, *The Letters of His Eminence William Cardinal O'Connell, Archbishop of Boston*, Volume I: *From College Days 1876 to Bishop of Portland 1901* (Cambridge, Ma.: Riverside Press, 1915), 129, 170, 214–16; O'Connell, *Recollections*, 148–49, 160–62; Robert W. Hayman, *Catholicism in Rhode Island and the Diocese of Providence, 1887–1921* (Providence: Diocese of Providence,1995); Donna Merwick, *Boston Priests, 1848–1910: A Study of Social and Intellectual Change* (Cambridge: Harvard University Press , 1973), 147–61.

37. Patrick Daly to Falconio, 27 April 1904, ASV, DAUS, IV, Liste Episcopali, 73; Gaffey, "Changing of the Guard," 231; O'Toole, *Militant and Triumphant*, 66.

38. Patrick Supple to Most Reverend Eminence [Girolamo Gotti], 7 May 1904, copy, ASV, DAUS, IV, Liste Episcopali 73. Supple sent a copy to Falconio (8 May 1904) and informed him that the letter was sent to both Gotti and Merry del Val. The date on this copy differs from that on the originals in APF (26 and 28 April respectively [Gaffey, "Changing of the Guard," 231, n. 15]).

39. Gaffey, "Changing of the Guard," 231–32.

40. Patrick Collins to Falconio, 23 April 1904; James R. Murphy to Falconio, 3 May 1904; Matthew Hale to Falconio, 7 May 1904—all in ASV, DAUS, IV, Liste Episcopali 73.

41. Gaffey, "Changing of the Guard," 232–36 (the quotation appears on 232–33). For Ireland's interest in the succession, see Ireland to William Byrne, telegram, 12 July 1904; Ireland to Byrne, telegram, 16 July 1904; Ireland to Matthew Harkins, telegram, 16 July 1904—all in AASMSU, RG 9, box 6. On Delany's support of O'Connell, see Stang to Falconio, 17 February

1906, ASV, DAUS, IV, Liste Episcopali 73.

42. O'Toole, *Militant and Triumphant*, 75–78 (the quotation is on 75). See also O'Leary, "O'Connell," 79–81. On the Americanists' continued espousal of cherished causes, see Neil T. Storch, "John Ireland's Americanism *After* 1899: The Argument from History," *Church History* 51 (December 1982): 434–44; Ede, *Lay Crusade*, 160–70; Ahern, *Life of Keane*, 337–38.

43. O'Leary, "Cardinal O'Connell," 81–82.

44. O'Toole, *Militant and Triumphant*, 75.

45. MacNutt to O'Connell, 5 May [1904], ADP, O'Connell Papers; Savelli-Spinola to O'Connell, 26 May 1904, ibid. (the first quotation is from here); [Umberto Benigni, Alphonse Jonckx, and Frédéric Speiser], Notes en Vue du Prochain Conclave, 27 août 1913, in Émile Poulat, *Intégrisme et catholicisme intégral: un réseau secret international antimoderniste: La "Sapinière" (1909–1921)*, (Tournai: Casterman, 1969), 329 (the second quotation is from here).

46. Satolli to O'Connell, 12 April 1904, ADP, O'Connell Papers; O'Connell to Pius X, feast of St. Pius V, [5 May] 1904, copy, ibid.; Falconio to O'Connell, 5 July 1904, ibid.; Ellis, *Gibbons*, 2:423–24, n. 154; MacNutt, *Papal Chamberlain*, 271.

47. Ireland to Byrne, 16 July 1904, telegram, AASMSU, RG 9, box 6; Byrne to Harkins, 16 July 1904, ibid.; Satolli to O'Connell, 5 October 1904, ADP, O'Connell Papers; *Boston Globe*, 23 July 1904; Finn, *Twenty-Four American Cardinals*, 277; John J. Delaney, *Dictionary of American Catholic Biography* (Garden City, N.Y.: Doubleday & Company, 1984), 509–10.

48. Byrne to Harkins, 19 July 1904, AASMSU, RG 9, box 6; Byrne to Harkins, 22 July 1904, ibid. (the quotation is here); *Boston Globe*, 26 July 1904.

49. *Boston Journal*, 27 July 1904; Byrne to Harkins, 27 July 1904, AASMSU, RG 9, box 6 (the second quotation is here); Byrne to Harkins, 30 July 1904, ibid.; Byrne to Harkins, 6 August 1904, ibid.; Byrne to Harkins, 8 August 1904, ibid.

50. *Boston Journal*, 27 July 1904; Byrne to Harkins, 30 July 1904, AASMSU, RG 9, box 6.

51. Satolli to O'Connell, 5 October 1904, ADP, O'Connell Papers; Gaffey, "Changing of the Guard," 233–34.

52. MacNutt, *Papal Chamberlain*, 279; O'Toole, *Militant and Triumphant*, 69–70.

53. Gaffey, "Changing of the Guard," 233. Information about the second petition (17 December 1904) is found in William Stang to Pius X, 5 June 1906, copy (in Latin), ASV, DAUS, IV, Liste Episcopali 73 (an English copy in AASMSU, RG 9, box 6), which recounts the history of the Boston succession.

54. O'Connell, *Recollections*, 235–62; Gaffey, "Changing of the Guard," 234–35; O'Toole, *Militant and Triumphant*, 70–71; Wayman, *Cardinal O'Connell*, 118–22.

55. The comments of Gotti and Vannutelli were made to Bishop Louis Walsh of Portland, Maine, during his *ad limina* visit to Rome in 1909 (Diary of Walsh, 18 and 20 [the quotation by Vannutelli is here] November 1909, ADP); O'Toole, *Militant and Triumphant*, 71–72 (the quotation by Agliardi is here); Gaffey, "Changing of the Guard," 235–36; Diary of Harkins, 7 December 1905 and 15 March 1906, copy, AUND.

56. The comments of Gotti, Vannutelli, Orban, and Genocchi were made to Walsh during his *ad limina* visit to Rome in 1909 (Diary of Walsh, 18, 20, 22 November, and 4 [the quotation by Pius X is here] and 14 [the quotation by Gotti is here] December 1909, ADP); Fogarty, *American Hierarchy*, 203 (the quotation by Edes is from here); O'Connell, *Recollections*, 262–63; O'Toole, *Militant and Triumphant*, 71–72; Gaffey, "Changing of the Guard," 235–36; Diary of Harkins, 7 December 1905 and 15 March 1906, copy, AUND.

57. Stang to Falconio, 10 February 1906, ASV, DAUS, IV, Liste Episcopali 73 (emphasis in original).

58. Quoted in Stang to Falconio, 17 February 1906, ASV, DAUS, IV, Liste Episcopali 73.

59. Diary of Harkins, 10 March 1906, copy, AUND.

60. O'Connell to Falconio, 17 March 1906, ASV, DAUS, IV, Liste Episcopali 73.

61. Stang to Pius X, 5 June 1906, copy (in Latin), ASV, DAUS, IV, Liste Episcopali 73, copy in AASMSU, RG 9, box 6; Stang to Falconio, 17 February 1906, ASV, DAUS, IV, Liste Episcopali 73; Gaffey, "Changing of the Guard," 235–36. O'Toole states that, save for Delany, all the suffragans signed the letter *(Militant and Triumphant*, 73). In fact, only Stang did, but as the quote above indicates, he was acting in the name of his colleagues.

62. Diary of Walsh, 29, 30, and 31 March 1909, 3 and 5 April 1909, ADP, emphasis in original; Walsh to O'Connell, undated draft [April 1909], ibid.; Kenneth B. Woodbury, Jr., "An Incident Between the French Canadians and the Irish in the Diocese of Maine in 1906," *New England Quarterly* 40 (June 1967): 266–67; J. Albert Foisy, *The Sentinellist Agitation in New England, 1925–1928* (Providence: Providence Visitor Press, 1930), 3–13; Mason Wade, "The French Parish and *Survivance* in Nineteenth-Century New England," *Catholic Historical Review* 36 (July 1950): 168–69; Dolores Liptak, R.S.M., *Immigrants and Their Church* (New York: Macmillan Publishing Company, 1989), 160–70; O'Toole, *Militant and Triumphant*, 44.

63. [Pierre Dupont, François Trudel, and Narcisse Charland to Williams, undated (late March or early April 1906), copy], AASMSU, RG 27, box 2; Woodbury, "An Incident Between the French Canadians and the Irish," 265–66; Adolphe Lacroix to Gotti, 10 May 1906, copy, AASMSU, RG 27, box 2

64. Lacroix to Gotti, 10 May 1906, copy, AASMSU, RG 27, box 2.

65. Lacroix to Stang, 20 May 1906, AASMSU, RG 27, box 2.

CHAPTER 3

1. Copy of the Contract Relative to the Seminary Made in Triplicate at Rome, 10 December 1883, AAB, St. John's Seminary file; Kauffman, "Sulpician Experience in the United States," Cushwa Conference, University of Notre Dame, 1985; Kauffman, *Tradition and Transformation*, 17–28.

2. Brief Notes on Archbishop O'Connell and the Sulpicians at Brighton Seminary, by Francis Havey, S.S., undated [June 1910], AASMSU, RG 9, box 6; Kauffman, "Sulpician Experience in the United States," Cushwa Conference, 1985; Kauffman, *Tradition and Transformation*, xv, 261 (the quotation is from here); O'Toole, *Militant and Triumphant*, 106–07; O'Leary, "O'Connell," 131–33.

3. Louis J. Rogier et al., eds., *The Christian Centuries*, 5 vols. (London: Darton, Longman, and Todd, 1964–1978), vol. 5: *The Church in a Secularized Society*, by Roger Aubert et al., 186–97, the quotation appears on 187; Aubert et al., *The Church in the Industrial Age*, 431–55; Bernard M. G. Reardon, ed., *Roman Catholic Modernism* (Stanford: Stanford University Press, 1970), 9–63; Gabriel Daly, O.S.A., *Transcendence and Immanence: A Study in Catholic Modernism and Integralism* (Oxford: Oxford University Press, 1980), *passim*; R. Scott Appleby, *"Church and Age Unite!": The Modernist Impulse in American Catholicism* (Notre Dame, Ind.: University of Notre Dame Press, 1992), 53–167; Michael V. Gannon, "Before and After Modernism: The Intellectual Isolation of the American Priest," in Ellis, ed., *The Catholic Priest in the United States: Historical Investigations* (Collegeville, Minn.: St. John's University Press, 1971), 326–31; Fogarty, *Vatican and American Hierarchy*, 190–91; Kauffman, *Tradition and Transformation*, 168–77, 204–23; Reher, *Catholic Intellectual Life*, 91–99.

4. O'Connell to Paul Chapon, S.S., 5 December 1907, AASMSU, RG 9 Box 6; Brief Notes

by Havey, undated [June 1910], AASMSU, RG 9, box 6; Notes by same, 15 August 1935, AASMSU, RG 9, box 6; O'Connell to Havey, 8 March 1910, ibid.; Kauffman, *Tradition and Transformation*, 230–31, 234; Ex Sacre Congregatione Episcoporum et Regularium, "Normae ad instaurandam institutionem et disciplinam in Seminariis Italiae as SS. D.N. Pio PP. X approbatae," *Acta Sanctae Sedis* 41 (1908): 221, 223. Although this decree pertained to Italy, the congregation applied it worldwide (Roger Aubert et al., *Church in the Industrial Age*, 416.)

5. Joseph Bruneau to Dyer, 2 January 1909, AASMSU, RG 10, box 15; Marie-François-Xavier Hertzog to Havey, 16 June 1909, ibid., RG 10, box 20.

6. Hertzog to Havey, 12 March 1909, AASMSU, RG 10, box 20 (the first quote is here); Herzog to Havey, 16 June 1909, ibid. (the second quote is here).

7. Hertzog to Edward Dyer, 17 April 1909, AASMSU, RG 10, box 20.

8. Brief Notes by Havey, 15 August 1935, AASMSU, RG 9, box 6 (the quotations are here); Dyer to Garriguet, 16 July 1909 copy, AASMSU, RG 10, box 16; Dyer to Garriguet, 3 August 1909, copy, RG 9, box 6; Diary of Walsh, 22 November 1909, ADP; Kauffman, *Tradition and Transformation*, 230–31.

9. George Leahy to O'Connell, 3 January 1910, AAB, St. John's Seminary file.

10. Havey, Contract between Archdiocese of Boston & Saint-Sulpice: Comments on the Interview between His Grace, Archbishop O'Connell and Very Reverend Father Garriguet, Superior General of the Sulpicians, held at Boston, 29 September 1910, AASMSU, RG 9, box 6. Hereafter cited as Contract-Comments.

11. Ibid.

12. Garriguet, Havey, and Francesco Hertzog, Interview with Monsignor, the Archbishop of Boston, 29 September 1910, AASMSU, RG 9, box 6; Michael Splaine and James P. E. O'Connell, Agreement reached by Roman Catholic archbishop of Boston and superior general of the Sulpicians, archbishop's house, Boston, 29 September 1910, AAB, St. John's Seminary file; O'Toole, *Militant and Triumphant*, 107–08; Kauffman, *Tradition and Transformation*, 235; John E. Sexton and Arthur J. Riley, *History of Saint John's Seminary, Brighton* (Boston: Roman Catholic Archbishop of Boston, 1945), 140–43.

13. Havey, Contract-Comments, AASMSU, RG 9, box 6.

14. O'Connell to Garriguet, 21 October 1910, copy, AASMSU, RG 9, box 6; Kauffman, *Tradition and Transformation*, 236.

15. Reply of Mr. Garriguet, Superior of St. Sulpice, to Mgr. O'Connell, Archbishop of Boston, undated [11 November 1910], copy, AASMSU, RG 9, box 6.

16. John Peterson to O'Connell, 27 October 1910, AAB, St. John's Seminary file; O'Connell to Peterson, 17 May 1911, ibid.; Peterson to O'Connell, 29 September 1911, AAB, ibid.; Ex Sacre Congregatione Episcoporum et Regularium, "Programma generale studiorum a Pio PP. X approbatum pro omnibus Italiae Seminariis," *Acta Sanctae Sedis* 40 (1907): 336–43.

17. Boston *Pilot*, 20 May 1911.

18. Dyer to O'Connell, 3 June 1911, copy, AASMSU, RG 10, box 16.

19. O'Toole, *Militant and Triumphant*, 7.

20. Thomas Beaven to Walsh, 27 April 1908, ADP, Walsh Papers; Beaven to Walsh, 15 May 1908, ibid.; Beaven to Walsh, 18 May 1908, ibid. For the announcement of O'Connell's presidency at the convocation, see the Boston *Pilot*, 16 May 1908.

21. O'Connell to Merry del Val, Satolli, and Martinelli, 8 December 1908, copy, AAB, O'Connell correspondence M850. This letter comes courtesy of Father Gerald Fogarty, S.J.

22. Diary of Walsh, 20 August 1908, ADP; O'Connell to Merry del Val, Satolli, and Martinelli, 8 December 1908, copy, AAB, O'Connell correspondence M850.

23. O'Connell to Merry del Val, Satolli, and Martinelli, 8 December 1908, copy, AAB, O'Connell correspondence M850. For the change by the bishops, see Diary of Walsh, 1 April 1909, ADP; *New York Herald*, 2 June 1913.

24. Diary of Walsh, 1 April and 14 May 1909, ADP (the quotation appears under the latter date); O'Connell to Beaven, 16 March 1909, AASMSU, RG 9, box 6.

25. Dyer to Garriguet, 16 July 1909, copy, AASMSU, RG 9, box 6; Dyer to Garriguet, 3 August 1909, copy, ibid.

26. Delaney, *Dictionary of American Catholic Biography*, 585; O'Toole, *Militant and Triumphant*, 54.

27. Walsh to Harkins, 26 November 1909, AASMSU, RG 9, box 6; Walsh to Harkins, 17 December 1909, AASMSU, RG 9, box 6; Diary of Walsh, 22 and 25 November 1909, ADP.

28. Walsh to Harkins, 26 November 1909, AASMSU, RG 9, box 6; Walsh to Harkins, 17 December 1909, AASMSU, RG 9, box 6; Diary of Walsh, 17 and 22 November 1909, ADP.

29. O'Connell to Merry del Val, 24 February 1910, copy, AASMSU, RG 9, box 6.

30. *New York Herald*, 2 June 1913.

31. Archbishop Bonaventura Cerretti, former auditor of the apostolic delegation, to Walsh, 5 July 1914, AASMSU, RG 9, box 6; Cerretti to Walsh, 11 November 1914, ibid.; Walsh, untitled notes [1914], ibid.; Beaven to Walsh, 20 December 1914, ibid.

32. Harkins to Benedict XV, 4 October 1918, copy, AASMSU, RG 9, box 6; Harkins to Cardinal Gaetano De Lai, 4 October 1918, copy, ibid.

33. Walsh Diary, 29 October 1911, ADP; Gaffey, "Changing of the Guard," 242; Fogarty, *American Hierarchy*, 205–06; O'Toole, *Militant and Triumphant*, 93–94.

34. Cerretti to Gaetano De Lai, 1 March 1912, copy, ASV, DAUS IX, Boston 71; O'Toole, *Militant and Triumphant*, 93–96.

35. O'Connell, *Sermons and Addresses*, 4:30–31.

36. Cerretti to De Lai, 1 March 1912, copy, ASV, DAUS, IX, Boston 71.

37. Ibid.

38. O'Connell, *Sermons and Addresses*, 4:78–81.

39. Cerretti to De Lai, 3 April 1912, copy, ASV, DAUS, IX, Boston 71.

40. Dyer to the editor of the *Pilot*, [March 1912], copy, AASMSU, RG 4, box 10; Boston *Pilot*, 23 March 1912.

41. William Starr to Thomas Gasson, S.J., 2 April 1912, copy, AASMSU, RG 4, box 10.

42. *Baltimore Catholic Review*, [June 1912], clipping, in AASMSU, RG 4, box 10.

43. Cerretti to Harkins, telegram, 9 April 1912, ASV, DAUS, IX, Boston 71; Harkins to Cerretti, telegram, 9 April 1912, ibid.; Cerretti to De Lai, 16 April 1912, copy, ibid.; Glazier and Shelley, *Encyclopedia of Catholic History*, 456; Delaney, *Dictionary of American Catholic History*, 151.

44. Cerretti to De Lai, 16 April 1912, copy, ASV, DAUS, IX, Boston 71.

45. Ibid.

46. Cerretti to Harkins, 18 April 1912, copy, ASV, DAUS, IX, Boston 71; Cerretti to Austin Dowling, telegram, 20 April 1912, ibid.; Dowling to Cerretti, telegram, 20 April 1912, ibid.; Harkins to Cerretti, 21 April 1912, ibid.

47. O'Toole, *Militant and Triumphant*, 96–98.

48. P. R. O'D., *How History Is Made, 1911–1912*, ASV, DAUS, IX, Boston 71.

49. W. A. R., untitled verse, ASV, DAUS, IX, Boston, 71.

1. Diary of Walsh, 29, 30, and 31 March 1909, 3 and 5 April 1909, ADP, emphasis in original; Walsh to O'Connell, undated draft [April 1909], ibid.; O'Toole, *Militant and Triumphant*, 54–55.

2. Diary of Walsh, 22 October 1909, and 1 June 1910, ADP; Walsh to O'Connell, undated [summer 1910], copy, ADP, Walsh papers; O'Toole, *Militant and Triumphant*, 54–55.

3. O'Toole, *Militant and Triumphant*, 95–96; Lord, Sexton, and Harrington, *Archdiocese of Boston*, 3:558–61.

4. O'Connell, *Sermons and Addresses*, 4:39–50; Boston *Pilot* 10 February 1912.

5. [M. J. Dwyer], *Charge of the Gold Brigade*, enclosure with Anonymous clergyman to Bonzano, undated [March-April 1912], ASV, DAUS, IX, Boston 71; Anonymous to Reverend and dear Father, 17 March 1912, ADP, Walsh papers (copy in ASV, DAUS, IX, Boston, 71); *Boston Globe*, February 1912, clipping in ADP, Walsh papers.

6. In addition to the three mentioned above, two more are located in ASV, DAUS, IX, Boston 71.

7. Untitled verse by S.P.H., [1912], ASV, DAUS, IX, Boston 71.

8. Anonymous clergyman to Bonzano, undated [March-April 1912], ASV, DAUS, IX, Boston 71; Quidam Sacerdos [a certain priest] to O'Connell, undated [circa 23 March 1912], copy, AASMSU, RG 9, box 6.

9. Quoted in Ireland to Walsh, 12 June 1914, AASMSU, RG 9, box 6.

10. Walsh, untitled notes [1914], AASMSU, RG 27, box 2.

11. O'Toole, *Militant and Triumphant*, 92–93.

12. Anonymous to Reverend and dear Father, 17 March 1912, copy, ADP, Walsh papers. See also a copy enclosed from an anonymous clergyman to Bonzano, 15 August 1912, ASV, DAUS, IX, Boston 71.

13. Anonymous to Reverend and dear Father, 17 March 1912, copy, ADP, Walsh papers.

14. Mullen to Bonzano, 12 June 1919, ASV, DAUS, IX, Boston 94; William Wolkovich-Valkavicius, "Cardinal and Cleric: O'Connell and Mullen in Conflict," *Historical Journal of Massachusetts* 13 (June 1985):129–33.

15. Anonymous to Reverend and dear Father, 17 March 1912, copy, ADP, Walsh papers; Mullen to Bonzano, 12 June 1919, copy, AASMSU, RG 9, box 6; O'Connell, *Sermons and Addresses*, 3:172 (this is decree thirteen of the 1909 archdiocesan synod establishing cathedraticum); Robert E. Sullivan, "Beneficial Relations: Toward a Social History of the Diocesan Priests of Boston, 1875–1944," in Robert E. Sullivan and James M. O'Toole, eds., *Catholic Boston: Studies in Religion and Community 1870–1970*, (Boston: Roman Catholic Archdiocese of Boston, 1985), 232. In 1912 the cathedraticum of New York was $12,500, equivalent to about $244,000 in 2006 (Cathedraticum Account: Chancery Office, AANY, O–2).

16. Anonymous to Reverend and dear Father, 17 March 1912, copy, ADP, Walsh papers; Mullen to Bonzano, 12 June 1919, ASV, DAUS, IX, Boston 94 (copy in AASMSU, RG 9, box 6, under the incorrect date of March 1919); O'Connell, *Sermons and Addresses*, 3:172 (this is decree thirteen of the 1909 archdiocesan synod, establishing the financial rights of pastors); O'Toole, *Militant and Triumphant*, 219, 220–21; Sullivan, "Beneficial Relations," 227–28; Lord, Sexton, and Harrington, *Archdiocese of Boston*, 3:681.

17. Mullen to Bonzano, 26 April 1919, ASV, DAUS, IX, Boston 94; Mullen to Bonzano, 12 June 1919, ibid. (copy in AASMSU, RG 9, box 6, under the incorrect date of March 1919); Mullen to Cerretti, [April 1920], enclosure with Mullen to Bonzano, 23 April 1920, ASV, DAUS,

IX, Boston 94 (copy in AASMSU, RG 9, box 6, under the cover letter Gillis to Walsh, 14 November 1920); *The Official Catholic Directory, 1910–1919* (New York, 1910–1919); Iustiniani Seredi, ed., *Codicis Juris Canonici Fontes*, 9 vols. (Vatican, 1935), 7:181.

18. Anonymous to Reverend and dear Father, 17 March 1912, ADP, Walsh papers; Mullen to Bonzano, 12 December 1914, ASV, DAUS, IX, Boston 71; Michael Doody to Bonzano, 10 June 1919, ibid, Boston 94; Mullen to Bonzano, 12 June 1919, ibid. (copy in AASMSU, RG 9, box 6); Mullen to Cerretti, [April 1920], enclosure with Mullen to Bonzano, 23 April 1920, ibid.; O'Connell, *Sermons and Addresses*, 3:173 (decree sixteen of the 1909 archdiocesan synod, mandating that all insurance be taken out through the chancery). See also James A. Walsh to Bonzano, 9 June 1919, ASV, DAUS, IX, Boston 94.

19. O'Connell, *Recollections*, 295; Anonymous to Reverend and dear Father, 17 March 1912, copy, ADP, Walsh papers; Mullen to Bonzano, 12 June 1919, ASV, DAUS, IX, Boston 94 (copy, AASMSU, RG 9, box 6); Mullen to Cerretti, [April 1920], enclosure with Mullen to Bonzano, 23 April 1920, ibid.; [Mullen], untitled brief, undated [December 1923 or January 1924], copy, AASMSU, RG 9, box 6; O'Toole, *Militant and Triumphant*, 83–84; Merwick, *Boston Priests*, 189–90; William E. Leuchtenburg, *The Perils of Prosperity, 1914–1932* (Chicago: University of Chicago Press, 1958), 70–71, 75.

20. Anonymous to Reverend and dear Father, 17 March 1912, copy, ADP, Walsh papers; Mullen to Cerretti, [23 April 1920], ASV, DAUS, IX, Boston 94; James A. Walsh to Bonzano, 9 June 1919, ibid.

21. Anonymous clergyman to Bonzano, undated [March-April 1912], emphasis in original, ASV, DAUS, IX, Boston 71.

22. Mullen to Bonzano, 12 June 1919, ASV, DAUS, IX, Boston 94; O'Toole, *Militant and Triumphant*, 85–56; James M. O'Toole, "Militant and Triumphant: William Henry O'Connell and Boston Catholicism, 1859–1944 (Boston College: unpublished doctoral dissertation, 1987), 126.

23. O'Toole, *Militant and Triumphant*, 180.

24. Mullen to Bonzano, 12 June 1919, ASV, DAUS, IX, Boston 94. See also O'Toole, *Militant and Triumphant*, 86.

25. Quoted in "A Petition with a Lesson," *Fortnightly Review* 31 (1 February 1924): 47; O'Toole, "Militant and Triumphant," 237–38. I have used O'Toole's doctoral dissertation here because it goes into more detail about the Keith inheritance than does his book.

26. An untitled, unsigned brief by Mullen, undated [December 1923 or early January 1924], AASMSU, RG 9, box 6; O'Toole, "Militant and Triumphant: William Henry O'Connell and Boston Catholicis, 1859–1944," (Boston College: unpublished doctoral dissertation, 1987), 237–38; Internal evidence clearly indicates that the untitled brief is from Mullen to Walsh. I have used O'Toole's doctoral dissertation here because it goes into more detail about the Keith inheritance than does his book.

27. "A Petition with a Lesson," 47–48; Mullen to Walsh, 20 December 1923, AASMSU, RG 9, box 6; Mullen to Walsh, 4 January 1924, ibid. At the expense of Patrick H. Callahan, a prominent layman, the *Fortnightly* was sent gratis to every Catholic bishop, newspaper, and institution in the country (Patrick Henry Callahan to Kenkel, 5 March 1925, AUND, Kenkel Papers, part 1, box 25).

28. Commonwealth of Massachusetts, Probate Court, Trustee's Inventory, A. Paul Keith, No. 184,536, 13 December 1923, copy, AASMSU, RG 9, box 6; O'Toole, "Militant and Triumphant," 238–41.

29. Wayman, *Cardinal O'Connell*, 191–95; O'Toole, *Militant and Triumphant*, 210–11, 221;

Lord, Sexton, and Harrington, *Archdiocese of Boston*, 3:560–66.

30. Walsh to Bonzano, 5 June 1914, with enclosure: Terna of the Consultors & Rectors, ASV, DAUS, IV, Liste Episcopali 73 (copy in AASMSU, RG 9, box 6).

31. Bonzano to Walsh, 13 June 1914, AASMSU, RG 9, box 6.

32. O'Connell to Harkins, 19 September 1912, ADP, Walsh papers; Harkins to O'Connell, 21 September 1912, copy, ibid.

33. O'Connell to Walsh, 31 October 1912, ADP, Walsh papers; Walsh to O'Connell, undated [November 1912], copy, AASMSU, RG 9, box 6. There is an earlier draft of the latter in ADP, Walsh papers.

CHAPTER 5

1. Ray Allen Billington, *The Protestant Crusade, 1800–1860: A Study of the Origins of American Nativism* (New York: Rinehart and Company, 1952), 53–108, 361–67; Tyler Anbinder, *Nativism and Slavery: The Northern Know Nothings and the Politics of the 1850s* (New York and Oxford: Oxford University Press, 1992), 115; David Potter, *The Impending Crisis, 1848–1861* (New York: Harper Colophon, 1976), 251–52; John Higham, *Strangers in the Land: Patterns of American Nativism, 1860–1925* (New York: Atheneum, 11975), 178–84; Gustavus Myers. *History of Bigotry in the United States*, ed. and rev. by Henry M. Christman (New York: Capricorn Books, 1960), 84–103, 192–99, 211–13.

2. *Menace*, 28 June 1913, 23 August 1913, 20 September 1913, 4 October 1913, 14 February 1914, and 20 June 1914; Higham, *Strangers in the Land*, 178–82; Myers, *History of Bigotry*, 192–99, 211–13.

3. *Menace*, 27 September 1913 and 4 October 1913; *New York Times*, 7 September 1913, 11:3; 15 September 1913, 1:8, 2:1; 16 September 1913, 1:8, 2:1; 17 September 1913, 2:3; 21 September 1913, II, 1:3; 23 September 1913, 5:3.

4. Cardinal Pietro Gasparri, Vatican secretary of state, to O'Connell, 22 April 1921, copy, AASMSU, RG 9, box 6 (this letter contains the information about the expulsion); William O'Connell to James E. O'Connell (editor of the *Boston Globe*), 4 March 1902, copy, ADP, O'Connell letter book (this letter states that the nephew was studying for Portland); Henry J. Brann, *History of the American College of the Roman Catholic Church of the United States* (New York: Benziger Brothers, 1910) 565; McNamara, *American College*, 835; Mullen to Cerretti, [April 1920], enclosure with Mullen to Bonzano, 23 April 1920, ASV, DAUS, IX, Boston 94; O'Toole, *Militant and Triumphant*, 176–78.

5. Episcopal Register, 1889–1907, p. 365, AAB; Register of Baptisms, Sacred Heart Parish, Lowell, Massachusetts, 1884–1900, p. 7, AAB; Mullen to Bonzano, 12 December 1914, ASV, DAUS, IX, Boston 71; Mullen to Cerretti, [April 1920], enclosure with Mullen to Bonzano, 23 April 1920, ibid., Boston 94 (the quotation is from here); O'Toole, *Militant and Triumphant*, 178–80.

6. Dyer to Harkins, 26 April 1909; Dyer to Walsh, 27 April 1909—both in ADP, Walsh Papers.

7. Mullen to Cerretti, [April 1920], enclosure of Mullen to Bonzano, 23 April 1920, ASV, DAUS, IX, Boston 94; O'Toole, *Militant and Triumphant*, 185.

8. O'Toole, *Militant and Triumphant*, 184.

9. Mullen to Bonzano, 6 December 1918, ASV, DAUS, IX, Boston 93.

10. Beaven to Falconio, 28 April 1913, copy, AASMSU, RG 9, box 6; Mullen to Cerretti, [April 1920], enclosure of Mullen to Bonzano, 23 April 1920, ASV, DAUS, IX, Boston 94; clip-

ping from the *Boston Globe*, [March 1913], ADP, Walsh Papers; Copy of letter sent to one of the Bishops of New England, attached to the clipping, undated, ADP, Walsh Papers; O'Toole, *Militant and Triumphant*, 185.

11. Copy of letter sent to one of the Bishops of New England, attached to the clipping, undated, ADP, Walsh Papers; Beaven to Falconio, 28 April 1913, copy, AASMSU, RG 9, box 6.

12. Beaven to Falconio, 28 April 1913, copy, AASMSU, RG 9, box 6.

13. *Menace*, 27 December 1913.

14. Walsh to Harkins, 14 February 1914, AASMSU, RG 27, box 2.

15. Quoted in Ireland to Walsh, 12 June 1914, AASMSU, RG 9, box 6.

16. [Benigni, Jonckx, and Speiser], Notes en Vue du Prochain Conclave, 27 août 1913, in Poulat, *Intégrisme et catholicisme intégral*, 330. The French original is as follows: ami d'enfance de Merry del Val, s'est imposé celui-ci, fait le romain, représente le romanisme en Amérique, très louche, arriviste par l'argent. The three were better disposed to four of O'Connell's supporters. They described Merry del Val as "The Terror!" (of the Modernists); Cardinal Gaetano De Lai as "Ours!"; Cardinal Willem Van Rossum as "Good, with us"; and Cardinal Basilio Pompili as "Very good, with us."

17. Gabriel Adriányi et al., *The Church in the Modern Age*, trans. by Anselm Biggs, Vol. 10 of *The History of the Church*, ed. by Hubert Jedin et al. (New York: Crossroad, 1981) 21–23; Walter Peters, *The Life of Benedict XV* (Milwaukee: The Bruce Publishing Company, 1959), 1–58, 102–110.

18. Mullen to Cerretti, [April 1920], enclosure with Mullen to Bonzano, 23 April 1920, ASV, DAUS, IX, Boston 94; Photocopy of marriage license, enclosure with Mullen to Bonzano, 17 December 1919, ibid; Bonzano to Gasparri, 7 April 1920, copy, ibid; An untitled, unsigned brief by Mullen, undated [December 1923 or early January 1924], AASMSU, RG 9, box 6; Office of the Surveyor of Customs, N.Y., N.Y., 30 August 1913, Hearing in the declaration and Baggage of D. Foss[a], accompanied by Mr. & Mrs. James Roe, first cabin passengers ex S.S. Lusitania, arrival of 29 August 1913, copy, ASV, DAUS, IX, Boston 94; O'Toole, *Militant and Triumphant*, 181–82.

19. Deposition of Florence Marlow, 20 March 1919, ASV, DAUS, IX, Boston 94; Memoradum of Doody, undated [March 1919], ibid.

20. Doody to Bonzano, 10 June 1919, ASV, DAUS, IX, Boston 94.

21. Mullen to Bonzano, 14 March 1919, ASV, DAUS, IX, Boston 94; Mullen to Cerretti, [April 1920], enclosure with Mullen to Bonzano, 23 April 1920, ibid.; Deposition of Florence Marlow, 20 March 1919, ibid.; Memorandum of Doody, undated [March 1919], ibid.; O'Toole, *Militant and Triumphant*, 185–86. O'Toole indicates that Florence did not know her husband was a priest until their marriage ended in 1918. However, both Doody and Bonzano, who conducted the investigation, stated that she lived with Toomey for some years after learning he was priest (Bonzano to Pietro Gasparri, 16 January 1921, ibid.).

22. Deposition of Florence Marlow, 20 March 1919, ASV, DAUS, IX, Boston 94. Mullen twice indicated that in 1916 or 1917, after O'Connell had moved to his new home on Rawson Road, he received an anonymous telegram informing him of the two marriages and the two ménages in New York City (Mullen to Bonzano, 14 March 1919, ibid.; Mullen to Cerretti, undated [April 1920], enclosure with Mullen to Bonzano, 23 April 1920, ibid.).

23. Statement of Joseph Pelletier, undated [1919], ASV, DAUS, IXBoston 94; Deposition of Joseph Pelletier, 26 April 1921, copy, AASMSU, RG 9, box 6.

24. Mullen to Bonzano, 6 December 1918, ASV, DAUS, IX, Boston 93; Mullen to Bonzano, 14 March 1919, ibid., Boston 94; Mullen to Cerretti, [April 1920], enclosure with Mullen to

Bonzano, 23 April 1920, ibid.; Deposition of Florence Marlow, 20 March 1919, ibid.; Bonzano to Gasparri, 16 January 1921, ibid. The first quotation is from the deposition; the next three are from Mullen to Cerretti.

25. Mullen to Bonzano, 14 March 1919, ASV, DAUS, IX, Boston 94; Mullen to Cerretti, [April 1920] (the second quotation is from here), enclosure with Mullen to Bonzano, 23 April 1920, ibid.; Mullen to Bonzano, 12 June 1919, ibid.; Mullen to Bonzano, 27 December 1920, ibid. (the first and third quotations are from here).

26. John J. Dunn to Bonzano, 25 March 1919, ASV, DAUS, IX, Boston 94; Dunn to Bonzano, 15 April 1919, ibid. O'Toole mistakenly values the property at $32,000 (*Militant and Triumphant*, 182).

27. Dunn to Bonzano, 20 April 1919, ASV, DAUS, IX, Boston 94; [Untitled Report of the Assistant District Attorney of New York], undated (April or May 1919), ibid. This report is in English. The archive also contains an Italian translation entitled *Raporto del Sostituto Procuratore Fiscale del Distretto di New York.*

28. Dunn to Bonzano, 20 April 1919, ASV, DAUS, IX, Boston 94; [Report of the Assistant District Attorney], undated (April or May 1919)], ibid.; Statement of Pelletier, undated [April 1919], ibid.

29. Deposition of Joseph C. Pelletier, 26 April 1921, copy, AASMSU, RG 9, box 6; Bonzano to Gasparri, 15 April 1920, copy, ASV, DAUS, IX, Boston 94 (the quotations are from here, wherein Bonzano recounts his recent interview with Pelletier).

30. Mullen to Bonzano, 15 May 1919, ASV, DAUS, IX, Boston 94.

31. James A. Walsh to Bonzano, 9 June 1919, ASV, DAUS, IX, Boston 94. Walsh had indeed seen a holograph of Supple's letter. Compare the quotations contained in this item with Supple to Gotti, 17 April 1904, ibid., IV, Liste Episcopali 73.

32. Ibid.

33. Ibid. With regard to word getting back to O'Connell, John Tracy Ellis, who during his studies at Harvard lived with Father John Sexton, author of the cardinal's first biography, written in 1926 to celebrate the twenty-fifth anniversary of O'Connell's consecration as a bishop, recounts a story told by his host. At a gathering of priests where the cardinal was being criticized, Sexton commented, "But remember, the bird has brains." Some time later, Sexton had to see O'Connell on business. As he was taking his leave, the cardinal said, "I understand that 'the bird has brains.'" Ellis remarks, "It was an illustration of how directly stories got back to headquarters" (*Catholic Bishops*, 76).

34. Bonzano to Gasparri, 7 April 1920, ASV, DAUS, IX, Boston 94.

35. Bonzano to De Lai, 14 September 1919, copy, ASV, DAUS, IX, Boston 94. In spring of 1918, O'Connell had sent De Lai "a generous check" that the Roman cardinal had used for the support of numerous charitable works throughout his diocese (De Lai to O'Connell, 16 April 1918), AAB, 2, Correspondence, 4:10.

36. Doody to Bonzano, 21 April 1920, with enclosure (summary of interview with Toomey), ASV, DAUS, IX, Boston 94; Mullen to Bonzano, 21 November 1919, ibid.; Mullen to Cerretti, [April 1920], enclosure with Mullen to Bonzano, 23 April 1920, ibid. With regard to O'Connell's avoidance of saying mass, Father Thomas McCarthy, who was investigating the cardinal for Bonzano in 1923, reported that when O'Connell visited the novitiate of the Sisters of St. Joseph in Framingham, he sent their chaplain away and then failed to say mass for the nuns the next morning (McCarthy to Walsh, 11 March 1923, AASMSU, RG 9, box 6).

37. Mullen to Bonzano, 17 December 1919, ASV, DAUS, IX, Boston 94.; Mullen to Bonzano, 12 January 1920, with enclosures, ibid.; Bonzano to Gasparri, 7 April 1920, ibid.; *Pilot*, 10 April 1920.

38. Mullen to Cerretti, [April 1920] enclosure with Mullen to Bonzano, 23 April 1920, ASV, DAUS, IX, Boston 94.

39. Ibid.; Mullen to Cerretti, 22 August 1920, copy AASMSU, RG 9, box 6 (the quotation is from here); O'Connell, *Recollections*, 209–11; O'Toole, *Militant and Triumphant*, 191–92.

40. Mullen to Cerretti, [April 1920], enclosure with Mullen to Bonzano, 23 April 1920, ASV, DAUS, IX, Boston 94.

41. See Mullen to Bonzano, 15 May 1919, ASV, DAUS, IX, Boston 94.

42. Boston *Pilot*, 8 May 1920; Walsh, Meeting of the Bishops of Boston, 21 April 1921, copy, AASMSU, RG 9, box 6; Daniel Feehan to Walsh, undated [October 1921], AASMSU, RG 9, box 6; John Tracy Ellis, *Catholic Bishops: A Memoir* (Wilmington, Del.: Michael Glazier, Inc.), 73; O'Toole, *Militant and Triumphant*, 193. Feehan had followed O'Connell to Rome and reported the outcome of the cardinal's meeting with the pope.

43. Gasparri to Bonzano, 10 June 1920, ASV, DAUS, IX, Boston 94.

44. Bonzano to Doody, 9 September 1920, copy, ASV, DAUS, IX, Boston 94; Gasparri to Bonzano, 24 October 1920, ibid.; Mullen to Cerretti, 22 August 1920, AASMSU, RG 9, box 6.

45. Mullen to Bonzano, 27 December 1920, ASV, DAUS, IX, Boston 94.

46. O'Connell to Gasparri, 18 September 1920, copy, ASV, DAUS, IX, Boston 94.

47. Diary of Walsh, 11 May and 19 July 1920, ADP.

48. Harkins et al. to Benedict XV, 31 July 1920, copy, AASMSU, RG 9, box 6.

49. Walsh to Cerretti, October 1920, draft, AASMSU, RG 9, box 6.

50. Walsh to Cerretti, 11 December 1920, copy, AASMSU, RG 9, box 6.

51. Mullen to Cerretti, 22 August 1920, copy, AASMSU, RG 9, box 6; John Nilan to Walsh, 29 September 1921, AASMSU, RG 9, box 6.

52. An untitled, unsigned brief by Mullen, undated [December 1923 or early January 1924], AASMSU, RG 9, box 6.

53. Gasparri to Bonzano, 24 October 1920, ASV, DAUS, IX, Boston 94.

54. J. P. E. O'Connell to W. H. O'Connell, 8 November 1920, AAB, Priests' Correspondence file; *Boston Herald*, 30 November 1920; Mullen to Bonzano, 11 December 1920, ASV, DAUS, IX, Boston 94; Mullen to Bonzano, 14 February 1921, ibid.; O'Toole, *Militant and Triumphant*, 193. See also an untitled, unsigned brief by Mullen, undated [December 1923 or early January 1924], AASMSU, RG 9, box 6. Internal evidence clearly indicates that the document is from Mullen to Walsh.

55. Mullen to Bonzano, 27 December 1920, copy, AASMSU, RG 9, box 6.

56. Bonzano to Gasparri, 16 January 1921, copy, ASV, DAUS, IX, Boston 94; Bonzano to Gasparri, 14 February 1921, ibid.

57. Gasparri to W. H. O'Connell, 22 April 1921, copy, AASMSU, RG 9, box 6.

58. Walsh to [Rice], 12–22 May 1921, AASMSU, RG 9, box 6.

59. Gasparri to W. H. O'Connell, 22 April 1921, copy, AASMSU, RG 9, box 6.

60. Ibid.

61. O'Toole, *Militant and Triumphant*, 206–07.

62. Ibid., 187.

63. J. P. E. O'Connell to W. H. O'Connell, 1 July 1918, copy, AAB, Priests' Correspondence file; J. P. E. O'Connell to Henry Cunningham, 9 September 1918, copy, ibid.

64. Mullen to Cerretti, 18 April 1920, ASV, DAUS, IX, Boston 94; O'Toole, *Militant and Triumphant*, 179–80.

CHAPTER 6

1. O'Connell to John Glennon, 8 February 1917, AASL, RG 9, D–O'Connell; Minutes of the Board of the Archbishops, 18 April 1917, AASL, Rg 9, U.S.A. hierarchy; Ede, *Lay Crusade*, 57–357; Mary Adele Francis Gorman, "Federation of Catholic Societies in the United States, 1870–1920" (University of Notre Dame, unpublished doctoral dissertation, 1962), 74–274; O'Leary, "Cardinal O'Connell," 127–28; Douglas J. Slawson, *The Foundation and First Decade of the National Catholic Welfare Council* (Washington, D.C.: The Catholic University of America Press, 1992), 12–13 (hereinafter cited as *NCWC*); Lynn Dumenil, *The Modern Temper: American Culture and Society in the 1920s* (New York: Hill and Wang, 1995), 40–55.

2. Peter Muldoon, Diary, 20 February 1919, ACUA, microfilm; William Russell, draft of James Gibbons to the hierarchy, 1 May 1919, AASMSU, RG 10, box 23; Louis Walsh to Russell, 7 February 1922, ADCh, 111–R6; *Report of the General Committee on Catholic Affairs and Interests Presented to the Catholic Hierarchy of America Assembled at The Catholic University, Washington, D.C., September 24, 1919, His Eminence, Cardinal Gibbons, Presiding* (n.p.: 1919); Slawson, *NCWC*, 45–57; Elizabeth McKeown, *War and Welfare: American Catholics and World War 1* (New York: Garland, 1988), 1–88; McKeown, "The National Bishops' Conference: An Analysis of Its Origins," *Catholic Historical Review*, 66 (October, 1980): 565–83; Michael Williams, *American Catholics in the War: National Catholic War Council, 1917–1921* (New York: Macmillan, 1921), 1–156. The quotation of Cerretti is found in the first four items cited above.

3. Slawson, *NCWC*, 57–83; McKeown, *War and Welfare*, Chapter V; McKeown, "The National Bishops' Conference," 565–83.

4. Slawson, *NCWC*, 57–83.

5. Quoted in *Minutes of the First Annual Meeting of the Hierarchy, September 1919*, 7–8, ACUA, NCWC General Secretary files; Slawson, *NCWC*, 47–57, 64–67, 123–24.

6. Slawson, *NCWC*, 64–67, 123–24; Kauffman, *Tradition and Transformation*, 258.

7. Thomas W. Spalding, *Premier See: A History of the Archdiocese of Baltimore, 1789–1989* (Baltimore: Johns Hopkins University Press, 1989), 157–58.

8. Slawson, *NCWC*, 93, 123–25.

9. Walsh to Bonzano, 17 November 1921, copy, AASMSU, RG 9, box 6. This letter rehearses the events leading up to the chairmanship debacle.

10. Walsh, Meeting of the Bishops of Boston, 21 April 1921, copy, AASMSU, RG 9, box 6; Nilan to Walsh, 29 September 1921, ibid.; Hickey to Walsh, 3 October 1921, ibid.; Feehan to Walsh, undated, ibid. Walsh's minutes and the three letters recount what transpired at the meeting. All four accounts are substantially the same, with some particulars individual to each. This and the following paragraphs attempt a reconstruction of the meeting based on these accounts.

11. Walsh, Meeting of the Bishops of Boston, 21 April 1921, copy, AASMSU, RG 9, box 6; Nilan to Walsh, 29 September 1921, ibid.; Hickey to Walsh, 3 October 1921, ibid.; Feehan to Walsh, undated, ibid.

12. Walsh, Meeting of the Bishops of Boston, 21 April 1921, copy, AASMSU, RG 9, box 6; Nilan to Walsh, 29 September 1921, ibid.; Hickey to Walsh, 3 October 1921, ibid.; Feehan to Walsh, undated, ibid.

13. Walsh, Meeting of the Bishops of Boston, 21 April 1921, copy, AASMSU, RG 9, box 6; Nilan to Walsh, 29 September 1921, ibid.; Hickey to Walsh, 3 October 1921, ibid.; Feehan to Walsh, undated, ibid.

14. Walsh to [Rice], 12–22 May 1921, AASMSU, RG 9, box 6; Bonzano to Gasparri, 25 Sep-

tember 1921, copy, ASV, DAUS, IX, Boston 104.

15. P. Charles Augustine, O.S.B., *A Commentary on the New Code of Canon Law*, 8 vols. (St. Louis: B. Herder Book Company, 1925–1936), 7:355–56, 380–84.

16. Walsh to [Rice], 12–22 May 1921, AASMSU, RG 9, box 6.

17. Deposition of Pelletier, 26 April 1921, copy, AASMSU, RG 9, box 6.

18. Walsh to [Rice], 12–22 May 1921, AASMSU, RG 9, box 6; Walsh to Bonzano, 17 November 1921, copy, ibid.

19. Walsh to [Rice], 12–22 May 1921, AASMSU, RG 9, box 6; Bonzano to Gasparri, 25 September 1921, copy, ASV, DAUS, IX, Boston 104; Walsh to Bonzano, 17 November 1921, copy, AASMSU, RG 9, box 6.

20. Diary of Walsh, 1 and 2 July 1921, ADP; Bonzano to Gasparri, 25 September 1921, copy, ASV, DAUS, IX, Boston 104; Walsh to Gasparri, 1 August 1921, copy, AASMSU, RG 9, box 6; Walsh to Bonzano, 17 November 1921, copy, AASMSU, RG 9, box 6.

21. Diary of Walsh, 24 and 27 July 1921, ADP; Walsh to Gasparri, 1 August 1921, copy, AASMSU, RG 9, box 6; Walsh to Bonzano, 17 November 1921, copy, AASMSU, RG 9, box 6.

22. Michael Curley to Walsh, 10 August 1921, AASMSU, RG 9, box 6.

23. Walsh to Benedict XV, 21August 1921, copy, AASMSU, RG 9, box 6. This letter bears two dates, 15 and 22 August, neither of which is correct.

24. Ibid.

25. Ibid.

26. Glennon to Walsh, 17 August 1921, AASMSU, RG 9, box 6.

27. Dowling to Walsh, 19 August 1921, AASMSU, RG 9, box 6. Dagon was the god of the Philistines. The Philistine lords and their idol were destroyed when Samson pulled down the temple.

28. Patrick Heffron of Winona to O'Connell, 26 September 1921, AAB, O'Connell Correspondence 7:1.

29. Schrembs to Walsh, 30 August 1921, AASMSU, RG 9, box 6.

30. Gasparri to Bonzano, 25 August 1921, ASV, DAUS, IX, Boston 104.

31. Bonzano to Gasparri, 9 September 1921, copy, ASV, DAUS, IX, Boston 104 (the second quotation is from here); Bonzano to Walsh, 4 September 1921, ibid.; Bonzano to Gasparri, 25 September 1921, copy, ibid. (the first quotation is from here).

32. Walsh to [Rice], 12–22 May 1921, AASMSU, RG 9, box 6

33. Diary of Walsh, 20 September 1921, ADP.

34. Bonzano to Gasparri, 25 September 1921, ASV, DAUS, IX, Boston 104 .

35. Diary of Walsh, 20 September 1921, ADP.

36. Bonzano to Gasparri, 25 September 1921, ASV, DAUS, IX, Boston 104.

37. Walsh to Bonzano, 30 November 1921, ASV, DAUS, IX, Boston 104.

38. "Annual Conference of the Hierarchy: Prelates Review Work of Welfare Council and Adopt Program for Coming Year," *NCWC Bulletin* 3 (October 1921): 2. With the exception of a single page, there are no minutes for this meeting, either published or in draft. Pertinent events have been reconstructed from other available sources. With regard to attendance, the *NCWC Bulletin* says that more than three score bishops were present (the number was probably somewhere in the low to mid sixties). The Directory of Divinity Hall (The Catholic University of America), September 1921 (ACUA, annual meeting of the hierarchy file) assigned rooms to forty-seven prelates. Five more can be accounted for by other sources, bringing the known total to fifty-two.

39. Diary of Walsh, 21 September 1921, ADP; Walsh to Bonzano, 30 November 1921, ASV,

DAUS, IX, Boston 104; Walsh to Gasparri, 30 November 1921, copy, AASMSU, RG 9, box 6.

40. Diary of Walsh, 21 September 1921, ADP; Walsh to O'Connell, 26 September 1921, draft, with enclosure; AASMSU, RG 9, box 6 (the first quote is from the enclosure; the third, fourth, and fifth quotes are from the draft); Feehan to Walsh, undated [October 1921], ibid. (the second quote is from here).

41. Diary of Walsh, 21 September 1921, ADP.

42. Busch to Hanna, 28 March 1922, AASF, NCWC papers; William Turner to Hanna, 5 May 1922, AASF, NCWC papers; W. H. O'Connell to Bonzano, 27 September 1921, copy, AAB, annual meeting of the hierarchy file; D. J. O'Connell to Walsh, 30 September 1921 and 8 October 1921, ADP, NCWC files; Slawson, *NCWC*, 100–06. A few prelates, like Joseph Busch of St. Cloud and William Turner of Buffalo, wanted to see the council restructured.

43. Diary of Walsh, 22 September 1921, ADP.

44. Ibid. Emphasis in original. The words "rule or ruin" are taken from Walsh's copy of the decree suppressing the NCWC. He had written on top: "Threat of Boston & Philadelphia now carried out—rule or ruin" (ADP, Walsh papers).

CHAPTER 7

1. Walsh to Bonzano, draft of a letter, September 1921, AASMSU, RG 9, box 6.

2. Walsh to Bonzano, 25 September 1921, ASV, DAUS, IX, Boston 104.

3. Patrick Heffron to Bonzano, 25 September 1921, ASV, DAUS, IX, Boston 104.

4. Heffron to O'Connell, 26 September 1921, AAB, O'Connell Correspondence 7:1.

5. O'Connell to Heffron, 1 October 1921, copy, AAB, O'Connell Correspondence 7:1.

6. Bonzano to Walsh, 4 October 1921, AASMSU, RG 9, box 6.

7. Walsh to Bonzano, draft of a letter, September 1921, AASMSU, RG 9, box 6.

8. Walsh to Bonzano, 30 November 1921, ASV, DAUS, IX, Boston 104.

9. O'Connell to Bonzano, 27 September 1921, ASV, DAUS, IX, Boston 104.

10. Bonzano to Gasparri, 25 September 1921, copy, ASV, DAUS, IX, Boston 104.

11. Walsh, Feehan, Rice, Nilan, and Hickey to O'Connell, November 1921, AASMSU, RG 9, box 6.

12. Walsh to Feehan, Rice, Nilan, and Hickey, 18 November 1921, copy, AASMSU, RG 9, box 6.

13. Archbishops and Bishops of the U.S. to Benedict XV, undated draft by Walsh, [probably November or December 1921], AASMSU, RG 9, box 6.

14. O'Connell to Merry del Val, undated [October 1921], copy, AAB, O'Connell Correspondence 7:10.

15. Merry del Val to O'Connell, 4 November 1921, AAB, O'Connell Correspondence 7:10.

16. Walsh to Gasparri, 30 November 1921, copy, AASMSU, RG 9, box 6.

17. Ibid.

18. Fenlon to Walsh, 29 September 1921, copy, AASMSU, RG 13, box 7; D. J. O'Connell to Walsh, 30 September 1921 and 8 October 1921, ADP, NCWC Papers; Minutes of the Administrative Committee, 27 January 1921, ACUA, NCWC General Secretary files.

19. Walsh to members of the administrative committee, 7 February 1922, with enclosure, The National Catholic Welfare Council, ADCh, 111–R6.

20. Muldoon to Walsh, 11 February 1922, ADP, NCWC Papers.

21. Michael Curley to Walsh, 23 February 1922, ADP, NCWC Papers.

22. Russell to Walsh, 28 February 1922, ADP, NCWC Papers.

23. Curley to Walsh, 23 February 1922, ADP, NCWC Papers.

24. Ibid.

25. O'Toole, *Militant and Triumphant,* 197.

26. Mullen to Walsh, 9 February 1922, AASMSU, RG 9, box 6.

27. Mullen to Walsh, 13 February 1922, AASMSU, RG 9, box 6. Neagle is quoted in this letter.

28. Peters, *Life of Benedict XV*, 268–74; Wayman, *Cardinal O'Connell*, 178–79.

29. Quoted in Christopher Kauffman, *Faith and Fraternalism: The History of the Knights of Columbus, 1882–1982* (New York: Harper and Row, 1982), 241–45; Francis Russel, "The Knave of Boston," *American Heritage* 27 (August 1976): 72–80; Leon Harris, *Only to God: The Extraordinary Life of Godfrey Lowell Cabot* (New York: Atheneum, 1967), 230–51.

30. O'Toole, *Militant and Triumphant*, 190; Mullen to Cerretti, [April 1920], enclosure with Mullen to Bonzano, 23 April 1920, ASV, DAUS, IX, Diocesi, Boston 94.

31. Diary of Walsh, 8 April 1922, ADP; Walsh to Curley, 9 April 1922, AASMSU, W271.1; Walsh to Muldoon, 11 April 1922, ACUA, NCWC General Secretary files; Kauffman, *Faith and Fraternalism,* 241–45.

32. Walsh to Muldoon, 27 May 1922, ACUA, NCWC General Secretary files.

33. Minutes of the Sixty-sixth Meeting of the Board of Trustees of The Catholic University of America, 20 September 1921, ACUA; Turner to O'Connell 6 April 1922, AAB, The Catholic University of America file; O'Connell to Gaetano Bisleti, 20 February 1922, copy, AASMSU, O250, also a copy in ACUA, Rector files; Los Angeles *Tidings*, 26 May 1922 (for copy of the decree); Blaise Dixon, T.O.R., "The Catholic University of America, 1909–1928: The Rectorship of Thomas Joseph Shahan" (Catholic University of America: unpublished doctoral dissertation, 1972), 212–14.

34. Thomas O'Neill, C.S.P., to Burke, 30 March 1922, ACUA, NCWC General Secretary files. Prelates in Rome at the time were O'Connell, Dougherty, Archbishop James Keane of Dubuque, and Bishop Thomas Walsh of Trenton.

35. Giovanni Genocchi to Hanna, 11 May 1922, AASF, NCWC file. The letter is in English.

36. Thomas O'Neill to Burke, 30 March 1922, ACUA, NCWC General Secretary files.

37. Muldoon to Burke, undated [14 July 1922], ACUA, NCWC General Secretary files. As a matter of fact, the archives of the Boston chancery contain an original of the decree of suppression, typed on Consistorial stationery and signed in ink by Cardinal Gaetano de Lai (AAB, Roman Congregations' correspondence: Consistorial). This is the only original of the decree the author has ever seen; all others are printed versions.

38. Muldoon to Schrembs, 30 April 1922, ADCl, Schrembs papers; Schrembs to Muldoon, 9 May 1922, ACUA, NCWC General Secretary files; J. H. Ryan to Burke, [25 May 1922], ibid. The latter two, sent from Paris and Rome, embody what Cerretti, then nuncio to France, knew about the suppression.

39. S. Congregatio Consistorialis, Decretum de Episcopalibus Conventibus in Foederatis Americae Septentionalis Statibus, 25 Februarii 1922, ACUA, NCWC General Secretary files.

40. Ibid.

41. Bonzano to hierarchy, 22 March 1922, with enclosure, AASF, NCWC file.

42. Muldoon, Diary, 25 March 1922, copy, ACUA, microfilm.

43. Walsh, Diary, 25 March 1922, emphasis in original, ADP.

44. Walsh to Bonzano, 25 March 1922, draft (never sent), ADP, NCWC papers.

45. Dowling to James H. Ryan, 27 March 1922, ACUA, NCWC General Secretary files.

46. Dowling to Muldoon, 27 March 1922, ACUA, NCWC General Secretary files. He had

similar words for Russell: "I think something should be done by the bishops to show their resentment of the imputation of schism which this Decree contains. It is not so unexpected as we say for we were without Roman representation & exposed to the slanders of the first comer" (Dowling to Russell, 27 March 1922, ADCh, 111–T5).

47. Hanna to Muldoon, 28 March 1922, copy, AASF, NCWC files.

48. Bernard Wall, *Report on the Vatican* (London: Weidenfeld and Nicolson, 1956), 60; Zsolt Aradi, *Pius XI: The Pope and the Man* (New York: Hanover House, 1958), 127; Thomas Morgan, *A Reporter at the Papal Court: A Narrative of the Reign of Pius XI* (New York: Longmans, Green and Co., 1937), 33–35; Robin Anderson, *Between Two Wars: The Story of Pope Pius XI (Achille Ratti, 1922–1939)* (Chicago: Franciscan Herald Press, 1977), 56–58.

49. Ryan to John Burke, Sunday, 11 [June 1922], ACUA, NCWC General Secretary files; Slawson, *NCWC*, chpt. 7.

50. Bonzano to O'Connell, 4 May 1922, AAB, O'Connell Correspondence; Bonzano to Dougherty, 4 May 1922, AAP, Dougherty Papers.

51. Quoted in Fogarty, *American Hierarchy*, 222.

52. O'Connell to De Lai, 10 May 1922, copy, emphasis in original, AAB, O'Connell Correspondence. Quoted in full in Fogarty, *American Hierarchy*, 222–23.

53. O'Connell to Merry del Val, 10 May 1922, copy, AAB, O'Connell Correspondence.

54. Ryan to Burke, 13 June [1922], ACUA, NCWC General Secretary files.

55. Slawson, *NCWC*, chpt. 7.

56. Schrembs to Gasparri, 24 June 1922, copy, ADCl, Schrembs papers; J. H. Ryan to Burke, 23 June 1922, ACUA, NCWC, General Secretary files; Instructiones S. Congregationis Consistorialis Circa Conventum Episcoporum Statuum Foederatorum Americae Septentrionalis mense Septembri A. 1922 Habendum, 4 July 1922, copy, ACUA, NCWC General Secretary files. Schrembs wrote Gasparri's instructions on the copy of his letter. Ryan summarized them in his.

CHAPTER 8

1. Bonzano to O'Connell, 1 August 1922, AAB, O'Connell Correspondence.

2. O'Connell to Bonzano, 5 August 1922, AAB, O'Connell Correspondence; Fogarty, *American Hierarchy*, 225. Two years later De Lai told Walsh that the NCWC was suppressed because there was a danger that it would exceed proper limits. It was thought best to cut short the whole thing and start over with guidelines (Walsh, Diary, 27 February 1924, ADP).

3. Gasparri to O'Connell, 16 July 1922, AAB, Roman Congregations Correspondence: Secretary of State; Pius XI to Gasparri, 28 June 1922, *Civilta Cattolica*, 1922, vol. 3, 170–71.

4. De Lai to O'Connell, 24 July 1922, AAB, O'Connell Correspondence 4:10.

5. O'Connell to De Lai, 11 August 1922, AAB, O'Connell Correspondence 4:10.

6. De Lai to O'Connell, 30 August 1922, AAB, O'Connell Correspondence 4:10.

7. Walsh, notes for 1922 meeting of the administrative committee and of hierarchy, ADP, NCWC Papers. The above elements were things Walsh would fight for. Others were more speculative. For example, he thought that the general secretary should be a bishop. In addition, the chairman of the administrative committee and several of its members ought to live near Washington to make it convenient to hold emergency meetings and to control lay department heads. Although these last ideas were enlightened, it does not seem he ever made them as suggestions.

8. Minutes of the administrative committee, 11 and 12 August 1922, ACUA, NCWC General Secretary files.

9. O'Connell to Hanna, 1 September 1922, copy, AAB, NCWC file, 1922.

10. O'Connell, Memorandum for Bishops' Meeting [1922], copy, AAB, Annual Meeting of Hierarchy file.

11. Diary of Walsh, 26 September 1922, ADP.

12. *Minutes of the Hierarchy, 1922*, 3–4, ACUA, NCWC General Secretary files.

13. Diary of Walsh, 27 September 1922, ADP; *Minutes of the Hierarchy, 1922*, 5–6, ACUA, NCWC General Secretary files.

14. Walsh to Curley, 2 October 1922, AASMSU, W272.

15. *Minutes of the Hierarchy, 1922*, 6, ACUA, NCWC General Secretary files.

16. Diary of Walsh, 28 September 1922, emphasis in original, ADP.

17. *Minutes of the Hierarchy, 1922*, 6–7, ACUA, NCWC General Secretary files.

18. Walsh to Curley, 2 October 1922, AASMSU, W272.

19. Dowling to Burke, 2 October 1922; Muldoon to Burke, undated [October 1922]—both in ACUA, NCWC General Secretary files.

20. Walsh to Curley, 2 October 1922, AASMSU, W272.

21. Curley to Walsh, 6 October 1922, AASMSU, RG 9, box 6; copy in AASMSU, W273.

22. Ibid.

23. Ibid.; Diary of Walsh, 17 November 1922, ADP.

24. Diary of Walsh, 5 January 1923, ADP; Thomas McCarthy to Walsh, 11 March 1923, AASMSU, RG 9, box 6; McCarthy to Walsh, 20 December 1923, AASMSU, RG 9, box 6.

25. McCarthy to Walsh, 12 August 1923, AASMSU, RG 9, box 6.

26. Fogarty, *American Hierarchy*, 225–26.

27. O'Connell to Dougherty, 13 December 1922, AAP, Dougherty Papers.

28. Dougherty to O'Connell, 15 December 1922, AAB, Annual Meeting of the Hierarchy file.

29. Slawson, *NCWC*, 206–07.

30. O'Connell to Hanna, 16 December 1922, copy, ACUA, NCWC General Secretary files.

31. Fogarty, *American Hierarchy*, 226.

32. Minutes of the administrative committee, 12 January 1923, ACUA, NCWC General Secretary files.

33. Ibid.; Diary of Walsh, 12 January 1923, ADP; Walsh to Curley, 5 February 1923, AASMSU, W273; Canon 250, no. 4, *Codex Juris Canonici* (Rome: Typis Polyglottis Vaticanis, 1919).

34. O'Connell to Hanna, 6 January 1923, AASF, NCWC files. O'Connell quoted De Lai as follows: "It is the mind of the Holy Father and mine that in place of 'Council' the name of 'Committee' be adopted."

35. O'Connell to Hanna, 30 January 1923, AASF, NCWC files.

36. Hanna to O'Connell, 14 February 1923, copy, AASF, NCWC files.

37. Minutes of the administrative committee, 12 April 1923, ACUA, NCWC General Secretary files.

38. J. A. Walsh to Bonzano, 9 June 1919, ASV, DAUS, IX, Diocesi, Boston 94; O'Toole, *Militant and Triumphant*, 113–17, 206. Louis Walsh made a similar point: "He [O'Connell] never had any genuine courage and his whole career proves it" (Walsh to Bonzano, September 1921, draft, AASMSU, RG 9, box 6.

CHAPTER 9

1. [Dyer], untitled and undated memorandum on the discourse with O'Connell, Washington, [21 September 1920], AASMSU, RG 10, box 16; Kauffman, *Tradition and Transformation*, 246–47.

2. [Dyer], untitled and undated memorandum on the discourse with O'Connell, Washington, [21 September 1920], AASMSU, RG 10, box 16.

3. O'Toole, "Militant and Triumphant," 250–51; O'Toole, *Militant and Triumphant*, 215; O'Toole, "The Role of Bishops in American Catholic History: Myth and Reality in the Case of Cardinal William O'Connell," *Catholic Historical Review* 77 (October 1991): 609; Sullivan, "Beneficial Relations," 231.

4. Joseph Nevins to Dyer, 23 September 1923, AASMSU, RG 10, box 21. Running twelve pages, the letter is a blow by blow account of the interview.

5. Ibid.

6. Ibid.

7. Minutes of the administrative committee, 24 September 1923, ACUA, NCWC General Secretary files.

8. *Minutes of the Hierarchy, 1923*, 8, AAB, Annual meeting of the hierarchy file.

9. Ibid., 19–20, AAB, Annual meeting of the hierarchy file; Dolores Liptak, R.S.M., *Immigrants and Their Church* (New York: Macmillan, 1989), 139; Bohdan P. Procko, "Soter Ortynsky: First Ruthenian Bishop in the United States, 1907–1916," *Catholic Historical Review* 58 (January 1973): 513–33.

10. Muldoon to Burke, 14 November 1923, ACUA, NCWC General Secretary files.

11. Diary of Walsh, 27 September 1923, ADP.

12. O'Connell to Fumasoni-Biondi, 1 October 1923, copy (emphasis in original), AAB, Annual meeting of the hierarchy file. The same event is recounted in O'Connell to Dougherty, 2 October 1923, AAP, Dougherty Papers.

13. O'Connell to Fumasoni-Biondi, 1 October 1923, copy, AAB, Annual meeting of the hierarchy file.

14. Ibid. Emphasis in original.

15. Ibid.

16. O'Connell to Dougherty, 2 October 1923, AAP, Dougherty Papers.

17. Ibid.

18. Dougherty to O'Connell, 6 October 1923, copy, AAP, Dougherty Papers.

19. Walsh to Feehan, Rice, Nilan, and Hickey, 2 December 1921, copy, AASMSU, RG 9, box 6.

20. Minutes of the administrative committee, 28 September 1923, ACUA, NCWC General Secretary files; Hanna to Samuel Stritch, 6 October 1923, copy, AASF, NCWC files; Fogarty, *American Hierarchy*, 228.

21. Quoted in Fogarty, *American Hierarchy*, 228.

22. O'Connell to Dougherty, 17 October 1923, emphasis in original, AAP, Dougherty Papers.

23. Hanna to Burke, 2 November 1923, ACUA, NCWC General Secretary files.

24. Mullen to Dyer, 8 January 1924, AASMSU, RG 9, box 6.

25. Suprema Sacra Congregatio S. Officii, Decretum: Damnatur Opus Cui Titulus "Manuel Biblique etc.," *Acta Apostolicae Sedis* 15 (31 December 1923): 615–19; Gerald P. Fogarty, *American Catholic Biblical Scholarship: A History from the Early Republic to Vatican II* (San Francisco: Harper and Row, 1989), 187.

26. De Lai to O'Connell, 25 December 1923, AAB, O'Connell Correspondence 4:10.

27. O'Connell to Merry del Val, 21 November 1923, copy, AAB, O'Connell Correspondence 7:10. For the Bonzano-O'Connell confrontation, see Curley to Walsh, 6 October 1922, copy, AASMSU, W273.

CHAPTER 10

1. Thomas McCarthy to Walsh, 20 December 1923, AASMSU, RG 9, box 6.

2. McCarthy to Walsh, 12 August 1923, AASMSU, RG 9, box 6.

3. Diary of Walsh, 12 December 1923, ADP.

4. An untitled, unsigned brief by Mullen, undated [December 1923 or early January 1924], AASMSU, RG 9, box 6. Internal evidence clearly indicates that the document is from Mullen to Walsh.

5. Ibid.; Mullen to Walsh, 6 January 1924, AASMSU, RG 9, box 6. For greater detail on many of the charges in this and the following paragraphs, see Mullen to Cerretti, [April 1920], enclosure with Mullen to Bonzano, 23 April 1920, ASV, DAUS, IX, Diocesi, Boston 94; Mullen to Bonzano, n.d. March 1919, copy, AASMSU, RG 9, box 6; McCarthy to Bonzano, 9 January 1923 [sic for 1924], AASMSU, RG 9, box 6.

6. An untitled, unsigned brief by Mullen, undated [December 1923 or early January 1924], AASMSU, RG 9, box 6. See also J. A. Walsh to Bonzano, 9 June 1919, ASV, DAUS, IX, Diocesi, Boston 94; Mullen to Cerretti, [April 1920], enclosure with Mullen to Bonzano, 23 April 1920, ibid.

7. An untitled, unsigned brief by Mullen, undated [December 1923 or early January 1924], AASMSU, RG 9, box 6.

8. McCarthy to Walsh, 9 January 1923 [sic for 1924], with enclosure, AASMSU, RG 9, box 6.

9. O'Connell to Merry del Val, 21 November 1923, copy, AAB, O'Connell Correspondence 7:10; Mullen to Walsh, 9 February 1924, with enclosure, AASMSU, RG 9 box 6; O'Toole, *Militant and Triumphant*, 198.

10. O'Connell to Fumasoni-Biondi, 21 December 1923, AAB, Apostolic Delegate Correspondence, 1923; Boston *Pilot*, 12 January 1924.

11. Boston *Pilot*, 12 January 1924; O'Connell to De Lai, 9 March 1923 and 16 April 1924, with enclosure, copies, AAB, O'Connell Correspondence 4:10; Wayman, *Cardinal O'Connell*, 200–02. For the attribution to Murphy, see Mullen to Walsh, 9 February 1924, with enclosure, AASMSU, RG 9, box 6.

12. O'Connell to Fumasoni-Biondi, 21 December 1923, AAB, Apostolic Delegate Correspondence, 1923; Mullen to Dyer, 8 January 1924, AASMSU, RG 9, box 6; Wolkovich-Valkavicius, "Cardinal and Cleric," 132 and 138 n. 17; Dowling to Burke, 7 February 1924, ACUA, NCWC General Secretary files. Dowling's remark appears later in this chapter.

13. McCarthy to Bonzano, 9 January 1923 [sic for 1924], copy, AASMSU, RG 9, box 6.

14. Mullen to Walsh, 9 February 1924, AASMSU, RG 9, box 6.

15. De Lai to O'Connell, 25 December 1923, AAB, O'Connell Correspondence 4:10.

16. O'Connell to De Lai, 16 April 1924, copy, with enclosure: list of payments for the *Passion*, AAB, O'Connell Correspondence 4:10.

17. Boston *Pilot*, 19 January 1924; O'Toole, "Militant and Triumphant," 313. Again, the dissertation contains information that was omitted from the published work.

18. *Boston Post*, 14 February 1924. On the automobile, see Mullen to Dear Monsignor, 15 February 1924, AASMSU, RG 9, box 6; Walsh, Diary, 23 February 1924, ADP.

19. London *Tablet*, 15 March 1924; Boston *Pilot*, 16 February 1924.

20. London *Tablet*, 15 March 1924; *Boston Post*, 15 February 1924.

21. London *Tablet,* 15 March 1924; *Boston Post*, 16 February 1924.

22. Mullen to Dear Monsignor, 15 February 1924, AASMSU, RG 9, box 6; Mullen to Walsh, 4 January 1924, ibid.

23. Walsh to Burke, 2 February 1924, ACUA, NCWC General Secretary files. Emphasis in original.

24. Diary of Walsh, 26 January 1924, ADP; Dowling to Burke, 7 February 1924, ACUA, NCWC General Secretary files.

25. Dowling to Walsh, 2 March 1924, AASMSU, RG 9, box 6.

26. Diary of Walsh, 18 February 1924, ADP, Emphasis in original.

27. O'Toole, "Militant and Triumphant," 221 (again, the dissertation is clearer on this point than the book).

28. Diary of Walsh, 21 February 1924, ADP.

29. Ibid. 23 and 24 February 1924.

30. Ibid., 25 February 1924.

31. Ibid., 27 February 1924. Emphasis in original.

32. Ibid., 28 February 1924. Emphasis in original, quoted in French.

33. Boston *Pilot*, 8 March 1924; O'Toole, *Militant and Triumphant*, 201.

34. Diary of Walsh, 11 March 1924, emphasis in original, ADP.

35. Walsh, Syllogism, 3 March 1924, emphasis in original, AASMSU, RG 9, box 6. This syllogism is attached to Walsh's later letter to Pius XI. The thirteen bishops named were John Williams, Denis Bradley, Matthew Harkins, Thomas Beaven, John Michaud, William Stang, John Brady, Louis Walsh, Daniel Feehan, Joseph Rice, John Nilan, William Hickey, and John Murray.

36. Diary of Walsh, 12 March 1924. Emphasis in original.

37. Walsh to Pius XI, undated [after 12 March 1924], copy, AASMSU, RG 9, box 6. Among the evidence that had disappeared was the Pelletier deposition and the letter from the suffragans in July 1920 petitioning Benedict XV to remove O'Connell (Diary of Walsh, 28 February 1924).

38. Walsh to Pius XI, undated [after 12 March 1924], copy, AASMSU, RG 9, box 6.

39. De Lai to O'Connell, St. William's day [25 June] 1924, AAB, O'Connell Correspondence 4:10.

40. Ibid.

41. Fumasoni-Biondi to Gasparri, 26 March 1925, copy, ASV, DAUS, IX, Diocesi, Boston 95. On the method of selecting bishops, see Fogarty, *American Hierarchy*, 208–09.

42. Fumasoni-Biondi to Gasparri, 26 March 1925, copy, ASV, DAUS, IV, Liste Episcopali 93.

43. Ibid.

44. Ibid.

CHAPTER 11

1. John A. Ryan, "Seek Amendment to Constitution on Child Labor," *NCWC News Service*, 26 June 1922; Francis L. Broderick, *Right Reverend New Dealer: John A. Ryan* (New York: Macmillan, 1963), 97–98, 126–27; Vincent McQuade, O.S.A., *The American Catholic Attitude on Child Labor Since 1891: A Study of the Formation and Development of a Catholic Attitude on a Specific Social Question* (Washington, D.C.: The Catholic University of America Press,

1938), 72–73.

2. Minutes of the administrative committee, 12 January 1923, ACUA, NCWC General Secretary files; Departmental Minutes, 18 January 1923, ACUA, NCWC General Secretary files.

3. Slawson, *NCWC*, 76–80; Douglas J. Slawson, "John J. Burke, C.S.P.: The Vision and Character of a Public Churchman," *Journal of Paulist Studies* 4 (1995–1996): 63–67.

4. Proceedings of the Third Annual Convention of the NCCW, Washington, 30 September to 3 October 1923, 538, 546–54, ACUA, NCWC NCCW files.

5. *New York Times*, 21 November 1923, 21; ibid., 24 December 1923, 21; Broderick, *New Dealer*, 128.

6. Quoted in McQuade, *Child Labor*, 79.

7. See Schrembs to Gertrude Gavin, 15 November 1924, copy, emphasis added, ADCl, Schrembs papers.

8. "Year's Labor Review Given by Social Action Department: Child Labor Amendment, Peace and Wages also Discussed in Weekly News Releases," *NCWC Bulletin* 6 (October 1924): 23. The Bishops' Program of Social Reconstruction (1919) had called for federal legislation against child labor. Since the Supreme Court had overturned each attempt at this, there was no recourse but to empower congress by constitutional amendment to enact such legislation. Hence, Ryan argued that the Program could be said to endorse an amendment. See "John A. Ryan and the Bishops' Program of Social Reconstruction" in Ellis, *Documents*, 585–603; Joseph McShane, *"Sufficiently Radical": Catholicism, Progressivism, and the Bishops' Program of 1919* (Washington, D.C.: The Catholic University of America Press, 1986).

9. Thomas R. Greene, "The Catholic Committee for the Ratification of the Child Labor Amendment, 1935–1937: Origin and Limits," *Catholic Historical Review* 74 (April 1988): 248-49; James M. O'Toole, "Prelates and Politicos: Catholics and Politics in Massachusetts, 1900–1970," in *Catholic Boston*, 29; McQuade, *Child Labor*, 74–78, 82–89. For O'Connell's view as it pertained to education, see O'Connell, "The Reasonable Limits of State Activity," *CEA Bulletin* 16 (November 1919): 62–66, also in *Catholic Educational Review* 17 (November 1919): 513–27.

10. Douglas J. Slawson, *The Department of Education Battle, 1918–1932: Public Schools, Catholic Schools, and the Social Order* (Notre Dame, Ind.: University of Notre Dame Press, 2005), chapters 1 through 5.

11. *Boston Herald*, 6 and 7 October 1924; *Christian Science Monitor*, 8 October 1924; *New Republic*, 29 October 1924; O'Toole, "Prelates and Politicos," 27–30; Wayman, *Cardinal O'Connell*, 220; McQuade, *Child Labor*, 97.

12. O'Toole, "Prelates and Politicos," 20–21; O'Leary, "O'Connell," 161–67.

13. *Boston Herald*, 8 October 1924.

14. *Christian Science Monitor*, 8 October 1924. For the Klan fight at the Democratic convention, see David M. Chalmers, *Hooded Americanism: The History of the Ku Klux Klan* (New York: New View Points, 1976), 202–12; Robert K Murray, *The 103rd Ballot: Democrats and the Disaster in Madison Square Garden* (New York: Harper & Row, 1976), 90, 104, 108–09.

15. *New Republic*, 29 October 1924.

16. Quoted in Gibbons to James Ryan, 23 October 1924, copy, ACUA, John A. Ryan Papers.

17. O'Connell to Schrembs, 14 October 1924, ADCl, Schrembs Papers.

18. Schrembs to O'Connell, 17 October 1924, copy, ADCl, Schrembs Papers; Schrembs to Muldoon, 17 October 1924, copy, ibid.; Schrembs to Burke, 17 October 1924, copy, ibid.

19. Schrembs to Gibbons, 28 October 1924, ADA, NCWC files.

20. John Ryan to Muldoon, 23 October 1924, copy, ACUA, John A. Ryan Papers.

21. Boston *Pilot*, 18 October 1924.

22. James Ryan to Gibbons, Sunday 1924, ADA, NCWC files.

23. James Ryan to Schrembs, 21 October 1924, copy, ACUA, NCWC J. H. Ryan Papers.

24. Burke to Schrembs, 22 October 1924, copy, ACUA, NCWC General Secretary files.

25. John Ryan to Muldoon, 23 October 1924, copy, ACUA, John A. Ryan Papers.

26. O'Connell to Curley, 24 October 1924, AASMSU, O276; copy in AAB, Catholic University files; Curley to O'Connell, 27 October 1924, AAB, Catholic University files; copy in AASMSU, O277.

27. Dowling to Hanna, 31 October 1924, AASF, NCWC files.

28. James Hennesey, *American Catholics: A History of the Roman Catholic Community in the United States* (New York: Oxford University Press, 1983), 233; Broderick, *New Dealer*, 157.

29. O'Connell to Curley, 2 November 1924, AASMSU, O278; copy in AAB, Catholic University files.

30. O'Connell to Muldoon, 3 November 1924, copy, ACUA, NCWC General Secretary files.

31. Curley to O'Connell, 10 November 1924, AAB, Catholic University files.

32. O'Connell to Curley, 12 November 1924, AASMSU, O281.

33. Burke to Hanna, 8 November 1924, with enclosure, AASF, NCWC files; Burke to Muldoon, 8 November 1924, copy, ACUA, NCWC General Secretary files.

34. Schrembs to Gavin, 15 November 1924, copy, ADCl, Schrembs Papers; see also Schrembs's copy of Slattery's motion and his ruling, handwritten on telegram paper in ADCl, Schrembs Papers.

35. Proceedings of the Fourth Annual Convention of the NCCW, 9 to 12 November 1924, 375–76, ACUA, NCWC NCCW files. For a less partisan assessment of the Catholic endeavor in defeating the amendment, see O'Toole, "Prelates and Politicos," 30–31.

36. Proceedings of the Fourth Annual Convention of the NCCW, 9 to 12 November 1924, 376–82, ACUA, NCWC NCCW files.

37. Ibid.

38. Ibid., 380–81.

39. Schrembs to Gavin, 15 November 1924, copy, ADCl, Schrembs Papers.

40. Gavin to Schrembs, 1 December 1924, ADCl, Schrembs Papers.

41. James Ryan, Memorandum on the Child Labor Amendment, 21 November 1924, copy, ACUA, NCWC General Secretary files; James Ryan to Burke, 9 December 1924, copy, ibid.

42. Fumasoni-Biondi to Gasparri, 26 March 1925, copy, ASV, DAUS, IV, Liste Episcopali, 93.

43. Ibid.

CHAPTER 12

1. Slawson, *Department of Education Battle*, 138–39, 143–46.

2. Ibid., 146–48.

3. *Minutes of the Hierarchy, 1925,* 8, ACUA, NCWC General Secretary files; Slawson, *Department of Education Battle*, 148; Slawson, *NCWC*, 250.

4. Minutes of the Administrative Committee, 17 September 1925, ACUA, NCWC General Secretary files; Slawson, *Department of Education Battle*, 148; Slawson, *NCWC*, 251.

5. Slawson, *Department of Education Battle*, 155–56; Slawson, *NCWC*, 251.

6. Wilfrid Parsons to Curley, 24 December 1925, AASMSU, P235; Slawson, *Department of Education Battle*, 156; Slawson, *NCWC*, 251.

7. Richard Haberlin to Burke, 28 December 1925, copy, AASF, NCWC files; Slawson, *Department of Education Battle*, 156.

8. "An Alarm and a Warning," *America* 34 (2 January 1926): 271; Slawson, *Department of*

Education Battle, 156–57.

    9. Slawson, *Department of Education Battle*, 158–60.

    10. *NCWC News Service*, 15 March 1926, extra; Slawson, *Department of Education Battle*, 160–68.

    11. Burke interview with O'Connell, 12 September 1926, ACUA, NCWC General Secretary files.

    12. Kenneth T. Jackson, *Ku Klux Klan in the City, 1915–1930* (New York: Oxford University Press, 1967), 226–28; Robert Alan Goldberg, "Hooded Empire: The Ku Klux Klan in Colorado, 1921–1932," (University of Wisconsin: unpublished doctoral dissertation, 1977), 118 and 131; Chalmers, *Hooded Americanism*, 127–29. In 1924, Phipps joined hands with the Klan to end a two-year power struggle for control of the Colorado Republican Party. He supplied the party with money, the Klan supplied him with votes.

    13. Burke interview with O'Connell, 12 September 1926, ACUA, NCWC General Secretary files.

    14. Ibid.

    15. Ibid.

    16. Ibid.

    17. Ibid.

    18. Muldoon to Burke, 17 November 1926, ACUA, NCWC General Secretary files.

    19. Quoted in O'Toole, "William O'Connell and Modern Episcopal Style," 178.

    20. O'Toole, *Militant and Triumphant*, 231; Slawson, *NCWC*, 286; "Decree on the Pastoral Office of Bishops in the Church," 28 October 1965, in Flannery, *Vatican Council II*, 586–88, 609–610.

    21. David H. McDonald to Fenlon, 23 April 1928, AASMSU, RG 9, box 6.

    22. O'Connell, *Sermons and Addresses*, 10:65.

    23. Gerald P. Fogarty, S.J., "Francis J. Spellman: American and Roman," in *Patterns of Episcopal Leadership* (New York: Macmillan, 1989), 217–18; O'Toole, *Militant and Triumphant*, 205.

    24. *New York* Times, 4 December 2003; Buffalo *News*, 5 December 2003; Boston *Pilot*, 5 December 2003; Boston *College Chronicle*, 29 April 2004; *Catholic News Agency*, 2 November 2005.

EPILOGUE

    1. O'Toole, "Militant and Triumphant," 278 n. 9. Again, the dissertation is more detailed than the published biography.

    2. Actually, the visit took place in 1904.

    3. O'Connell, *Recollections*, 128–29.

    4. Satolli to O'Connell, 12 April 1904, ADP, O'Connell Papers; MacNutt to O'Connell, 5 May 1904, ibid.; Savelli-Spinola to O'Connell, 26 May 1904, ibid.

    5. Satolli to O'Connell, 5 October 1904, ADP, O'Connell Papers; Finn, *Twenty-Four American Cardinals*, 277; Delaney, *Dictionary of American Catholic Biography*, 509–10; Ireland to Byrne, telegram, 12 July 1904, AASMSU, RG 9, box 6; Ireland to Byrne, telegram, 16 July 1904, ibid.; Ireland to Harkins, telegram, 16 July 1904, ibid.; *Boston Globe*, 23 and 26 July 1904; *Boston Journal*, 27 July 1904.

    6. Finn, *Twenty-Four American Cardinals*, 277; Delaney, *Dictionary of American Catholic Biography*, 509–10.

    7. O'Toole, *Militant and Triumphant*, 251–52.

Participants in the Saga

Agliardi, Antonio. A professor of William O'Connell during the latter's student days in Rome, he was created a cardinal and became a promoter of his former pupil.

Beaven, Thomas. A suffragan of Boston, he served as bishop of Springfield, Massachusetts, from 1892 until his death in 1920.

Bonzano, Giovanni. Successor of Diomede Falconio, he served as apostolic delegate to the United States from 1912 until 1922 when he was created a cardinal.

Burke, John. A Paulist priest, he was general secretary of the National Catholic Welfare Council/Conference from 1920 until his death in 1936.

Byrne, William. Vicar general of the Boston archdiocese under John Williams, he was pastor at St. Joseph's parish in the West End when William O'Connell was a curate there.

Cerretti, Bonaventura. A Vatican diplomat, he served in the Apostolic Delegation to the United States under both Diomede Falconio and Giovanni Bonzano. After his return to Rome, he served in the Secretariat of State as secretary of the Congregation for Extraordinary Ecclesiastical Affairs.

Corrigan, Michael. An anti-Americanist conservative, he was archbishop of New York City from 1885 until his death in 1902.

Cunningham, Henry V. A Catholic layman, he was attorney for William O'Connell.

Curley, Michael. Successor of James Gibbons, he served as archbishop of Baltimore from 1921 until his death in 1947. He was an early supporter of the National Catholic Welfare Council/Conference.

De Lai, Gaetano. A cardinal in Rome, he was secretary of the Consistorial Congregation, which had charge of the American Catholic church from 1908 onward. He was a supporter of William O'Connell and was one of the "Zealots."

Doody, Michael. A chancellor of the archdiocese of Boston under John Williams, he was pastor of St. Mary of the Annunciation parish in Cambridge.

Dougherty, Dennis. Cardinal archbishop of Philadelphia, he sided with William O'Connell in opposition to the National Catholic Welfare Council/Conference.

Dowling, Austin. Successor of John Ireland, he was archbishop of St. Paul from 1919 until his death in 1930. As a priest, he had been on the faculty with the Sulpicians at St. John's Seminary in Brighton from 1894 until 1897. As archbishop, he chaired the Department of Education of the National Catholic Welfare Council/Conference from 1919 to 1930.

Dunn, William. A Boston physician, he was a notorious homosexual. He joined William O'Connell on a walking tour of Switzerland and Bavaria. He left his estate to a male companion, whose identity was suppressed by O'Connell's attorney.

Dyer, Edward, S.S. Vicar general and later provincial of the Sulpicians in the United States, he was rector of St. Mary's Seminary in Baltimore and one of the masterminds behind the formation of the National Catholic Welfare Council/Conference.

Falconio, Diomede. Successor of Sebastiano Martinelli, he served as apostolic delegate to the United States from 1902 until 1911.

Feehan, Daniel. A suffragan of Boston, he succeeded William Stang as bishop of Fall River, Massachusetts, in 1907, a position he held until his death in 1934.

Fossa, David. *See* Toomey, David.

Fossa, Florence. Wife of David Fossa, she became the whistle-blower.

Fumasoni-Biondi, Pietro. Successor of Giovanni Bonzano, he served as apostolic delegate to the United States from 1922 to 1932.

Gasparri, Pietro. A cardinal in Rome, he served as secretary of state under both Benedict XV and Pius XI.

Gasson, Thomas. A Jesuit priest, he was president of Boston College from 1907 to 1914.

Gavin, Gertrude. Daughter of railroad baron James J. Hill of the Great Northern, she was president of the National Council of Catholic Women.

Gibbons, Edmund. Bishop of Albany, New York, he chaired the Legal Department of the National Catholic Welfare Council/Conference from 1921 until well into the 1930s.

Gibbons, James. A supporter of the Americanist movement, he was archbishop of Baltimore from 1877 until his death in 1921. He was created a cardinal in 1886, and by virtue of his longevity became dean of the American hierarchy and de facto primate (head) of the American church.

Gotti, Girolamo. A cardinal in Rome, he was prefect of the Congregation for the Propagation of the Faith, which had charge of the American Catholic church until 1908.

Guertin, George. A suffragan of Boston, he served as bishop of Manchester, New Hampshire, from 1907 until his death in 1931.

Haberlin, Richard. A priest of the archdiocese of Boston, he served first as secretary to Cardinal William O'Connell and then as chancellor of the archdiocese after the departure of James Percival Edward O'Connell from that position.

Hanna, Edward. Archbishop of San Francisco, he chaired the administrative committee of the National Catholic Welfare Council/Conference from 1919 to 1935.

Havey, Francis, S.S. A Sulpician priest, he was an alumnus of St. John's Seminary in Brighton. He later became rector of that institution and held that position at the time William O'Connell dismissed the Sulpicians from it.

Harkins, Matthew. A suffragan of Boston, he served as bishop of Providence, Rhode Island, from 1887 until his death in 1921.

Heffron, Patrick. Bishop of Winona, Minnesota, he refused to take part in a proposed walkout from the convention of the hierarchy in 1921 if William O'Connell presided.

Hertzog, François-Xavier. A priest in Rome, he was the procurator general (Vatican representative) for the Sulpician Fathers.

Hickey, William. A suffragan of Boston, he was coadjutor bishop and administrator of the diocese of Providence, Rhode Island, from 1919 until 1921 when Bishop Matthew Harkins died. Thereupon, Hickey became bishop of Providence, a position he held until his death in 1933.

Ireland, John. Leader of the Americanist movement, he was archbishop of St. Paul from 1884 until his death in 1918.

Keane, John. A supporter of the Americanist movement, he was rector of The Catholic University of America in Washington, D.C., from 1888 until removed by papal order in 1896. From 1896 to 1899, he served in Rome as a consultor to the Congregation for the Propagation of the Faith. In 1900, he was appointed archbishop of Dubuque and served there until his death in 1918.

MacNutt, Francis. An Indiana layman, he had been a classmate of Raphael Merry del Val, Jr., in the seminary, but departed for marriage and a career. He later became a diplomatic agent for the Vatican and lived in the American colony at Rome. He became a friend of William O'Connell when the latter was rector of the American College.

Martinelli, Sebastiano. Successor of Francesco Satolli, he served as apostolic delegate to the United States from 1896 until 1901 when he was created a cardinal.

Merry del Val, Rafael, Sr. Spanish ambassador to the Vatican, he was the father of Cardinal Raphael Merry del Val, Jr.

Merry del Val, Raphael, Jr. One of the private secretaries of Pope Leo XIII, he became secretary of state under Pope Pius X, who created him a cardinal. With the accession of the less conservative Benedict XV, Merry del Val resigned from the Secretariat of State and became head of the Holy Office, the Vatican department charged with maintaining pure doctrine. He had befriended William O'Connell during the latter's tenure as rector of the American College and became his patron. He was also one of the "Zealots."

Muldoon, Peter. Bishop of Rockford, Illinois, he chaired the Social Action Department of the National Catholic Welfare Council/Conference from 1919 until 1926.

Mullen, John. Rector of the Boston cathedral under Archbishop John Williams, he had been banished to the parish in Hudson, Massachusetts, by William O'Connell. He was a confirmed opponent of the latter.

Nilan, John. A suffragan of Boston, he served as bishop of Hartford, Connecticut, from 1910 until his death in 1934.

O'Connell, Denis. A supporter of the Americanist movement, he served as rector of the American College in Rome from 1885 to1895 when he was compelled to resign. From 1895 to 1903, he was vicar of Santa Maria in Trastevere, Rome. Consecrated a bishop in 1903, he became rector of The Catholic University of America in Washington, D.C. In 1912, he was appointed bishop of Richmond. He was unrelated to William Henry O'Connell.

O'Connell, James P. E. Nephew of William O'Connell, he served first as his uncle's secretary and then as chancellor of the archdiocese of Boston until his excommunication from the church in 1921. He had been secretly married since 1913 and lived part-time in New York City under the assumed name Roe.

Pelletier, Joseph. A Catholic layman, he was district attorney of Boston from 1906 until 1922.

Regan, Agnes. An educator with a long career public schools, she was executive secretary of the National Council of Catholic Women.

Rice, Joseph. A suffragan of Boston, he served as bishop of Burlington, Vermont, from 1910 until his death in 1938.

Roe, James. *See* O'Connell, James P. E.

Russell, William. Bishop of Charleston, South Carolina, he was the mastermind behind the formation of the National Catholic Welfare Council/Conference and chaired its Press Department from 1919 until 1921.

Ryan, James H. An Indiana priest, he served as executive secretary of the Department of Education of the National Catholic Welfare Council/Conference from 1921 until 1928 when he became rector of The Catholic University of American in Washington, D.C.

Ryan, John A. A Minnesota priest, he served as director of the Social Action Department of the National Catholic Welfare Council/Conference from 1920 to 1944.

Satolli, Francesco. Professor of theology at several Roman universities in the late 1870s and early 1880s. He became titular archbishop of Lepant in 1888 and was appointed first apostolic delegate to the United States in 1893. Created a cardinal in 1896, he returned to Rome, where he served until his death in 1910. He taught William O'Connell theology in Rome and later became his patron.

Savelli-Spinola, Antonio. A Roman friend of William O'Connell, he was a consultor for the Congregation for the Propagation of the Faith.

Schrembs, Joseph. Bishop of Toledo, Ohio, and later of Cleveland, he chaired the Department of Lay Activities of the National Catholic Welfare Council/Conference from 1919 to 1934.

Supple, Patrick. A priest of the archdiocese of Boston, he was initially close to William O'Connell both in Portland and in Boston, but later broke with him.

Stang, William. A suffragan of Boston, he served as bishop of Fall River, Massachusetts, from 1904 until his death in 1907.

Tampieri, Sante. A Roman friend of William O'Connell, he was a functionary in the Congregation for the Propagation of the Faith while his companion was rector of the American College.

Toomey, David. A priest of the archdiocese of Boston, he was editor of the *Pilot* until 1919 when he departed from the church. Secretly married in 1914, he lived part-time in New York under the assumed name Fossa.

Van Rossum, Willem. A Vatican cardinal, he was prefect of Propaganda Fide after Gotti. He was also one of the "Zealots."

Walsh, Louis. A suffragan of Boston, he had succeeded William O'Connell as bishop of Portland, Maine, a position he held until his death in 1924. He taught with the Sulpicians at St. John's Seminary in Brighton from 1884 until 1897.

Williams, John. A sympathizer of the Americanist movement, he served as archbishop of Boston from 1866 until his death in 1907.

Wort, Frankie Johnson. A woman of unknown religion, she was wife of James P. E. O'Connell.

Bibliography

MANUSCRIPT COLLECTIONS

Archives of the Archdiocese of Boston
    Annual Meeting of the Hierarchy files
    Apostolic Delegate Correspondence
    The Catholic University of America files
    National Catholic Welfare Conference files
    Priests' Correspondence
    Roman Congregations Correspondence
    Saint John's Seminary files
    William Henry O'Connell Correspondence
Archives of the Archdiocese of New York
    Cathedraticum Account
Archives of the Archdiocese of Philadelphia
    Dennis Dougherty Papers
Archives of the Archdiocese of San Francisco
    National Catholic Welfare Conference files
Archives of the Archdiocese of St. Louis
    American Hierarchy files
Archives of The Catholic University of America
    Annual Meeting of the Hierarchy file
    John A. Ryan Papers
    National Catholic Welfare Conference files
        General Secretary files
        James H. Ryan Papers
        National Council of Catholic Women files
    Nolan-Dixon Collection
    Peter Muldoon Diary
    Rector's Office files
Archives of the Diocese of Albany
    NCWC files
Archives of the Diocese of Charleston
    William Russell Papers
Archives of the Diocese of Cleveland
    Joseph Schrembs Papers
Archives of the Diocese of Portland
    Louis Walsh Papers
    NCWC Papers
    William Henry O'Connell Papers
Archives of the Congregation for the Propagation of the Faith
    Acta della Congregazione (Acts of the Congregation)
Archivio Segreto Vaticano (Vatican Secret Archives)
    Diocesi Boston (Boston Diocese)
    Liste Episcopali (Bishops Lists)
Archives of the University of Notre Dame
    Frederick Kenkel Papers

Matthew Harkins Diary
Associated Archives at St. Mary's Seminary & University (Baltimore)
Michael Curley Papers
Record Group 4: St. Charles' Seminary Papers
Record Groups 9 and 27: Louis Walsh Papers
Record Group 10: Edward Dyer Papers

SECONDARY SOURCES

Adriányi, Gabriel, et al. *The Church in the Modern Age*. Translated by Anselm Biggs. Vol. 10 of *The History of the Church*. Edited by Hubert Jedin and John Dolan. New York: Crossroad, 1981.

Ahern, Patrick H. *The Life of John J. Keane, Educator and Archbishop, 1839–1918*. Milwaukee: Bruce Publishing Company, 1955.

Ahlstrom, Sydney E. *A Religious History of the American People*. New Haven, Conn.: Yale University Press, 1972.

Anbinder, Tyler. *Nativism and Slavery: The Northern Know-Nothings & the Politics of the 1850s*. New York: Oxford University Press, 1992.

Anderson, Robin. *Between Two Wars: The Story of Pope Pius XI (Achille Ratti, 1922–1939)*. Chicago: Franciscan Herald Press, 1977.

Appleby, R. Scott. *"Church and Age Unite!": The Modernist Impulse in American Catholicism*. Notre Dame, Ind.: University of Notre Dame Press, 1992.

Aradi, Zsolt. *Pius XI: The Pope and the Man*. New York: Hanover House, 1958.

Aubert, Roger, et al. *The Church between Revolution and Restoration*. Trans. by Peter Becker. Vol. 7 of *The History of the Church*. Edited Hubert Jedin and John Dolan. New York: Crossroad, 1981.

_____. *The Church in the Age of Liberalism*. Trans. by Peter Becker. Vol. 8 of *The History of Church History*. Edited by Hubert Jedin and John Dolan. New York: Crossroad, 1981.

_____. *The Church in the Industrial Age*. Trans. by Margit Resch. Vol. 9 of *The History of the Church*. Edited by Hubert Jedin and John Dolan. New York: Crossroad, 1981.

_____. *The Church in a Secularized Society*. Translated by Janet Sondheimer. Vol. 5 of *The Christian Centuries: A New History of the Catholic Church*. Edited by Louis Rogier et al. New York: Paulist Press, 1978.

Augustine, P. Charles, O.S.B. *A Commentary on the New Code of Canon Law*, 8 vols. St. Louis: B. Herder Book Company, 1925–1936.

Barry, Colman. *The Catholic Church and German Americans*. Milwaukee: Bruce Publishing Company, 1953.

Billington, Ray Allen. *The Protestant Crusade, 1800–1860: A Study of the Origins of American Nativism*. New York: Rinehart and Company, 1952.

Broderick, Francis L. *Right Reverend New Dealer: John A. Ryan*. New York: Macmillan, 1963.

Broderick, John F., S.J., ed. and trans. *Documents of Vatican Council I, 1869–1870*. Collegeville, Minn.: The Liturgical Press, 1971.

Browne, Henry J. *The Catholic Church and the Knights of Labor*. Washington, D.C.: The Catholic University of America Press, 1949.

Buetow, Harold A. *Of Singular Benefit: The Story of Catholic Education in the United States*. New York: Macmillan Company, 1970.

Chalmers, David M. *Hooded Americanism: The History of the Ku Klux Klan*. New York: New

View Points (reprint of Quadrangle Books, Inc., 1968), 1976.

Chinnici, Joseph P., O.F.M., ed. *Devotion to the Holy Spirit in American Catholicism*. New York: Paulist Press, 1985.

_____. *Living Stones: The History and Structure of Catholic Spiritual Life in the United States*. New York: Macmillan Publishing Company, 1989.

Codex Juris Canonici. Rome: Typis Polyglottis Vaticanis, 1919.

Curran, R. Emmett. *Michael Augustine Corrigan and the Shaping of Conservative Catholicism in America, 1878–1902*. New York: Arno Press, 1978.

_____. "Prelude to 'Americanism': The New York Accademia and Clerical Radicalism in the Late Nineteenth Century," *Church History* 47 (March 1978): 48–65.

Daly, Gabriel, O.S.A. *Transcendence and Immanence: A Study of Catholic Modernism and Integralism*. Oxford: Clarendon Press, 1980.

Delaney, John J. *Dictionary of American Catholic Biography*. Garden City, N.Y.: Doubleday & Company, 1984.

Dixon, Blaise, T.O.R. "The Catholic University of America, 1909–1928: The Rectorship of Thomas Joseph Shahan." Catholic University of America: unpublished doctoral dissertation, 1972.

Dolan, Jay P. *American Catholic Experience: A History from Colonial Times to the Present*. Garden City, N.Y.: Doubleday & Company, 1985.

Dumenil, Lynn. *The Modern Temper: American Culture and Society in the 1920s*. New York: Hill and Wang, 1995.

Ede, Alfred J. *The Lay Crusade for a Christian America: A Study of the American Federation of Catholic Societies, 1900–1919*. New York: Garland Press, 1988.

Ellis, John Tracy. *Catholic Bishops: A Memoir*. Wilmington, Del.: Michael Glazier, Inc., 1984.

_____, ed. *Documents of American Catholic History*. 2nd ed. Milwaukee: Bruce Publishing Company, 1962.

_____. "James Gibbons of Baltimore." In Gerald P. Fogarty, S.J., ed. *Patterns of Episcopal Leadership*. New York: Macmillan and Company, 1989.

_____. *The Life of James Cardinal Gibbons, Archbishop of Baltimore, 1834–1921*, 2 vols. Milwaukee: Bruce Publishing Company, 1952.

Ex Sacre Congregatione Episcoporum et Regularium. "Programma generale studiorum a Pio PP. X approbatum pro omnibus Italiae Seminariis." *Acta Sanctae Sedis* 40 (1907): 336–43.

Farina, John. *An American Experience of God: The Spirituality of Isaac Hecker*. New York: Paulist Press, 1981.

Farrell, John T. "Archbishop Ireland and Manifest Destiny." *Catholic Historical Review* 33 (October 1947): 295–301.

Finn, Brendan A. *Twenty-four American Cardinals: Biographical Sketches of Those Princes of the Catholic Church Who Either Were Born in America or Served at Some Time*. Boston: Bruce Humphries, 1947.

Flannery, Austin, O.P., ed., *Vatican Council II: The Conciliar and Post Conciliar Documents*. Northport, N.Y.: Costello Publishing Company, 1977.

Fogarty, Gerald P., S.J. *American Catholic Biblical Scholarship: A History from the Early Republic to Vatican II*. San Francisco: Harper and Row, 1989.

_____. "Francis J. Spellman: American and Roman." In Gerald P. Fogarty, ed. *Patterns of Episcopal Leadership*. New York: Macmillan and Company, 1989.

_____. *The Vatican and the American Hierarchy from 1870 to 1965*. Wilmington, Del.: Michael Glazier Press, 1985

_____. *The Vatican and the Americanist Crisis: Denis J. O'Connell, American Agent in Rome, 1885–1903*. Rome: Università Gregoriana, 1974.

Foisy, J. Albert. *The Sentinellist Agitation in New England, 1925–1928*. Providence. R. I.. Providence Visitor Press, 1930.

Gaffey, James. "The Changing of the Guard: The Rise of Cardinal O'Connell of Boston." *Catholic Historical Review* 59 (July 1973): 225–44.

Gannon, Michael V. "Before and After Modernism: The Intellectual Isolation of the American Priest." In John Tracy Ellis, ed. *The Catholic Priest in the United States: Historical Investigations*. Collegeville, Minn.: Saint John's University Press, 1971.

Gavin, Donald P. *The National Conference of Catholic Charities, 1910–1960*. Milwaukee: Bruce Press, 1962.

Glazier, Michael, and Thomas Shelley, eds. *The Encyclopedia of American Catholic History*. Collegeville, Minn.: The Liturgical Press, 1997.

Goldberg, Robert Alan. "Hooded Empire: The Ku Klux Klan in Colorado, 1921–1932." University of Wisconsin: unpublished doctoral dissertation, 1977.

Gorman, Mary Adele Francis. "Federation of Catholic Societies in the United States, 1870–1920." University of Notre Dame, unpublished doctoral dissertation, 1962.

Gower, Joseph F. "Democracy as a Theological Problem in Isaac Hecker's Apologetics." In Thomas M. McFadden, ed., *America in Theological Perspective*. New York: Seabury Press, 1976.

Greene, Thomas R. "The Catholic Committee for the Ratification of the Child Labor Amendment, 1935–1937: Origin and Limits." *Catholic Historical Review* 74 (April 1988): 248–69.

Gregory XVI, *Mirari Vos* (1832). In Colman J. Barry, O.S.B., ed. *Readings in Church History*, 3 vols. New York: Newman Press, 1965, 3:37–44.

Halsey, William M. *The Survival of American Innocence: Catholicism in an Era of Disillusionment, 1920–1940*. Notre Dame,Ind.: University of Notre Dame Press, 1980.

Hayman, Robert W. *Catholicism in Rhode Island and the Diocese of Providence, 1886–1921*. Providence: Diocese of Providence, 1995.

Hecker, Isaac T. *The Church and the Age: An Exposition of the Catholic Church in View of the Needs and Aspirations of the Present Age*. New York: Catholic Book Exchange, 1896.

Hennesey, James. *American Catholics: A History of the Roman Catholic Community in the United States*. New York: Oxford University Press, 1983.

Higham, John. *Strangers in the Land: Patterns of American Nativism, 1860–1925*. New York: Atheneum, 1975.

Ireland, John. *The Church and Modern Society: Lectures and Addresses*, 2 vols. St. Paul: Pioneer Press, 1905.

Jackson, Kenneth T. *Ku Klux Klan in the City, 1915–1930*. New York: Oxford University Press, 1967.

Jorgenson, Lloyd P. *The State and the Non-Public School, 1825–1925*. Columbia: University of Missouri Press, 1987.

Kauffman, Christopher J. *Faith and Fraternalism: The History of the Knights of Columbus, 1882–1982*. New York: Harper and Row, 1982.

_____. "The Sulpician Experience in the United States: From Gallicanism to Americanism." Paper delivered at the Cushwa Conference on American Catholicism, Notre Dame University, 4 October 1985.

_____. *Tradition and Transformation in Catholic Culture: The Priests of Saint Sulpice in the United States from 1791 to the Present*. New York: Macmillan Publishing Company, 1988.

Kirk, Martin J., C.F.M. *The Spirituality of Isaac Thomas Hecker: Reconciling the American Character and the Catholic Faith*. New York: Garland Publishing, Inc., 1988.

Lackner, Joseph H., S.M. "Bishop Ignatius Horstmann and the School Controversy of the 1890s." *Catholic Historical Review* 75 (January 1989): 73–90.

LaFeber, Walter. *The American Search for Opportunity, 1865–1913*. Vol. II of *The Cambridge History of American Foreign Relations*, ed. by Walter I. Cohen. New York: Cambridge University Press, 1995.

Langlois, Edward J., C.S.P. "Isaac Hecker's Political Thought." In John Farina, ed., *Hecker Studies: Essays on the Thought of Isaac Hecker*. New York: Paulist Press, 1983.

Leuchtenburg, William E. *The Perils of Prosperity, 1914–1932*. Chicago: University of Chicago Press, 1958.

Liptak, Dolores, R.S.M. *Immigrants and Their Church*. New York: Macmillan Publishing Company, 1989.

Lord, Robert H., John E. Sexton, and Edward T. Harrington. *History of the Archdiocese of Boston In the Various Stages of Its Development, 1604 to1943*, 3 vols. New York: Sheed and Ward, 1944.

McAvoy, Thomas, C.S.C. *The Great Crisis in American Catholic History, 1895–1900*. Chicago: H. Regnery Co., 1957.

McKeown, Elizabeth. "Catholic Identity in America." In Thomas McFadden, ed., *America in Theological Perspective*. New York: Seabury Press, 1976.

_____. "The National Bishops' Conference: An Analysis of Its Origins," *Catholic Historical Review*, 66 (October, 1980): 565–83.

_____. *War and Welfare: American Catholics and World War I* (New York: Garland, 1988).

McNamara, Robert F. *The American College in Rome, 1855–1955*. Rochester, N.Y.: The Christopher Press, 1956.

MacNutt, Francis. *A Papal Chamberlain: The Personal Chronicle of Francis Augustus MacNutt*. Edited by John J. Donovan. New York: Longmans, Green, and Company, 1936.

McQuade, Vincent, O.S.A. *The American Catholic Attitude on Child Labor Since 1891: A Study of the Formation and Development of a Catholic Attitude on a Specific Social Question*. Washington, D.C.: The Catholic University of America Press, 1938.

McShane, Joseph. *"Sufficiently Radical": Catholicism, Progressivism, and the Bishops' Program of 1919*. Washington, D.C.: The Catholic University of America Press, 1986.

Mead, Sidney. "American Protestantism Since the Civil War." *Journal of Religion* 26 (January 1956): 1–16.

Meiring, Bernard J. *Educational Aspects of the Legislation of the Councils of Baltimore, 1829–1884*. New York: Arno Press, 1978.

Merwick, Donna. *Boston Priests, 1848–1910: A Study of Social and Intellectual Change*. Cambridge, Mass.: Harvard University Press , 1973.

Morgan, Thomas. *A Reporter at the Papal Court: A Narrative of the Reign of Pius XI*. New York: Longmans, Green and Co., 1937.

Moynihan, James H. *The Life of Archbishop John Ireland*. New York: Harper and Brothers, 1953.

Murray, Robert K. *The 103rd Ballot: Democrats and the Disaster in Madison Square Garden*. New York: Harper & Row, 1976.

Myers, Gustavus. *History of Bigotry in the United States*. Edited and revised by Henry M. Christman. New York: Capricorn Books, 1960.

Nuesse, C. Joseph. "Thomas Joseph Bouquillon (1840–1902), Moral Theologian and Precursor of the Social Sciences in The Catholic University of America." *Catholic Historical Review* 72 (October 1986): 603–06.

O'Brien, David J. "An Evangelical Imperative: Isaac Hecker, Catholicism, and Modern Society." In John Farina, *Hecker Studies: Essays on the Thought of Isaac Hecker*. New York: Paulist

Press, 1983.

_____. *Public Catholicism*. New York: Macmillan, 1989.

O'Connell, Marvin R. *John Ireland and the American Catholic Church*. St. Paul: Minnesota Historical Society Press, 1988.

O'Connell, William Henry. *The Letters of His Eminence William Cardinal O'Connell, Archbishop of Boston*, Volume I: *From College Days, 1876, to Bishop of Portland, 1901*. Cambridge, Mass.: Riverside Press, 1915.

_____. *Recollections of Seventy Years*. Boston: Houghton Mifflin, 1934.

_____. *Sermons and Addresses of His Eminence William Cardinal O'Connell, Archbishop of Boston*, 11 vols.. Boston: The Pilot Publishing Company, 1915 and 1938.

O'Leary, Robert Aidan. "William Henry O'Connell: A Social and Intellectual Biography." Tufts University: unpublished doctoral dissertation, 1980.

O'Toole, James M. *Militant and Triumphant: William Henry O'Connell and the Catholic Church in Boston, 1859–1944*. Notre Dame, Ind.: University of Notre Dame Press, 1992.

_____. "Militant and Triumphant: William Henry O'Connell and Boston Catholics, 1859–1944." Boston College: unpublished doctoral dissertation, 1987.

_____. "The Name That Stood for Rome: William O'Connell and the Modern Episcopal Style. In Gerald P. Fogarty, S.J., ed. *Patterns of Episcopal Leadership*. New York: Macmillan Publishing Company, 1989.

_____. "Prelates and Politicos: Catholics and Politics in Massachusetts, 1900–1970." In Robert E. Sullivan and James M. O'Toole, eds. *Catholic Boston: Studies in Religion and Community 1870–1970*. Boston: Roman Catholic Archdiocese of Boston, 1985.

_____. "The Role of Bishops in American Catholic History: Myth and Reality in the Case of Cardinal William O'Connell." *Catholic Historical Review* 77 (October 1991): 595–615.

Paterson, Thomas G., et al. *American Foreign Relations*, 2 vols. 4th ed. Lexington, Mass.: D. C. Heath, 1995.

Peters, Walter. *The Life of Benedict XV*. Milwaukee: The Bruce Publishing Company, 1959.

Pius IX. *Syllabus of Errors* (1864). In Colman J. Barry, O.S.B., ed. *Readings in Church History*, 3 vols. New York: Newman Press, 1965, 3:70–74.

Potter, David. *The Impending Crisis, 1848–1861*. New York: Harper Colophon, 1976.

Poulat, Émile. *Intégrisme et catholicisme intégral: un réseau secret international antimoderniste: La "Sapinière" (1909–1921)*. Tournai: Casterman, 1969.

Procko, Bohdan P. "Soter Ortynsky: First Ruthenian Bishop in the United States, 1907–1916." *Catholic Historical Review* 58 (January 1973): 513–33.

Reardon, Bernard M. G., ed. *Roman Catholic Modernism*. Stanford, Calif.: Stanford University Press, 1970.

Reher, Margaret Mary. *Catholic Intellectual Life in America: A Historical Study of Persons and Movements*. New York: Macmillan Publishing Company, 1989.

_____. "The Church and the Kingdom of God in America." Fordham University: unpublished doctoral dissertation, 1972.

Reilly, Daniel F., O.P. *The School Controversy (1891–1893)*. Washington, D.C.: The Catholic University of America Press, 1943.

Reilly, Mary Lonanm. O.S.F. *A History of the Catholic Press Association, 1911–1968*. Metuchen, N.J.: Scarecrow Press, 1971.

Rippley, La Vern J. "Archbishop Ireland and the School Language Controversy." *U.S. Catholic Historian* 1 (Fall 1980): 1–16.

Rosenberg, Emily S. *Spreading the American Dream: American Economic and Cultural Expansion,*

1890–1945. New York: Hill and Wang, 1982.

Salvaterra, David L. *American Catholicism and the Intellectual Life, 1880–1950*. New York: Garland Publishing Company, 1988.

Seredi, Iustiniani, ed. *Codicis Juris Canonici Fontes*, 9 vols. Vatican, 1935.

Sexton, John E., and Arthur J. Riley. *History of Saint John's Seminary, Brighton*. Boston: Roman Catholic Archbishop of Boston, 1945.

Slawson, Douglas J. *The Department of Education Battle, 1918–1932: Public Schools, Catholic Schools, and the Social Order*. Notre Dame, Ind.: University of Notre Dame Press, 2005.

_____. *The Foundation and First Decade of the National Catholic Welfare Council*. Washington, D.C.: The Catholic University of America Press, 1992.

_____. "John J. Burke, C.S.P.: The Vision and Character of a Public Churchman." *Journal of Paulist Studies* 4 (1995–1996): 47–93.

Spalding, Thomas W. *Premier See: A History of the Archdiocese of Baltimore, 1789–1989*. Baltimore: Johns Hopkins University Press, 1989.

Storch, Neil T. "John Ireland's Americanism *After* 1899: The Argument from History." *Church History* 51 (December 1982): 434–44.

Strong, Josiah. *Our Country: Its Possible Future and Its Present Crisis*. New York: Baker & Taylor Company for the American Home Missionary Society, 1885 and 1891.

Sullivan, Robert E. "Beneficial Relations: Toward a Social History of the Diocesan Priests of Boston, 1875–1944." In Robert E. Sullivan and James M. O'Toole, eds. *Catholic Boston: Studies in Religion and Community 1870–1970*. Boston: Roman Catholic Archdiocese of Boston, 1985.

Suprema Sacra Congregatio S. Officii. Decretum: Damnatur Opus Cui Titulus "Manuel Biblique etc." *Acta Apostolicae Sedis* 15 (31 December 1923): 615–19.

Vatican II. *Dignitatis Humanae* (1965). In Austin Flannery, O.P., *Vatican Council II: The Conciliar and Post Conciliar Documents*. Northport, N.Y.: Costello Publishing Company, 1975.

Wall, Bernard. *Report on the Vatican*. London: Weidenfeld and Nicolson, 1956.

Wangler, Thomas. "The Birth of Americanism: 'Westward the Apocalyptic Candlestick,'" *Harvard Theological Review* 65 (July 1972): 415–36.

_____. "Emergence of John J. Keane as a Liberal Catholic and Americanist (1878–1887)." *American Ecclesiastical Review* 166 (September 1972): 457–478.

_____. "John Ireland and the Origins of Liberal Catholicism in the United States," *Catholic Historical Review* 56 (January 1971): 617–29.

_____. "John Ireland's Emergence as a Liberal Catholic and Americanist: 1875-1887," *Records of the American Catholic Historical Society of Philadelphia* 81 (June 1970): 67–82

Wayman, Dorothy. *Cardinal O'Connell of Boston: A Biography of William Henry O'Connell, 1859–1944*. New York: Farrar, Straus and Young, 1955.

Williams, Michael. *American Catholics in the War: National Catholic War Council, 1917–1921*. New York: Macmillan, 1921.

Williams, William Appleman. *The Contours of American History*. New York: W. W. Norton and Company, 1988.

Wolkovich-Valkavicius, William. "Cardinal and Cleric: O'Connell and Mullen in Conflict." *Historical Journal of Massachusetts* 13 (June 1985): 129–39.

Woodbury, Kenneth B, Jr. "An Incident Between the French Canadians and the Irish in the Diocese of Maine in 1906," *New England Quarterly* 40 (June 1967): 260–69.

Zwierlein, Frederick J. *The Life and Letters of Bishop McQuaid*, 3 vols. Rochester, N.Y.: The Art Print Shop, 1925–1927.

Index

Douglas J. Slawson is an author, educator and lecturer. He holds a doctorate in history from The Catholic University of America and a Master of Divinity from De Andreis Institute of Theology. His previous book, *The Department of Education Battle, 1918–1932*, won the Cushwa Prize awarded by the Cushwa Center for the Study of American Catholicism at the University of Notre Dame. He is also author of *The Foundation and First Decade of the National Catholic Welfare Council*, co-author of *Church and Slave in Perry County, Missouri, 1818–1865*, and co-editor of *The American Vincentians: A Popular History of the Congregation of the Mission in the United States, 1815–1987*. His articles have appeared in *The Catholic Historical Review*, *Church History*, *The Americas*, *The Missouri Historical Review*, *Lo Straniero*, *Vincentian Heritage*, and *The Encyclopedia of American Catholic History*. He has served as a professor of history at St. John's Seminary in California and St. Thomas Theological Seminary in Colorado. Dr. Slawson is currently professor of history at National University in San Diego.